RE-DRESSING AMERICA'S
FRONTIER PAST

John Runk (1878–1964), Loc#1719 Neg#1719, Minnesota Historical
Society. John Runk grew up in Stillwater, Minnesota. As a
youngster, he worked in various phases of the logging industry but
also always demonstrated a creative side. He opened a photography
business in his hometown in 1899 and over the next several years
introduced inventions and innovations to the art. He never married
and was known as something of a loner, but was also involved with
the lives of the members of his extended family. A large collection of
his photographs, including a series of himself in female clothing,
ended up at the Minnesota Historical Society. More on his life can
be found in Allison Drtina, comp., *John Runk, Photographer: The
Life, Family and Legacy of John Runk, Jr.* (Stillwater, MN:
Washington County Historical Society, 2008).

RE-DRESSING

AMERICA'S

FRONTIER PAST

Peter Boag

UNIVERSITY OF CALIFORNIA PRESS

Berkeley   Los Angeles   London

University of California Press, one of the most distinguished
university presses in the United States, enriches lives around
the world by advancing scholarship in the humanities, social
sciences, and natural sciences. Its activities are supported by
the UC Press Foundation and by philanthropic contributions
from individuals and institutions. For more information,
visit www.ucpress.edu.

University of California Press
Berkeley and Los Angeles, California

University of California Press, Ltd.
London, England

Library of Congress Cataloging-in-Publication Data

Boag, Peter.
  Re-dressing America's frontier past / Peter Boag.
    p. cm.
  Includes bibliographical references and index.
  isbn 978-0-520-27062-6 (cloth : alk. paper)
    1. Transvestites—West (U.S.)—History—19th century.
    2. Gender identity—West (U.S.)—History—19th
century. 3. Homosexuality—West (U.S.)—History—19th
century. I. Title.
  HQ77.2.U6B63   2011
  306.77'8097809034—dc22

                                         2011009443

Manufactured in the United States of America

20 19 18 17 16 15 14 13 12 11
10 9 8 7 6 5 4 3 2 1

John A. Baures
1962–1996

The publisher gratefully acknowledges the generous support of the Humanities Endowment Fund of the University of California Press Foundation.

CONTENTS

List of Illustrations   *ix*

Acknowledgments   *xi*

Introduction. A Trip Along the Pike's Peak Express:
Cross-Dressers and America's Frontier Past   *1*

PART ONE.   "Females in Male Attire, and Males in Petticoats":
Remembering Cross-Dressers in Western American and
Frontier History

1. "Known to All Police West of the Mississippi": Disrobing the
    Female-to-Male Cross-Dresser   *23*
2. "I Have Done My Part in the Winning of the West": Unveiling
    the Male-to-Female Cross-Dresser   *59*

PART TWO.   "The Story of the Perverted Life Is Not Attractive":
Making the American West and the Frontier Heteronormative

3. "And Love Is a Vision and Life Is a Lie": The Daughters
    of Calamity Jane   *95*
4. "He Was a Mexican": Race and the Marginalization of
    Male-to-Female Cross-Dressers in Western History   *130*
5. "Death of a Modern Diana": Sexologists, Cross-Dressers,
    and the Heteronormalization of the American Frontier   *159*

Conclusion. Sierra Flats and Haunted Valleys: Cross-Dressers
and the Contested Terrain of America's Frontier Past   *189*

Notes   *197*
Index   *249*

ILLUSTRATIONS

1. Harry Allen, 1912 / 24
2. Milton Matson, 1895 / 49
3. Jack Garland, 1897 / 51
4. Bert Martin, 1900 / 60
5. Joe Monahan, 1904 / 96
6. Idaho's Owyhee Mountains gold-rush district, 1869 / 99
7. Pearl Hart, 1899 / 113
8. Tom King, 1895 / 119
9. Jennie Stephens, 1897 / 121
10. Mrs. Nash, 1878 / 131
11. Mexican cart, 1869 / 132
12. *Narrative of Lucy Ann Lobdell*, 1855 / 160

ACKNOWLEDGMENTS

I started imagining *Re-Dressing America's Frontier Past* while working on *Same-Sex Affairs: Constructing and Controlling Homosexuality in the Pacific Northwest* (Berkeley: University of California Press, 2003). That book was about men. My research turned up relatively little on women, though I did come across some tidbits about female-to-male cross-dressers. I planned that one day I would use that material as the basis for an article, which I did. But as I immersed myself in that project, I expanded my regional and temporal scope and soon turned up more material on female-to-male cross-dressers than I had anticipated. To my great surprise, considering how few male-to-female cross-dressers I came across doing my research for *Same-Sex Affairs*, I found a remarkable amount of source material on them as well. *Re-Dressing America's Frontier Past* is the result.

This project has been a great deal of fun, made much more so by those who helped me along the way. I owe much to my friends Ross Bunnell and Clayton Koppes. They read early drafts of my entire book, offered thoughtful comments, and made perceptive suggestions that I incorporated herein. Early on Kristine Stilwell, Tom Cook, and Robin Henry shared some of their own research with me. Lori Lahlum identified some illustrations for me, including those that appear on this book's cover and as its frontispiece. Dee Garceau, Catherine Cocks, Gregory Nobles, Susan Armitage, Matthew Sutton, Lisa Duggan, Louis Warren, Renée Laegreid, and the late Peggy Pascoe provided comments on different portions or iterations of this book or its proposal. Elizabeth Jameson took a great deal of care with a later draft. Her wonderful insights crucially influenced this book.

A number of people provided me moral support, wrote recommendations for grants, made available their considerable knowledge and imagination as I discussed with them my ideas, helped with research questions, or otherwise afforded me all manner of inspiration. These include Virginia DeJohn Anderson, Martha Hanna, Mark Pittenger, Marcia Yonemoto, Fred Anderson, John Wunder, Anne Butler, Richard Maxwell Brown, Lisa Pollard, James Potter, Sandy Schackel, Judy Austin, Brian DeLay, Susan Kent, Catherine Mason, and my parents. Thea Lindquist, history librarian at the University of Colorado, Boulder; Lou Vyhnanek, humanities and social science librarian at Washington State University; and John Doerner, historian at the Little Bighorn Battlefield National Monument, all supported my research. David Rich Lewis and Colleen O'Neill published my article out of which this book grew, "Go West Young Man, Go East Young Woman: Searching for the *Trans* in Western Gender History," in *Western Historical Quarterly* 36, no. 4 (Winter 2005): 477–97. That article is reproduced in bits and pieces throughout this book with permission. I especially thank Niels Hooper, my editor at the University of California Press. He pushed me over several years to write this book. Likewise, the editorial staff at California, which has now seen me through three books, has been a pleasure to work with. My life partner, Brent Owens, has now endured the research and writing of two of these. Through each he has been boundless in his encouragement and support.

Finally, throughout this project I gathered most of my inspiration from the memory of a boy I once knew. He was a gentle soul and deserved a world far gentler than ours. It is to him that I dedicate this work.

A Trip Along the Pike's Peak Express

Cross-Dressers and America's Frontier Past

In the mid-nineteenth century, the *New York Tribune*'s Horace Greeley ex-
horted young American men bereft of family and friends to go West to build
their homes and make their fortunes.[1] In 1859 the journalist traveled to the
region to observe the fruits of his advice. He did not necessarily find there
what he had hoped. On the Great Plains en route to the Rocky Mountains,
for example, he learned that hundreds of prospectors had recently gone bust
at the Colorado gold-diggings, deserted the region in droves, and consequently faced unemployment and other sufferings. Greeley reported his encounter with only one such individual, a young clerk with whom he had
supped at Station 9 of the Pike's Peak Express and who, "having frozen his
feet on the winter journey out, had had enough of gold-hunting, and was going
home to his parents in Indiana." The morning following Greeley's repast with
the clerk, and only after they had departed in opposite directions, the New
Yorker learned something astonishing about his new acquaintance: "I was ap-
prised by our conductor," exclaimed Greeley, "that said clerk was a woman!"[2]

Horace Greeley's clerk and other people like him are my subjects in *Re-
Dressing America's Frontier Past*. I focus on the era 1850 to 1920—roughly
from the heyday of the California gold rush to just after the last of the western (continental) territories became states in the union. I have two principal
goals. One is to *re-dress* America's frontier past—recovering its cross-dressers
and exploring what their transgressive sexual and gender identities meant to
their societies and communities. In doing so, I reveal that cross-dressers
were not simply ubiquitous, but were very much a part of daily life on the

frontier and in the West. I suspect that readers will be as amazed as I was with the number and variety of cross-dressers who found a home on the proverbial range—as astonished perhaps as Horace Greeley *claimed* to be when he encountered the gender-changing clerk in 1859 along the Pike's Peak Express. In fact, my surprise led me to a self-reflexive project that metamorphosed into the second goal of my study: how and why did such a large group of people so visible and so much a part of daily life in the nineteenth-century West become so forgotten that their rediscovery was such an unexpected thing?

I was prompted to this question during the early phase of my research when a high-profile public event occurred that starkly exposed the relationship between the American West and transgressive sexual and gender activities. That event was the Hollywood release of the full-length motion picture *Brokeback Mountain*, based on Annie Proulx's short story by the same title, in the late fall of 2005.[3] The film depicts a love and sex affair between two Wyoming cowboys (they are really sheepherders but are popularly identified as cowboys) during the second half of the twentieth century. The film sparked something of a national debate: everyone from late-night Hollywood talk show hosts to *New York Times* reporters sought answers to the question—some through what passed as humor and others needing "investigative" journalism—as to whether there really was such a thing as a gay cowboy.[4]

And why not? Generations of these Americans had grown up on Hollywood's hyper-masculine and hyper-heterosexual western actors and characters—actors such as Tom Mix, Gary Cooper, John Wayne, Alan Ladd, Glenn Ford, Kirk Douglas, Paul Newman, Clint Eastwood, Charles Bronson, and Chuck Connors, to name but a few; and characters such as Jesse James, George Custer, Daniel Boone, Buffalo Bill, Davy Crockett, "Wild Bill" Hickok, Butch Cassidy, Wyatt Earp, and a string of entirely fictional lawmen, gunslingers, and especially cowboys. They had also been imbued with Madison Avenue images of the Marlboro Man and the pulp heroes of Zane Grey and Louis L'Amour novels. Through these fictional and real-life characters and people, popular cultural outlets had long shaped the American imagination about the masculine, heterosexual West. After years of such fare, popular audiences who considered *Brokeback Mountain* simply found it incongruous and therefore uproariously laughable that homosexuality could exist within what was popularly understood to be the classic West—not just as a place, but as a culture represented by the iconic cowboy.

And yet fully two generations before *Brokeback Mountain*, Alfred Kinsey found and reported in his eyebrow-raising *Sexual Behavior in the Human Male* that the highest frequencies of homosexuality in America that he un-covered were in fact in rural communities in the most remote parts of the country, particularly in the West. Ranchmen, cattle men, prospectors, lum-bermen, and farmers—the most virile and physically active groups of men— Kinsey found, commonly engaged in same-sex sexual activities, probably, Kinsey further remarked, much like their pioneer forebears had. "This type of rural homosexuality," Kinsey concluded, "contradicts the theory that homosexuality in itself is an urban product."[5]

The sexual reality of the American West that Kinsey uncovered and made publicly known in the 1940s differs considerably from popular under-standings and memories about sexuality and gender in the Old West and on the frontier. My second goal, then, is to explain how and why this is so. In *redressing* America's frontier past, I posit that the roots of the answer can be found before Hollywood stepped into the fray and, more precisely, in the history of cross-dressing. Cross-dressers linked two monumental events that occurred at the tail end of the nineteenth century. One was the so-called closing of the frontier. The other was the development of our modern gender and sexual system—that is, the creation of the categories of homosexual and heterosexual, the division of people into these categories, and the identifica-tion of cross-dressing with the former. At the intersection of these two events at the turn of the twentieth century, cross-dressers crossed from one to the other: from the frontier to modern homosexuality. In doing so, they left behind them a wholly heterosexualized and unambiguously gendered American West. It is worth outlining these events here.

After all the facts and figures were in from the 1890 U.S. federal census, the superintendent of that enterprise declared that population growth and redistribution made it impossible for him to trace, as he had in previous years, an unbroken frontier line from north to south across the western por-tion of the continent. This signaled to him that the American frontier had vanished.[6] Later historians have shown time and again that the superinten-dent's 1890 definition of what constitutes the frontier was entirely arbitrary (he had defined it as a line marking off an area where population density dropped below two people per square mile). The same historians have fur-ther demonstrated that the frontier of late nineteenth-century popular imagination was nothing more than the product of popular imagining. Still, what happened in 1890 and the years surrounding that date was very real and meant a great deal to a large and influential sector of the American populace. By 1890 Americans were grappling with all sorts of troubling issues that seemed to be products of the same forces that caused the imagined frontier to disappear: rapid urbanization, industrialization, the rise of impersonal corporations, terrible economic depression, the depletion of natural resources, and any number of social problems and worries, such as women's growing independence, mass immigration of peoples of diverse racial and ethnic backgrounds, frightening labor unrest, and the spread of extreme squalor in the shadow of growing fortunes of unprecedented vastness.

Reeling from and trying to make sense of all this, many Americans looked into their own past—their so-called frontier past—for solace, escapism, and in some cases examples of alternative ways of living that might be useful in the modern era. Some did these things through purchasing, reading, and thus fueling the mass market for western dime novels and other regional literature that sensationalized frontier life. Others did so through attending any number of the era's live shows that depicted the wildness of the West and that sported bison herds, real live Indians and cowboys, shooting demonstrations, and even reenactments of Custer's Last Stand. Yet others found escapism and celebration of the nation's western past through viewing and patronizing the growing number of artists who filled galleries and museums with paintings and sculptures depicting monumental western landscapes and romanticized versions of western life. And a host of Americans began traveling to the West to experience what they felt were the last vestiges of its wildness, woolliness, and pristine environmental conditions, elements of the frontier that were just then receding into memory. Such responses show that however real or imaginary it was, the frontier epoch could be identified and separated from the dawn of the twentieth century—that is, from the modern era that had only just commenced and was defined by its complexities, changes, uncertainties, and hard realities.

At the very moment when Americans memorialized the frontier, social understandings of gender and sexuality were undergoing profound alteration, so much so that by the last years of the 1800s there emerged what historians have termed the "modern" sexual and gender system. Prior to the nineteenth century, the western world held to what is known as the one-sex model, as the historian Thomas Laqueur has ably demonstrated.[7] Accordingly, males and females were viewed as just different forms of the same sex.

They had, it was believed, the same sex organs; only the addition of a certain measure of heat turned them to the exterior of the body, forming a male, while sex organs that remained inside denoted the body of a woman. Significant alterations in knowledge systems as related to political developments led to the two-sex model replacing the one-sex model by the year 1800. The two-sex model maintained that the sexes were not different in degree, but rather they were so different as to be complete opposites. This set up in our "modern" thinking the notion of a binary sex system—that is, a system composed of two distinctly different sexes.

Corresponding to the binary two-sex system was the binary two-gender system. It held that feminine behaviors, actions, and feelings reside in the female body. Masculine behaviors, actions, and feelings reside in the male body. That is, gender (how one acts, the tasks one performs, how one carries and comports oneself, how one dresses, and even the feelings one is supposed to have) corresponds to biology. Among the feelings one has, of course, are sexual desires. Under the two-sex/two-gender system, a male-bodied person would have sexual desires for a woman. A female-bodied person would have sexual desires for a man (if she had any sexual desires at all—there was something of a debate about this at various times in the nineteenth century).[8] Under the two-sex model, then, body, gender, and sexual desire should all conform to each other. And that, moreover, is how nature determined it.

But what about people with female bodies who acted and behaved in masculine ways and people with male bodies who acted and behaved in feminine ways, especially, for example, in the clothing they chose to wear? The numbers of such people seemed only to be increasing in the latter years of the nineteenth century. The broader western world came to believe that these people's gender had become reversed or inverted from their physical sex. Such reversal was also believed to be manifest in sexual desire: the sexually inverted female (a manly woman) and the sexually inverted male (an effeminate man), it was thought, would have sexual desires for, respectively, a feminine woman and a masculine man. Accordingly, medical science developed the term "sex invert" to refer to such people and used it interchangeably with "homosexual," a term likewise coined in the latter part of the 1800s. "Sex invert/homosexual" as a term and concept evolved in direct contrast to "heterosexual."[9] By the end of the nineteenth century, therefore, not only did we have a binary sex and a binary gender system, but we also had a binary sexuality system composed of homosexuality and heterosexuality.

Homosexuals/sexual inverts were understood to be neither normal nor natural—some sort of physical, psychological, or neurological disease or disorder or personal vice must have interfered with nature to cause such a monstrous problem. As I explain in detail in Part II of this book, medical theory of the day at times went beyond individual malady to link the etiology of homosexuality to general social decay, degeneration, and the stresses and strains of modern living. Thus, homosexuality was understood as an unfortunate by-product of modernization. As such, it seemed that it could be neither associated with nor found on the early frontier, an era and place conceived of as unimpaired by all the troubles of the modern period.

So what, then, to do about all the people in America's recent frontier and western past and even present who did cross-dress and thus in doing so raised questions about transgressive sexual and gender identities understood as modern? In Part II of this book I demonstrate that through broad social projects some of these cross-dressers were re-imagined as heterosexuals, their legacies transformed. In Chapter 3 I explain that this was what principally happened in the case of female-to-male cross-dressers. I argue that myths developed in response to the closing of the frontier were embedded with powerful ideas about gender, tropes informed by the knowledge that the West and the frontier had been primarily male places. They held that a woman in the West might only have made it on her own had she disguised herself as a man. Once the frontier had closed, this myth easily made it possible to return western cross-dressing women (who might otherwise now raise concerns about sex and sexuality) to "normal" womanhood—that is, to heterosexuality and to appropriate gender behaviors. Americans undertook this project in part through inventing in the popular press and in dime novels fictionalized and idealized sexual and gender biographies for past and present female-to-male cross-dressers of the frontier and West.[10]

Male-to-female cross-dressers' effeminacy and sexuality ran diametrically counter to what the frontier and the American West symbolized already at the end of the nineteenth century. Thus, they represented a more serious problem. The western gender myths that could contain, explain, and rehabilitate female-to-male cross-dressers could not do the same in the case of male-to-females. The latter could be dealt with only through their exclusion from the frontier and the Old West. In Chapter 4 I explain that the public imagination by the end of the nineteenth century came to associate male-to-female cross-dressing and male effeminacy more generally with nonwhite/non-Anglo races. Accomplishing this stripped the male-to-female cross-dresser from America's frontier history along with its Asians, Mexicans, Indians, and other nonwhite/non-Anglo peoples. This rendered America's frontier past not only a white place and time, but a heterosexual one as well.

The turn-of-the-twentieth-century popular projects that heterosexualized some western cross-dressers and eliminated others from the frontier also had their scholarly counterpart—particularly at the intersection of the discipline of history and the science of sex, a topic that I focus on in Chapter 5. When Americans at the end of the nineteenth century romanticized their frontier past, professional historians also got into the act. In 1893, Frederick Jackson Turner, a University of Wisconsin professor, took note of the findings made by the census superintendent. From these he wrote his singularly influential "The Significance of the Frontier in American History."[11] Like his inspirational source, Turner claimed that the frontier had disappeared in 1890. He went beyond that determination to argue that a four hundred–year epoch that had commenced with the voyage of Christopher Columbus had now come to an end and that the United States had entered a new era. Somewhat differently from the census, he defined the frontier as the point where civilization meets savagery. He then expansively declared that all of American history could be explained by the frontier's continuous retreat westward. From a very narrow but altogether contemporary perspective, Turner saw American history as a story of Europeans moving triumphantly westward. In confronting and subduing savagery, they became Americans. That is, this process instilled in westering pioneers those qualities and characteristics viewed as distinctly American in nature, things like democracy, freedom, independence, and equality. Turner's heroes, in keeping with popular opinion, were white men, the most important being farmers who married and had children and built successive communities that became towns and then turned into cities. Turner's "frontier thesis" provided what in time became the most definitive, if not emblematic, white and heterosexual statement from his generation about the end of the frontier era and what that frontier meant to the United States, its people, and its institutions.[12]

The ideas that informed Turner were strikingly similar to the notions that informed scientists and medical experts of the day, the so-called sexologists who theorized, explained, and thereby helped to create modern sexuality at the precise moment the frontier vanished. Working from the same premises as Turner, late nineteenth-century American sexologists broadly claimed that sexual inversion/homosexuality, as products of modernity, could not be found in early American history, specifically on its frontier. They further forcefully argued that frontier conditions secured heterosexuality in westering Americans.

Notions of the frontier therefore played a foundational role in the development of modern sexuality. Likewise, transgressive sexuality and gender identities notably represented in the person of the cross-dresser have played a critical role in how western and frontier American history and myth have been conceived, imagined, and written since the 1890s. Because the frontier and the American West have been fundamental to how Americans (at least, that is, Americans who have traditionally been the socially dominant group) have understood and defined themselves, I further assert that cross-dressers have been functionally central to the American national narrative. These might seem odd, even counterintuitive claims considering my other contention that cross-dressers have been largely forgotten in western and frontier myth and history precisely because of their transgressive sexual and gender identities. But I follow the Foucauldian reasoning that in trying to forget, re-imagine, and expunge cross-dressers, nineteenth-century western and frontier history and myth have been written and conceived in direct opposition to the myriad cross-dressers of our past. In Part II of this book I reveal how and why this happened.

This book, however, is about more than how and why cross-dressers and the transgressive sexual and gender identities they represented have been marginalized, expunged, and forgotten in western history. A few years ago queer theoretician Ki Namaste pointed out that for all the recent outpouring of scholarship on "drag, gender, performance, and transsexuality," those who produced it "have shown very little concern for those who identify and live as drag queens, transsexuals, and/or transgenders."[13] *Re-Dressing America's Frontier Past* takes seriously this omission in cross-dressing studies. I have designed Part I of this book to recover the lives of cross-dressers in western and frontier history. In two chapters, one on women who dressed as men and the other on men who dressed as women, I examine the reality of cross-dressers' lives, explore how they understood their own gender and sexual identities, consider the ways in which their societies and communities viewed them, and analyze how they both affirmed and challenged the gender and sexual categories of their society. To help accomplish these tasks, I begin each chapter with an extended meditation on the life history of a particular western cross-dresser. This strategy, in addition to recovering the subjectivity of cross-dressers, also serves to draw attention to critical issues that the chapter following that biography analyzes in greater depth. In preparation for the deployment of this method, I here offer the reader a lengthy biography that amplifies and informs the tasks that I set out to accomplish in Part I.

Edna Bamford, a descendant of pioneers who arrived in Oregon in 1861, married Albert Hart, a more recent arrival to Oregon from Kansas, at the home of her parents in the Willamette Valley town of Oakville in 1888. Both Albert and Edna had business educations. Both business and family reversed their westward migration, taking them from Oregon back to Albert's Kansas not long after their nuptials. Albert prospered as a merchant in the Great Plains town of Halls Summit, becoming a respected business leader within just a few short years. Tragically, a typhoid epidemic prematurely claimed his life in the summer of 1892. Not quite two years before, on 4 October 1890, Edna had given birth to the couple's only child. Thankfully for his heirs, when Albert departed this world he left them a nice estate. Edna packed up herself, her inheritance, and her toddler and soon returned to Oregon, where her parents yet resided.[14]

Edna and Albert's child was born with a female body. The two parents christened her Alberta Lucille. Perhaps they had some premonition in choosing their daughter's patronymic, but in any case she widely became known as Lucille. When she grew into childhood in rural Oregon, she increasingly preferred what society then considered to be boyish pursuits. She played games such as horse and wagon and reenacted Civil War scenes with wooden guns. She had something of a passion for pocketknives and liked chopping with an ax—an accident even took the tip of one of her fingers; the remaining appendage she bandaged and hid from her mother. In time, Hart took up camping, tennis, hiking, rowing, and hunting. She also became an avid football fan. Likewise, because she despised domestic work, she instead took to boys' chores about the family farm at the same time that she set aside toying with dolls. She soon came to insist that she was the "man of the family" despite the fact that her mother remarried when Hart had not yet turned five. She also began behaving as such. For example, when Hart and her mother traveled anywhere in their buggy, she demanded to sit on the right side and take the reins. Hart forever intensely disliked her stepfather, but she idolized her grandfather, following him everywhere and listening to him talk politics and

agriculture with other men of the neighborhood. She particularly liked adventure stories and listened in rapt attention to those told by local men who
in years past and present traveled as far as the Klondike and as close as eastern Oregon to prospect for gold. Hart fantasized that one day she would do
the same. Always regarding herself as a boy, she early claimed that she would
be one if only her family would permit her to cut her hair and wear trousers.
During these years Hart also fell hopelessly in love with a string of domestic
servants whom the family employed. In her daydreaming she advanced from
imagined scenes in which she petted and kissed such women to fantasies in
which she had erotic relations with them, always seeing herself in what she
and her society understood to be the male role.[15]

Homeschooled when in the country, just before seventh grade Hart and
her mother and stepfather moved into Albany so that the girl might enter
upon a more routine education. Hart did not do particularly well at first. But
when students began taunting and teasing her for being skinny and unat-
tractive, she buried herself in her studies and soon became the best student
of the lot. When she graduated from high school in 1908, Hart had the highest grades in her class. During these years she developed a series of crushes
on female teachers and students she came to know.[16]

She next entered Albany College (today Lewis & Clark College and now
located in Portland), where she studied for two years. She continued to excel
in her work and became a class leader. Albany College's yearbook described
her as athletic and her command of English "fierce." It also revealed that her
dream was to live a life of "blessed spinsterhood," though the annual's editors
felt this "will be *only* dreams."[17] In fact, Hart formed a close relationship with
classmate Eva Cushman, the "society butterfly" who represented the class in
all its interclass organizations. The school's annual observed that Cushman
did not pay much attention to the boys. Another student publication took
note of her and Hart's relationship, reporting that they joked about being in
love and that they even planned to marry one day.[18] With a third classmate,
Hart and Cushman decided, "as part of their duty to the world and the rising
generation—to discard all rats and artificial puffs, and to adopt the dress-
reform style of clothing. They have not yet worn their new costumes in public, though they contemplate doing so."[19] Hart and Cushman were inseparable
by day, typically attending all functions in each other's company, and they
usually spent one night of the week together. Early in their relationship they
engaged in petting, but in time they became intensely sexual. During the

summers when Cushman was away (her parents resided elsewhere in Oregon), Hart daily wrote love letters to her.[20]

In the fall of 1910, Hart entered Stanford University. By then she had come into her inheritance from her father. She could afford to take Cushman with her, paying her lover's way as Cushman's parents could not, and all the while maintaining their affair discreetly. At Stanford, Hart began experimenting with certain articles of men's clothing and undertook what society considered to be more masculine activities—for example, drinking and smoking. These Cushman could not tolerate and their affair began to change; their love slowly subsided, though their relationship persisted for some years. Meanwhile, Hart began making regular trips to San Francisco, in fact almost every weekend, where she fell in love with the city's cabarets, cafés, theaters, and concerts. She occasionally visited the Tenderloin entertainment district and there developed a relationship with a dance-hall girl. They sometimes met at the San Franciscan's apartment, where they had sexual relations.[21]

Hart spent rather lavishly during these years, what with her trips to San Francisco and also supporting herself and Cushman. Thus, when she left Stanford in 1912 with a bachelor of science degree, she had exhausted her inheritance and faced mounting debt. She moved to Portland and found employment in a real estate office and then in a wholesale and retail butchery. In her spare time she typed, cleaned, worked wood, and built furniture. She slowly climbed out of debt but then borrowed again in order to enter the University of Oregon's Medical College, also in Portland, in 1913. Hart was the only woman in her class. As such, she experienced harsh hazing. But when she completed her medical degree in 1917, much as she had done years before to spite her classmates who had then taunted her for her looks, she did so with the highest honors in her class.[22] During these years Hart's relationship with Cushman finally ended and she had a string of intense emotional and sexual affairs with other women, each one ending for some reason or another, and some resulting in considerable misery for Hart. At one time, as a result of failed love, Hart even contemplated suicide. She tried a sexual relationship with a man, but it so disgusted her that during their first attempt to sleep together, she abruptly left in the middle of the night. That was the end of that.[23]

While in medical school Hart began perusing professional books to learn more about her gender and sexual feelings. What she read, not surprisingly, considering the era, only caused her despair. But after a period of self-condemnation, and once she had completed her studies, Hart sought professional help.[24] She turned to the rather progressive Portland physician J. Allen Gilbert, who began treating her psychologically and then medically. In fact, when Hart initially sought Gilbert's treatment, she did so ostensibly for a phobia related to the noise of shotgun fire. During their early visits, Gilbert suspected more was going on in Hart's life and one day confronted her with a question about sexuality. Hart's rather awkward response and abrupt departure led Gilbert to conclude that she would probably never return to him. But two weeks later, and after a great deal of soul-searching on her part, as Gilbert explained it, Hart "made up her mind that this was her chance to meet the difficulty and correct it, if possible; at least, to do the best for the condition that could be done."[25]

Upon consideration, Hart explained to Gilbert that she did not want any treatment that might deprive her of her masculine ambitions and tastes, as she did not want to exchange her male mental makeup for that of the "female type of mind."[26] Since Gilbert could not assure her that psychological therapy would not alter Hart's psyche, the two decided on another course: to accept the situation and move forward with completing Hart's physical and sartorial transformation into a man. Gilbert removed Hart's uterus to relieve her of the painful menstrual cramps from which she had suffered for some time, and to eliminate altogether the inconvenience of the menstrual cycle. They also thought sterilization precautionary, as it would prevent any pregnancy that might blow her cover, even though pregnancy was unlikely in Hart's case. Hart then cut her hair. She chose the name Alan, a variation on her first name. She also changed her wardrobe. Then, as Gilbert would straightforwardly put it in 1920, though all this happened in 1917, she "made her exit as a female and started as a male with a new hold on life and ambitions worthy of her high degree of intellectuality."[27]

Hart's own words, related in a remarkable 1918 interview with his hometown newspaper, confirm what Gilbert described two years later. When a reporter caught up with him at his mother's home in Albany and asked him about his "sex change," Hart explained that "I had to do it. . . . For years I had been unhappy. With all the inclinations and desires of the boy I had to restrain myself to the more conventional ways of the other sex. I have been happier since I made this change than I ever have in my life, and I will continue this way as long as I live. . . . There can be no dual sex in a person. It is either one or the other. I have long suspected my condition, and now I know."[28]

The news spread quickly. Henry Waldo Coe, a medical doctor and somewhat conservative editor of Portland's *Medical Sentinel*, reported on this "AMAZING SEX DISCOVERY" made by the Albany press. Calling this a "serious matter [that] means more than . . . gratifying the desire of a female to play the male role," Coe demanded that the doctor who operated on Hart publish his findings in a medical journal.[29] In fact, Gilbert would do just that, but a couple years later, when a suitable time had passed for any developments to appear in Hart's life and treatment that might add completeness to the picture.[30]

To be sure, Coe was partly interested in the science of it all. More, his concern revolved about the possibility that Hart, as a man, now qualified for the draft, as America was by then committed to the European war. "If Dr. Hart is of the male sex and representatives of our government say she is a male," Coe decreed, "we must accord to the doctor all the privileges of a male. If the findings should be that the doctor is of the female sex, a monstrous, inconceivable joke has been played on the children of our state who have heard the case discussed."[31] In fact, concerns that women who masqueraded as men might find their way into America's armed forces were not isolated to Coe. By now many had heard famous stories of women who had dressed as men and fought in the Civil and the Spanish-American Wars. And in fact, not long before Hart's story came to light, a Portland newspaper carried a sensational item about Samuel Ackerman, reportedly a woman from Toledo, Ohio, who had lived as a man for years and had even married a woman. Ackerman failed to register for the current draft, as he thought his female body would be discovered. Just before authorities moved in to apprehend this "slacker," Ackerman instead took his life.[32]

Upon exiting Gilbert's Portland office in 1917, Hart set out on a long medical career, one that, at least early on, had its share of difficulties for someone who had changed sexes. Sooner or later the news caught up with him. One of Hart's first appointments, already that November, was at the city hospital in San Francisco. A former Stanford classmate there soon recognized him and went about telling Hart's story. Because of the unwanted notoriety (though he had the support of hospital administration), Hart found that he had little choice but to resign his position. In the summer of 1918, Hart began a short stint as a doctor in Gardiner on the Oregon coast, but something (lost from the historical record) led him to leave under a cloud shortly thereafter. He then found a series of jobs across the West and Midwest in places such as Huntley, Montana; Thermopolis, Wyoming; Albuquerque, New Mexico; Rockford, Illinois; Spokane, Washington; Tacoma, Washington; and Boise, Idaho, all within the space of a few years.[33]

Whether problems associated with his "sex change" led to his quick turnover at these other locales is unclear, but in this light it is worth considering the following. Hart, an extraordinarily accomplished man, eventually published four novels, each related to medicine and each in its own way based on his own experiences. A minor subplot of his second, *The Undaunted* (1936), set in the fictional Northwest city of Seaforth, revolves about Sandy Farquhar, a homosexual male and, like Hart, a radiologist. In telling this character's difficult employment history, Hart undoubtedly drew upon his own. He wrote that Farquhar "stuck it out" in medical school, despite "a fellow there who'd known him in college and spread the word about Sandy." But henceforth for Farquhar, "when it came to outrunning gossip he found he couldn't do it. He went into radiology because he thought it wouldn't matter so much in a laboratory what a man's personality was. But wherever he went, scandal followed him sooner or later. . . . His story would get around and then he'd be forced to leave. 'Resigning by request' was the way he put it."[34] Because of such torment, in time Sandy suicided.

Although earlier in life Hart had considered ending it all just like his fictional Sandy, instead he persisted. He continued his studies, earning a master of science degree in radiology at the University of Pennsylvania in 1930 and a master's degree in public health at Yale. He finally found job security in the Connecticut Department of Health's tuberculosis office. He started there in 1945 and when he died in 1962 was serving as its director.[35] The pattern of Hart's personal life after leaving Gilbert's office followed somewhat the trajectory of his professional one. On 7 February 1918, under his grandfather's name, Hart married Inez Stark in Martinez, California. Inez followed her husband through his successive jobs until 1923, when she coldly left him and refused his several attempts at reconciliation. They soon divorced. Hart then found a loving relationship, his last, with Edna Ruddick. They married on 15 May 1925, in New York City. Edna survived him in death. Upon his passing, Hart's body was quietly shipped away for cremation and his ashes eventually spread on the waters of Puget Sound in Washington state.[36]

Alan Hart's biography highlights various issues that I consider in Part I. Two of the more tangled are how turn-of-the-twentieth-century cross-dressers understood themselves and how broader society and specific communities perceived their cross-dressers' sexual and gender identities. It seems clear that Hart was something more than merely a cross-dresser; both he and those around him thought this so. Medical science, at least through the eyes of the rather progressive J. Allen Gilbert, thought him a homosexual; the doctor even entitled his professionally published article about Hart "Homo-Sexuality and Its Treatment." Hart's well-documented life, however, reveals no precise term that he applied to himself. Gilbert did claim that Hart accepted his condition as "abnormal inversion"; Hart likely spoke to Gilbert using this and the term "homosexual," as they both appear in the medical record.[37] Hart also read scientific books that would have used those same terms and he referred to his fictional Sandy Farquhar as a homosexual.

What is clear is that Hart thought himself to be a man. In this light it might seem appropriate to consider him a transsexual.[38] Of course, such a term did not exist as such during the years of Hart's early life and when he underwent his "sex change." The concept of transsexual—a person who emotionally and psychologically feels that s/he belongs to the sex opposite of what his/her body socially indicates—only crystallized in the 1940s and 1950s, near the end of Hart's life, when advances in medical technology allowed such individuals the ability to surgically reshape their bodies so that their corporeality would correspond to their feelings of who they were. Since the middle of the twentieth century, transsexual identity has expanded to include those who choose not to, or are unable to, surgically change their bodies to conform with their gender identity. In the last quarter of the twentieth century, a broader concept of transgender emerged. Transgender includes the expansive definition of transsexual, but it also embraces a whole set of people who, perfectly satisfied with their bodies, nevertheless identify with the gender opposite of the one that society normally assigns to them; it also counts people who truly transcend normative gender categories—those who see themselves as neither female nor male.[39]

Transsexual was not existent as such at the turn of the twentieth century; nevertheless, that era had the concept of sexual inversion. It collapsed together the later developed notions of transsexual and transgender with (the also later more fully developed ideas of) homosexuality and even transvestism. The concept of transvestite—a desire of some people to dress as the opposite sex for reasons not linked to their gender or sexual identity—began to emerge in the scientific literature only right at the dawn of the twentieth century. Although used interchangeably with "sexual inversion" into the early years of the twentieth century, "homosexual" slowly became associated more with the object of someone's sexual desire than with how someone behaved in her/his gender comportment. J. Allen Gilbert's use of the term "homo-sexuality" alongside "abnormal inversion" in 1920 clearly shows that the former was tinged with the belief that it had something to do with gender presentation at that date.

Broader society at the time utilized terms and concepts similar to the medical profession's sexual inversion, notably man–woman and woman–man. Such terms really clue us in to how a society that held to a two-sex/two-gender model tried to come to grips with cross-dressers. Like science's sex invert, woman–man and man–woman show that society might actually perceive that a person could combine the two sexes otherwise thought to be mutually exclusive. I present any number of examples of this. But I also show that in keeping with the definitiveness of the two-sex model, nineteenth-century society and a cross-dresser's community at times closely scrutinized the cross-dresser's body in order to establish that s/he was either female or male. Henry Waldo Coe's and the Albany reporter's consideration of Alan Hart exposes this clearly. The journalist explained that Hart grew up as a girl but one day discovered his "fundamental sex organs are male."[40] Such a discovery accounts for Coe's incredulity and his demand that government representatives examine Hart's body to determine if he were really a man.[41]

I also show that cross-dressers' views on their own gender and sexual makeup varied as much as public opinion and differed as much as there were varieties of cross-dressers. Hart, whom this study holds up as transsexual, affirmed the two-sex/two-gender model. He voiced to his hometown newspaper, it will be recalled, that "there can be no dual sex in a person. It is either one or the other."[42] Hart knew he had been born with a female body, but he also knew himself to be male. In time he dressed and fully comported himself as such. Although he may have had difficulties at times with how society viewed him, evidence exposes that those surrounding him could believe him to be a man. Again, the Albany reporter evinced this: "The reporter talked with Dr. Hart this afternoon . . . and had he not known that Dr. Hart once was known as a woman he would never have given the matter a thought. Dressed in a natty, green suit, hair cut close, Dr. Hart looks the part of a man."[43]

Along these lines, queer theoretician Judith Butler pointed out some years ago that "gender is an identity tenuously constituted in time, instituted in an exterior space through a *stylized repetition of acts.*" These acts, Butler further explained, work to construct an identity, a "performative accomplishment which the mundane social audience, including the actors themselves, come to believe and to perform in the mode of belief."[44] Accordingly, when an individual in history chose certain articles of clothing and acted in ways commensurate with an idealized gender—feminine or masculine—that individual became the gender that s/he performed and her/his society viewed her/him as. When successfully wearing the clothing of the opposite sex, female-to-male and male-to-female cross-dressers in the history of the nineteenth-century West (and elsewhere) actually became, in the eyes of their society, men and women, respectively. In this way, a cross-dresser affirmed the two-gender/two-sex system.

On the other hand, and as Butler also remarked, gender "ought not to be construed as a stable identity or locus of agency from which various acts follow."[45] As such, cross-dressers could also undermine the stability of the two-sex/two-gender system, most notably when some mishap revealed the cross-dresser to have a body that did not correspond to her/his clothing (that is, gender performance).[46] Social and communal reactions recorded at those moments provide windows into period understandings of gender and, in some cases, sexuality. We can also at these times occasionally catch glimpses of how cross-dressers might understand themselves as either a person who was a male or a female, or a person who was a mix of the two sexes, or alternatively as a person who was neither male nor female. In all these cases cross-dressers subverted the binary sex/gender system, but they also oddly confirmed it.

Among the places where such moments of revelation are best recorded is in the mass-circulation press. Today newspapers are declining in importance as sources people turn to for their news. But during the place and time that this book covers, the mass-circulation press was the fundamental source of news, outside of gossip, for Americans, though it should be added that local newspapers were also filled with all sorts of gossip. In the nineteenth century any town of any size had at least one newspaper, in many cases two. The mass-circulation press is not without its limitations as a historical source, however. This book clearly demonstrates that. Nevertheless, because the mass-circulation press more than any other source provided constant news about cross-dressers, it serves as the most abundant and richest source for understanding a community's collective views on such people. Used carefully, and when possible with other sources—for example, the varied types of documents available in the case of Alan Hart—newspapers can also provide clues to how cross-dressers understood themselves.[47] I therefore employ the mass-circulation press extensively, complicating this source when needed.

The mass-circulation press also makes possible another of my tasks in Chapters 1 and 2: to show how communities and broader society reacted to the cross-dresser beyond questions of his/her gender and sexuality, though these two concerns were never far from mind. The press's coverage of Alan Hart reveals that period medical doctors, for example, could accept and support the cross-dresser as well as deride and condemn him. Some of Hart's employment history was also carried in the press. What there is of it demonstrates that he might gain support from some employers, and yet he might also be dogged by rumormongers apparently interested in titillating fellow workers. The news story about him from his hometown in 1918, furthermore, discloses that a community, or at least in this case a news reporter from a local community, could respond with objectivity to the cross-dresser. In this case the journalist plainly pointed out that "the story sounds unbelievable, but the facts are supported by documentary evidence of such a character that there is no use poo-poohing or denying" that Hart changed his sex.[48]

Before commencing our trip into cross-dressing history, I would like to clarify a few terms that I employ along the way. First, I regrettably use "cross-dresser" to refer to a large group of varied people—at one end of the spectrum individuals like Alan Hart and at the other end those who took on the garb of the opposite sex for purposes unrelated to either sexuality or gender identity. The term "cross-dresser" repeats the assumption that two immutable poles of gender and sexuality exist, and when one person from one gender and one sexuality historically took on the guise of a person of the other gender and the other sexuality, that person actually engaged in "crossing." In fact, as Alan Hart and myriad other "cross-dressers" have told us, such an act was not crossing at all but was something that came naturally to them, as they really felt themselves to be other than the sex their bodies suggested them to be.

Second, I have adopted feminine and masculine pronouns for cross-dressers according to how individuals likely viewed themselves. Therefore, I typically utilize "he," "him," and "his" (as well as the person's masculine name) when discussing biographical details of a female-to-male cross-dresser when evidence suggests that is the way he understood himself. Sometimes I switch from one gender to the other, depending on what was going on in the biography of the individual at a particular time. For example, in this introduction I began by referring to Alan Hart using feminine pronouns but switched to masculine when he finally made the decision that he was indeed a man and decided to live as such. Sometimes I put quotation marks around such pronouns when that is how sources referred to the individual, but at the time the individual seems to have thought about himself/herself differently. Sometimes I use gendered pronouns simultaneously and interchangeably when it is pretty clear that the person to whom they apply felt her/himself to be both male and female or neither.

Third, I often refer to the "progress narrative." My premise is not that all cross-dressers have been forgotten in western history; I contend that when historians, antiquarians, and the broader public have remembered them, notably female-to-male cross-dressers, they have been averse to considering the complex gender, sexual, and social meanings and realities of these people (for reasons I have outlined earlier in this introduction). In doing so, western writers have invoked the progress narrative. It normalizes the cross-dresser by maintaining that "she" changed her clothing for some purpose related to securing personal advancement in a world with a deck that was otherwise stacked against her. For example, she might have dressed in male attire to pass herself off as a man so that she could obtain better-paying employment. Perhaps she wanted to succeed in a profession that her biological sex excluded her from. Maybe she desired to follow her husband or male lover into a milieu, such as the army, which excluded women. Or a woman might also find that dressing in men's clothing could provide her safety when traveling in a male-dominated society. Humanities scholar Marjorie Garber pointed out a few years ago that the progress narrative impedes the recovery of transsexuality or transgenderism in the lives of cross-dressers.[49] Since *Re-Dressing America's Frontier Past* seeks to retrieve transgressive sexuality and gender identity in cross-dressing, I often conjure the progress narrative in it, usually to point out its limitations and inapplicability.[50]

Finally, as every American historian knows, "frontier" and "West" are problematic terms and concepts. The West might best be understood as a place, though a place that admittedly has moved around a lot and has vague boundaries.[51] In this book I consider the region classically known as the trans-Mississippi West, but sometimes I narrow my scope to the trans-Missouri West and alternately broaden my vision to include the northern Mexican borderlands and western Canada. One prevalent definition of "frontier" in

American history is that it is a process. But what it has been a process of is something that has been highly debated.[52] I at times search for the frontier as far east as New York. I also often use that term interchangeably with the West and I do so for a couple reasons. First, it is pretty clear that in the late nineteenth century (the period that I am most concerned with), the broad American public and even American sexologists understood that the West they knew was also the place where the last frontier (that they imagined) actually existed, however much it was also disappearing. Second, I am most interested in how Americans imagined the frontier and the West, in particular how they imagined them as related to who they were as a heterosexual nation. This was a process, a process about a place. And it is reflected in the vignette with which I commenced this introduction. When Horace Greeley implored young American men to "go West," he meant the West as a place. But by pairing that place with the verb "to go," he was referring to a process. Moreover, he saw both the place "the West" and the movement to it as male in nature. Along the Pike's Peak Express that he followed into his male West, Greeley encountered an otherwise nondescript fellow, a clerk heading in the opposite direction, to the East. As the male clerk moved out of the West, however, he changed into a cross-dressed woman. The clerk thus underwent a process, a process that linked two regions—the West and the East—into a binary relationship that, like the binaries of female and male, masculine and feminine, and homosexual and heterosexual, tell a great deal about how we have constructed America's geographical and historical past and have used cross-dressers to do so.

PART ONE

"Females in Male Attire, and Males in Petticoats"

*Remembering Cross-Dressers in Western American
and Frontier History*

"Known to All Police West of the Mississippi"

Disrobing the Female-to-Male Cross-Dresser

For the late spring, the evening of 3 June 1912 was unusually warm and dry in Portland, Oregon, when police there led a raid on the Yale rooming house located in a lower east-side working-class neighborhood. For their efforts, the authorities nabbed a recent arrival from Seattle who, over the years, had passed under the assumed names of Harry Allen and Harry Livingstone. Along with Allen, the police arrested Isabelle Maxwell, a known prostitute, also from Seattle, who posed as his wife and supported him on her earnings. Police had been keeping tabs on the pair for a while and during the raid reportedly discovered a telegram from Allen to Maxwell, asking her to come to Portland from Seattle. Since Allen apparently had transported Maxwell across state lines for immoral purposes, he had, in the eyes of the authorities, transgressed the Mann Act.[1] Passed by Congress in 1910, this statute was intended to curb the so-called white-slave trade, more a perceived than real problem, but one that had recently created something of a national hysteria.

Taken immediately before local authorities, Allen endured fierce questioning before the arrival of special agent Charles Pray, a federal officer who investigated white-slave cases. Within moments, Pray recognized Allen—just a few months before in Spokane, when Pray worked there as a U.S. deputy marshal, Allen had come before him, accused of selling bootleg whiskey on an eastern Washington Indian reservation. Well acquainted with Allen, Pray of course knew his given name. When the special agent called the captive by it, the prisoner broke down: "I am not a white slaver," he sobbed, "and I am not Harry Allen. I am Nell Pickerell, and I have been posing as a man for more

FIGURE 1. Harry Allen, 1912. From 1900 until his death in 1922, Seattle's Allen (sometimes Harry Livingstone) often made newspaper headlines across the nation. In June 1912 he was arrested in Portland, Oregon, as a man. When authorities determined to their satisfaction that he was actually a woman, the local press had a field day with the story. During the height of the excitement he was pictured here by a local paper and identified by his birth name, Nell Pickerell. Image courtesy of Oregon Historical Society, #105333.

than 12 years." The shocking revelation dumbfounded the local arresting authorities; they claimed that the suspect's disguise had been perfect, complete with "long stride and basso voice."[2] Federal authorities soon dropped the white-slave charges. But the local court, in lieu of an ordinance that criminalized the wearing of clothes more appropriate to the opposite sex, convicted Allen of vagrancy and sentenced him to ninety days in the city jail.[3]

Portland newspapers had a field day with the incident, not so much at the police department's expense, but rather because of Allen's arresting story. They marveled at his masculine characteristics, namely his way of walking, his speech pattern, his ability to swear, and his ease at drinking and smoking. They worked over his employment history, noting the various men's jobs he had performed through the years: bronco busting, bartending, barbering, and longshoring. They crooned over his remarkable ability to sing in a deep voice and his proficiency at playing several instruments—the piano, the violin, the guitar, and the slide trombone. The most sensational daily of the lot sponsored a debate on the question: "Should Nell be jailed for not wearing [a] skirt?" Soon realizing they had in their midst a person "known to the police of cities throughout the Northwest as the most skillful male impersonator that has operated on the Pacific Coast," journalists dug up yet more about him and his past, including his previous brushes with the law, dating back several years and across the region for cross-dressing, bootlegging, saloon brawling, and horse stealing.[4]

Considering all these details, the press boldly dubbed Allen "one of the most notorious male impersonators in the United States." That might have stretched it a bit, but in fact newspapers near and far had reported on him, making the most scurrilous statements and employing the purplest of prose, since at least 1900, when Allen had not even reached eighteen years of age.[5] For example, in June 1900 Minnesota's *Saint Paul Globe* carried the article "Wickedest Spot in the World," about Tunnel City, a Great Northern Railroad shantytown located in Washington's Cascade Range where construction workers labored on a three-mile passageway through the mountains. The paper described the camp's denizens and their effect on Tunnel City as the "scum of the West.... Murderers fleeing from justice, desperate and lawless hoboes, driven thither by the Western winter, ramblers and bunco men; saloon-keepers whose home-manufactured whiskey drives their patrons into a frenzy, and the most degraded women that Pacific seaport towns can supply, combine in making the camp an inferno." Despite the abundance of colorful Tunnel City reprobates whose lives, behaviors, and antics the *Saint Paul Globe* might have dished up to a shocked middle-class audience, the paper called out only one by name for consideration: the "incorrigible" Nell Pickerell, whose one ambition in life "is to act like a man."[6]

A few years later, on 23 February 1908, even the *Washington (D.C.) Times* carried an illustrated story on Pickerell in its Sunday magazine supplement.[7] Somewhat exaggerating its subject's celebrity, the paper contended that Pickerell "is known to all police west of the Mississippi." The article was more a cautionary tale of what happens when a woman masquerades as a man and trifles with the affections of others of her sex: the bulk of the piece focused on two suicides, Dolly Quappe and Hazel Walters, who, only after hopelessly falling for Pickerell, had become morbidly distraught upon learning their lover's true sex.[8]

> The first of her victims to end her disappointed life declared her infatuation knew no bounds. She was madly, raptu[r]ously in love with the attractive "Harry" Livingstone. The girl in man's garb played with the misguided member of her own sex as an angler with a big speckled trout until at last the secret was whispered in her ear. Her life seemed worth nothing when she learned the truth.
>
> "I love you, Harry, even though you have been to me a living lie," she cried, and shot herself to death.
>
> The second victim within a short space of a few weeks, hu[r]ried herself upon the rocks of destruction to the siren song of this woman who plays with life and death. Like a wrecker upon the beach, she placed false lights upon the shore to lure upon the treacherous sands the ships that sail the angry seas. Hazel Walters felt the lure of the girl's false personality, and in her delirium of madness drank a liquid that ended forever the disappointment that filled her life.

The *Washington Times* obscured little in describing Allen as "clever in the art of love making" to other women. Somewhat more tame than its meaning today, making love at the turn of the twentieth century nevertheless was something that society appropriately reserved for opposite sex couples, as it involved petting, romance, and perhaps declarations of intentions. Of course, such reporting salaciously called into question Allen's sexual and gender makeup. In that vein, the remainder of the piece focused on his convincing masquerade, suggesting that he had nearly become the opposite sex. Other news stories over the years likewise noted the same. Allen "is just as much like a man as can be," were the words of one, while another discovered that he "has arm[s] like a man . . . hard as nails, and exceptionally well developed."

"As a harvest hand," reported yet another, "she proved her ability to smoke, drink and frequent saloons," while another claimed Allen could "fight as good a fight as any man of her size." "She wears her hair closely cropped," maintained another, "and has the strength and rugged features of a workingman." When a Portland reporter visited him in the city jail in June 1912, he asserted that "the moisture in Nell Pickerell's eyes . . . was the only hint of the fact that she is a woman." Another jail scene rendered Allen a "lone 'man' among the women prisoners, strutting about with 'his' hands in 'his' pockets or hooking 'his' thumbs in 'his' suspenders, or adjusting 'his' tie."[9]

Over the years some newspapers went only so far in claiming that Allen had actually become a man, typically adding tidbits that still positioned femininity as somehow related to, or the cause for, Pickerell's sartorial switch. Some reported, for example, that "she" had once loved a man, if unwisely, married him, and had a child. When the relationship soured, it was "her" husband's treachery that likely led Pickerell later to flirt with women.[10] While one speculated that he took to men's clothing when a mere child due to the bicycle craze at that time, and a boy's short pants made riding easier, another theorized that Allen simply revolted against sartorial customs that prescribed the most uncomfortable and impractical getups for women. Such possibilities aside, the same source further feminized him when it reported one of his own explanations for why he wore men's clothes as a "typical woman's" non-reason: "because I want to."[11] The police, on the other hand, claimed Allen wore male attire "to better conceal her work in the underworld."[12] But the most common explanation given for Allen's masquerade proved also the most conventional trope for why women of the day passed as men: to more easily secure better paying employment. Even Allen at times said it was so.[13]

Social science of the day also worked to feminize and normalize Allen's wardrobe and behaviors. By sheer coincidence—and the historian's good luck—the very summer of Allen's incarceration in Portland, twenty-five-year-old Miriam Van Waters, an anthropology graduate student at Clark University in Worcester, Massachusetts, happened to be in Portland, her hometown, collecting data at the local jail for her doctoral thesis, "The Adolescent Girl Among Primitive People." Among the incarcerated, Van Waters encountered Allen, who supplied her with some of her most important evidence. A budding social reformer and women's rights advocate, Van Waters argued that any number of adolescent girls caught up in the penal system of the day were simply energetic and independent young women who, had they lived in "primitive" societies, such as those of the American Indian, would have been ushered into roles acceptable for such people where dressing and behaving in ways associated more with males were actually valued and supported. In turn-of-the-twentieth-century western civilization, however, such women tended to end up before the law for activities deemed unacceptable, even criminal. The fault in matters where a woman like Allen found "herself" in jail, in Van Waters's mind, lay not with the individual, but rather with modern society.[14] Specifically in Allen's case, Van Waters confidently concluded that "her criminal record appears to be the result of discrimination."[15]

Considering the dissertation's determinations, it comes as little surprise that in relating Allen's life history as "Case I" of her study, Van Waters labored to recapture certain elements of her subject's "normal" womanhood and even heterosexuality, despite also having to relate here and there Allen's masculine characteristics and adventures (and despite being a lesbian herself).[16] How much of Allen's life Van Waters reimagined, or Allen veiled when recounting it, is of course impossible to know; Van Waters's biographical sketch likely blended the two. For example, Van Waters told of Allen's marriage in her teens to an older man, a union that produced a child. (In fact, Allen never seems to have married and when she did give birth in 1898, the boy's father went unlisted and the child's birth was registered as illegitimate.)[17] When Allen's "husband" deserted "her," in Van Waters's recapitulation, Allen went to work as a domestic servant and waitress, but unable to earn enough, only then did he assume the identity of a man and find work on farms and cattle ranches, in lumber camps, and around freight depots and dock yards, earning "a man's full wages."[18] Steadfastly refusing to wear women's clothing, Van Waters asserted, it was impossible for Allen "to earn an honest and adequate living while dressed as a woman."[19] (On the other hand, Van Waters also offered hints that Allen had taken to male activities, chores, and clothing well before adulthood.) Of the reports that Allen ruined girls and that two even suicided as a result, Van Waters claimed them to be little more than apocrypha. Rather, in Van Waters's telling, Allen's life had early introduced him to women of the underworld, with whom he grew sympathetic. He took some in, returned others to their homes, and generally looked after their welfare. Supplementing this charitable assessment for Allen's interest in these women, Van Waters definitively asserted at once that Pickerell "does not exhibit homo-sexual tendencies" and reaffirmed later that he "lacks the excitability of the usual homosexual type."[20] (And yet elsewhere Lola G. Baldwin, superintendent of the Portland Police Department Women's Protective Division when Allen served time there in 1912, explained in her official reports that her charge had "an almost insane mania for making love to girls, when dressed in men's clothing" and that "she" and Isabelle Maxwell "lived together as man and wife.")[21]

Although Van Waters's findings support Allen's relatively "normal" womanhood and sexuality, and other sources of the day sometimes worked to conventionalize his behaviors, in fact most information offered up at the time, whether through news reports or the occasional legal and social science file, clearly indicated to an anxious public that Allen was, to use the common term of the time, a sexual invert. As such, "she" might have been a lesbian. Typically in the late nineteenth century and even well into the twentieth, working-class women (and somewhat later, certain middle-class women) who had same-sex desires expressed their interests by dressing as men and adopting elements of a male persona.[22] Some working-class lesbians in the early twentieth century (and beyond) also found themselves as sex workers or otherwise associated with them, as did Allen.[23]

More appropriately, Allen was a sexual invert and all that it implied. Within this expansive category, he may have leaned more toward what we now understand as transsexual or transgendered; evidence points to the fact that he saw himself as male, something that the era's term "sexual invert" could mean. In a 1912 interview, Allen maintained that as a result of living for many years as a man, he had experienced a "change of sex."[24] Even earlier he reportedly claimed to have "always played with the boys and wanted to be one of them. . . . I did not like to be a girl; did not feel like a girl, and never did look like a girl. I seemed to have nothing in common with my own sex. My hair was short and coarse. My shoulders were broad and square like a man's. . . . I put on men's clothing, and have not discarded them since."[25] He supposedly never acted as mother to his son, whose grandmother raised him, the two maintaining that the child's mother died and that Allen was in fact his uncle.[26]

Even those near Allen, and in some cases those from afar, questioned his femaleness. Particularly striking is the Portland jail matron's statement from 1912: "She looks and talks and walks and acts like a man," she recited. "Why, every time I go into the room where she is, although I know all about her, I can't help feeling that there is a man in the room. I went in there in night attire one evening, and she sat there in her street clothes, and I nearly screamed with the feeling that I had blundered into the presence of a man in dishabille."[27]

One perceptive reader of the *Portland News* in 1912 wrote a letter to the editor with only thinly veiled meaning: "A woman who is ashamed of her sex so that she masquerades in male attire," this reader argued, "should be shunned. This old story about more wages because she wears men's clothes is not the main part of the drama at all. There is many a good man who would marry such a woman as Nell Pickerell, but she will not have it that way."[28]

In Seattle in December 1922, Allen died at age forty from syphilitic meningitis. The *Post-Intelligencer* carried the obituary, which summarized his long and colorful criminal career, his varied masculine jobs, and the considerable consternation he caused the police over the years. Forever "ashamed" of being born female, the paper asserted, Allen "grew indignant when her sex was mentioned." The article included a picture of the deceased, reproduced at other times over the years, showing him wearing a derby hat, suit jacket, collared shirt, and necktie. The caption said he had been "masquerading for years as a man." The headline read NELL PICKERELL MAN-GIRL, DIES.[29] As was true with other reports about Allen over the years, this one at the conclusion of his life sprinkled throughout it uncertainty over his gender and sexual identity.

Even in death Allen remained robed in mystery, impossible for either the media or its readers to precisely categorize and comprehend. Did Allen don male clothes for economic reasons, or because *he* saw himself as a male, or because *she* wished to contest custom and law? Was Allen male or female, or a sexual invert? Did Allen's close relationships with women include a sexual component? Or did Allen simply have great sympathy for them, doing what he could with the limited means and opportunities available to him to assist them?

Such unanswered questions that hovered about Allen in life and in death make him a particularly suitable introduction to this chapter. In it I first examine the myriad reasons, in keeping with the progress narrative, that news and other period sources found, surmised, and reported for why a woman might take to male clothing. I note along the way that the press's penchant for contextualizing western female-to-male cross-dressers within the exigencies (whether real or imagined) of the American West contributed to the power of the progress narrative as explanatory tool for later historians who have considered such women in this region. Period press reports about Allen, after all, persistently embedded "her" within the western milieu or identified "her" with the region: "she" was "known to all police west of the Mississippi"; "she" was among the "scum of the West" who transformed Tunnel City into such a wicked place, a "western winter" driving "her" and other western characters (ramblers, bunco men, saloon-keepers) thither; "she" engaged in saloon brawls, bootlegging on reservations, bronco busting, and horse stealing; one period sociologist asserted that Allen's cross-gendered behaviors might best be compared to those of American Indians. Just as in life Allen's sexuality and gender complicated explanations for "her" switch to male clothing, I then seek to complicate the progress narrative by providing sexual and emotional reasons to account for at least some of the motivations compelling women to dress as men in the nineteenth-century West.

In early December 1908, right about the time when the young Harry Allen saw his local notoriety become national infamy, a considerably older Sammy Williams of Manhattan, Montana, complained of feeling ill and took to his bed. Well known and very popular throughout Gallatin County, where he had labored as a lumberjack and then a cook in logging camps for some eighteen years, Williams died on the tenth of the month, probably from apoplexy. He was about eighty. The next day the undertaker announced to a dumbfounded community that Williams was a woman. Sensational stories began circulating about him and his past. News items carried the odd report of people's occasional suspicions over the years about the deceased. For example, at times some locals had apparently "laughingly commented" that Williams had never developed a beard and that his voice was a bit weak. And yet, Williams's disguise proved otherwise flawless—he even chewed tobacco in order to complete it—so much so that no one ever really seemed to seriously doubt that Williams was anything but what he presented.[30]

This story, like so many others of its ilk during the era, circulated widely: the news of Sammy Williams quickly spread via wire service from Montana to California and then across the nation to Florida.[31] Boise's *Idaho Statesman* carried a particularly thoughtful editorial, titled "Handicapped by Sex," about the Williams case and its social ramifications. The author noted that in putting on men's clothing a woman might enjoy increased prerogatives, freedoms, and especially earning power. The piece detailed how little money a woman could really expect to make compared to a man even when working the same job. "Bound down as they are by social, domestic and other restrictions," the author opined, "it is . . . a marvel that more women have not adopted the course of 'Sammy' Williams. . . . It is a great deal quicker and more success-ful a process than any equal suffrage law that was ever framed."[32]

Plainspoken and matter-of-fact, not to mention rather forward in its thinking, the editorial focused, in keeping with the progress narrative, on the seemingly logical and pragmatic reasons that a woman might dress as a man. Oddly, however, the opinion piece did suggest that Sammy Williams was a rarity. In fact, from the time Williams first donned men's apparel and arrived in the West some fifty years prior to his death, news article after news article about female-to-male cross-dressers both near and far circu-lated constantly in the region's newspapers.

Such articles demonstrate that such women had a ubiquitous presence in the West. Even the *Idaho Statesman*, despite declaring its surprise that more women did not, like Williams, dress as men, reported a number of such sto-ries, at times carrying items on the well-known cross-dressing Civil War–veteran, feminist, and Medal of Honor–recipient Mary Walker from back East, and at other times running single pieces detailing women throughout history who disguised themselves as men and lived as such for years.[33] Just weeks before the Sammy Williams item, the newspaper presented its readers with an article about Canada's Mary Johnson, who arrived in California in the 1890s only to find it impossible to support herself, and so became Frank Woodhull. "I put on a man's suit of clothes," Woodhull divulged, "learned to walk, talk and work like a man and ever since then life has been so much more easy and pleasant."[34] A little earlier the same year, the *Statesman* told of Emma Carson, a young woman from Weiser, Idaho, arrested in Tekoa, Washington, for dressing as a man and hanging about local saloons.[35]

Editorial notes here and there in the western press evince the omnipres-ence of women who dressed as men already in the earliest years of western American settlement. "Good looking girls in male attire," warned the *Moun-tain Democrat* in Placerville, California, in 1857, "are dangerous counter-feits."[36] A few years later, in 1878, the Central City, Colorado, *Weekly Register-Call* asserted that the "mania for females to appear in male attire has struck . . . the state in a bad way."[37]

From curt editorial notes, to observations jotted down by curiosity seek-ers, to full-blown feature stories, nineteenth-century sources typically found reasons for these female-to-male masquerades in the exigencies of western

American settlement. When the editor of the *San Diego Herald* sought a boy to do menial office chores, his help-wanted ad also broadcast that "no young woman in disguise need apply." Western observer Albert Richardson, who reported this incident, elaborated that such a warning was "needful in mining country. I encountered in the diggings several women dressed in masculine apparel, and each telling some romantic story of her past life. One averred that she had twice crossed the plains to California with droves of cattle."[38]

One of the earliest recorded rationales for a woman to wear men's clothing in the West was the ease it provided as she traveled both to and through the region, whether on her own or in the company of others. While sailing on an Ohio River steamer in 1851, a "lady correspondent" for Massachusetts's *Lowell Courier* encountered four daughters of a respectable Philadelphia merchant named Springer who were clad in male attire. Their father having met with economic reversal back East, the girls accompanied him, bound for Independence, Missouri, their jumping-off point, for their planned trip across the plains to California. Aboard ship, they had already donned male clothing, garb the correspondent described as fashionable gentlemen's suits. Once they set out from Missouri, they intended to exchange these for rougher men's attire more suitable for wagon travel, but in the meantime, they had chosen a nicer masculine wardrobe, as they still found themselves in civilized regions.[39]

Safety also provided reason for women to become men as they traveled by themselves to and through the West. In Nampa, Idaho, in June 1893, for example, a lad climbed aboard a stagecoach en route to the nearby mining town of DeLamar. Claiming to be on his way from Ireland to visit his brother, the youth settled in for the last leg of his journey by perching himself in the box between the driver and a fellow traveler, Mr. A. A. Fraser. The men on either side of him exchanged several colorful yarns about life in the West that caused uproarious laughter between the two but drew little more than a smile from the boy, which the two men thought rather odd. The next day, to his considerable embarrassment, Fraser met the "boy" on a DeLamar street; he had now been transformed into an attractive twenty-year-old woman clad in a neatly fitting dress. The brother of the transatlantic and transcontinental traveler reportedly explained that his sister had adopted her disguise "as she was afraid to make the long trip . . . alone and unprotected in her customary costume."[40]

In addition to dressing as men to travel to or within the West, some women did so simply because they loved the adventure of wandering, an activity that otherwise excluded women. In the fall of 1896, the peripatetic Mrs. Georgie McRay spoke to the Kansas City press while beginning a seasonal layover there. Some forty years old and the daughter of a Pennsylvania farmer, she reported that early in life she had desired to travel, so she put on men's clothing and headed West. By the time of this interview, she had been to places such as Montana, Indian Territory, Arkansas, and Wisconsin. "I like the life I am now leading," she explained, "as it gives me a chance to see the country."[41] In explaining that McRay's "habit of tramping hither and thither has probably reached a chronic stage and is now beyond cure," reporters all but labeled her a hobo. In fact, by the first years of the twentieth century, when hoboing became chronic in America as a result of periodic economic downturns, newspapers typically used the term "hobo" or "tramp" to describe many cross-dressing women who rode the western rails.[42]

Whether as hoboes or not, throughout western history women traveled to the region in men's clothing to benefit from the opportunities the region afforded males. Take the example of Cathy Williams, a former Missouri slave who creatively altered her name to William Cathay and, in St. Louis in 1866, joined the 38th Infantry, a segregated African-American unit. Although the western military provided considerable hardships, especially for black recruits, congressional expansion of troop requirements in 1866 due to Mexican-border and Native American hostilities opened opportunities for African-American men, especially when few good alternatives were available.[43] Williams perhaps could see this and so joined up. From Missouri, the Buffalo Soldiers that she was now one of spent time at Forts Riley and Harker in Kansas and then marched the old Santa Fe Trail to New Mexico, where they served duty at Forts Union and Bayard. On occasion people have wondered about the efficacy of military intelligence and efficiency; Williams's story does nothing to assuage concerns. While a soldier, she received treatment for illness and injury in military hospitals on five separate occasions. Only during the last did those who attended her discover her true sex. She was then discharged on 14 October 1868. As for her reason to join the otherwise all-male military, she straightforwardly told the press, "I wanted to make my own living and not be dependent on relations or friends."[44]

For a brief moment during the earliest years of western settlement, specifically in mining areas, women could find, compared to elsewhere, relatively remunerative employment in respectable womanly trades (e.g., sewing, cooking, and housekeeping for the predominantly male populace) due to the old law of supply and demand—their female gender and the skills associated with it were in short supply. And yet, one of the most lucrative, albeit less honorable trades a woman could find during early years was in fact in the world's oldest profession. In this trade, ironically, many women donned male clothing. They did so not to disguise their sex, but rather to cheaply advertise it—often western women sex-workers wore men's clothing as by custom it provided an indication to others of the wearer's occupation. Among such women were the nine prostitutes of the Williams Creek district of western Canada's Cariboo gold rush who, according to an 1862 news item, put on "great airs" when they would "dress in male attire and swagger through the saloons and mining camps with cigars or huge quids of tobacco in their mouths, cursing and swearing, and look like anything but the angels in petticoats heaven intended them to be. Each has a revolver or a bowie-knife attached to her waist, and it is quite a common occurrence to see one or more women dressed in male attire playing poker in the saloons or drinking whisky in the bars."[45]

Nellie King, who had an "unsavory reputation in Minneapolis," blended feminine adornments with male attire when she made her western debut. After leading her once-respectable sister into life in a bagnio in Minnesota, she then appeared out of nowhere in the previously tranquil hamlet of Frankfort, Dakota Territory. Racing up and down the streets alternately in a training sulky and on the back of Kentucky steeds, King terrorized locals by displaying firearms, with which she maintained she could protect herself. Her true purpose for coming to town remained something of a mystery. Perhaps she was simply taking stock in hopes of setting up shop. In any case, during her forays into the street, King made "no effort to conceal her identity as a woman, wearing bracelets while otherwise dressed as a man."[46]

Some women who lived in working-class neighborhoods of large western cities where prostitution readily found a niche dressed as men and became friends, protectors, and even partners of women who made a living selling their bodies. That may have been the case of Harry Allen, for example, whom Miriam Van Waters explained did much to get women out of the demimonde. Perhaps the most infamous cross-dressing ally of western female sex workers was San Francisco's Jeanne Bonnet, reportedly a "man hater" who refused to keep company with her sworn enemies.[47] Arrested repeatedly in the 1870s for dressing as a male, Bonnet explained that she took on male garb for convenience: she worked as a frog catcher, a job for which women's apparel simply would not do. But whether on the job or not, Bonnet continuously wore men's clothing, driving local authorities to distraction. She befriended the demimonde's Blanche Beunon and induced her to leave her lover, Arthur Deneve. Angry and jealous, Deneve worked with his friend Emert Girard to kidnap Beunon's child, perhaps out of spite, perhaps in hopes of forcibly luring back his estranged lover. But Girard himself sought more, desiring to avenge his friend and pledging one day to "blow out the brains of these two harlots." Meeting up on a San Francisco street one day, Girard and Bonnet had a verbal exchange in which Bonnet pointed to Beunon and exclaimed, "Do you see that woman there? Well, her lover ran off with nine thousand dollars of her money, and I am going to induce all women to shake their lovers—such men as you are—for if they do not they will all be robbed."[48] A short time later, Bonnet and Beunon removed to nearby San Miguel. In the evening of 14 September 1876, shortly after Bonnet hopped into bed while Blanche, seated on its edge, undressed herself, several shots crashed through the boudoir's window, missing Beunon entirely but finding their way into Bonnet's body. She died shortly thereafter. Although evidence pointed to Girard and Deneve, it could never be proven and the perpetrator(s) of her murder, what local papers called an assassination, went unpunished. Any number of women from San Francisco's red-light district turned out for Bonnet's funeral.[49]

While some female sex workers in the West donned male clothing to advertise their trade, contradictorily other women saw early on that men's clothing could provide access to gainful employment without having to resort to prostitution. Such was the case for Marie Susie, a Frenchwoman who once explained that when she first arrived in San Francisco in 1850 she could not find "anything to do . . . and not wishing to lead a life of prostitution" she instead "dressed in men's clothes and went to work in the mines."[50] The habit became tradition. Years later, in 1915, the press discovered Bessie Martini operating a boat launch on the Sacramento River, and sometime before then picking hops and clearing land, all the while disguised as a man and accordingly drawing a man's pay for her labors. "I didn't like the kind of life some girls lead in a city," she explained. "I want to make an honest living."[51]

Women in the West might also dress as men to visit venues or parts of a city otherwise off-limits to a respectable woman. In 1903, San Francisco police arrested three male-garbed "lady tourists" in Chinatown. They explained that they only wanted to see the area for themselves and they understood that ladies as ladies could not do so.[52] A few years later, Eleanor Howard offered to a San Francisco judge a justification for her male dress, after her apprehension on the Barbary Coast, that mirrored her 1903 Chinatown-tourist counterparts. "She said that she was told," the papers reported, "the only way for a girl to see the Barbary Coast was in male attire."[53] In Carson City, Nevada, in 1881, "a woman arrayed in male attire" that only a few could see through, visited a gambling house to play "buck the tiger." She reportedly pocketed $300 within fifteen minutes and then disappeared.[54]

Innumerable western women also camouflaged themselves in order to perpetrate serious offenses or to disguise themselves after having broken the law. Such cases also made up an abundance of the earliest reports, dating from the 1870s through the 1890s, of women who dressed as men in the West. For example, in 1876 "Tom Johnson" came under arrest near Waco, Texas. He had arrived from the "frontier" sometime before and had become quite popular with the "young ladies of the neighborhood." Then some misfortune revealed Tom to be Ruth. Arrested as such, a few days later Johnson was set free by the justice of the peace, who could find no law forbidding a woman from dressing as a man. During the episode, Johnson explained she came from Comanche County and assumed the "disguise on account of having killed a Mexican in Brownwood," an apparent non-crime in Texas as it did not entail her continued incarceration or re-arrest.[55]

A Salmon, Idaho, rancher by the name of Harvey tutored his six daughters in the art of stage robbery. Dressed as men, they took down a number of targets in the early 1890s. So as not to attract attention, this family of cross-dressing bandits shipped back to the East for sale whatever non-tender they recovered. Not certain of the outlaws' identities but suspicious of Harvey, the sheriff laid a successful trap for them in the spring of 1892. Their capture reportedly caused quite the sensation.[56] This story is likely apocryphal, dreamt up on a slow news day to help fill a leftover column. But as such, it demonstrates yet again the penchant of the press to place cross-dressing women at the heart of certain episodes entirely western in nature.

Sometimes women dressed as men in order to commit murder, or acted as accomplices in the crime. In 1912, seventeen-year-old Winnie Brownell of

Culdesac, Idaho, cut her hair short and donned male attire not so much to disguise herself in committing her crime, but to accompany her twenty-five-year-old husband on foot for a hundred-mile trek to exact revenge on her stepfather, A. Neeves, who she claimed had abused her on several occasions. The Brownells located their prey at a ranch outside Colfax, Washington. When the opportunity presented itself, the two approached the house and sprung their deadly trap. Brownell shot his stepfather-in-law five times. But because Winnie wanted to do the actual killing, while her stepfather lay struggling on the porch she fired one final shot directly into his head.[57]

The major crime the press most often reported for cross-dressing women was their involvement with horse stealing, an offense easily cast as western. A sheriff's posse in Lake County, Colorado, shot a horse thief on the upper reaches of the Arkansas River during a chase in the summer of 1878. When they examined the body, they learned their victim was a woman dressed as a man. She rode a blooded mare, wore pants and boots, and carried two six-shooters and a bowie knife in her belt. Employing regional parlance, authorities reported she had shown "true grit."[58] In another episode, this one in 1892, two ranchers from Sierra County, Texas, missed a number of horses and tracked them and the thieves to the Rio Grande. In a pitched gun battle, they killed one rogue and injured a second. The third they captured. To the surprise of the ranchers (and the excitement of the local press), their captive turned out to be Alice Parker, a Texan, whom the press pawned off as particularly western by calling her the "Kid" and noting the huge six-shooter she carried in her belt.[59]

Many western women also donned male attire for some reason related specifically to their relationships with men. Several news reports from the day described women in the East who took to men's clothing to track to the West a "man who betrayed her" and then absconded to the region.[60] Others described horrific episodes in which abused women from the East were clothed as men by their husbands or paramours, probably to help disguise their kidnapping, and then forcibly taken to the West as little more than captives.[61] Papers might also describe western women who were found in male clothing as seeking a way to escape from a husband for whatever reason.[62]

Other women might change to men's clothing and head West to escape from families who disapproved of their choice in marriage. On 20 September 1878, for example, as an alderman and the police chief walked along the Brazos River in Waco, Texas, they spied a boy whose appearance raised suspicions, and took him in for questioning. To their consternation, they quickly learned that their prisoner was a young woman. She explained she came from a wealthy and prominent family in Missouri. When a brother-in-law there objected to her planned marriage, she and her intended fled to Texas, where they soon married anyway. Some weeks before the city officials discovered her walking aimlessly along the Brazos, "hearing that her relatives were on her track, she was obliged to adopt this disguise to escape from them and save herself and her husband from their wrath."[63]

On the other hand, some western marriages came to naught over crossdressing. In Laramie County, Wyoming, in 1906, Anna Duxsted demanded a divorce, claiming that, among other things, "her husband compelled her to wear men's clothing and to tend his flocks of sheep during the severe winter weather." In a cross-petition, Mr. Duxsted denied the charge and complained bitterly of Anna's extreme cruelty toward him, frequently attacking him with her fists and even threatening to shoot him. On one occasion, Mr. Duxsted's petition contended, Anna "stabbed him with a table fork because he asked her if she had oatmeal for dinner."[64]

The Duxsted incident—a vignette involving cross-dressing, marriage, and what passes for love—is apparently no exception to the old rule that every story has two sides. Among the more interesting of this genre concerns a woman dubbed "Bronco Liz," a name ripe with regional color. Both versions of the tale agree in their conclusion that, in March 1889, Liz shot and killed her husband, Charles Skeels. How the two stories arrive at this conclusion is a different matter. One claims that Liz and Charles met in the Coeur d'Alene, Idaho, mining district. At the time, Skeels was married with two children, but his affections for Liz led him to dump his wife and dress his newly intended in men's clothing in order to run away with her. As such, the two made their way first to Charles's father's nearby ranch, then to Choteau, Montana, and finally to Moscow, Idaho. There they married in 1888, Charles in the meantime having secured a divorce from his first wife. Shortly thereafter the newlyweds removed to Spokane and soon Charles's wandering eye fell upon a variety actress named Frankie Howard. Early one morning, Liz tracked him to a building known as Actors Flat, where he and Frankie had spent the night. As he exited his love nest, Liz shot him three times.[65]

The alternate tale holds that Bronco Liz took an obsessive interest in Charles, pledging to marry him despite the fact that he already had a wife, not to mention two children. To ward off Liz's bold advances, Charles sought refuge at his father's ranch. But Liz donned men's clothing, secretly followed her love interest, quietly taking a job as a cowboy and then ranch foreman as she plotted her next move. Before she made it, however, Charles caught wind of Liz's presence and escaped to the Coeur d'Alene mining country. Doggedly, Liz tracked him thither, this time taking on a job as a mule-team driver, again disguised as a male, to get closer to him. Soon again catching wind of Liz's proximity, Charles this time lit out for Montana and then for Moscow, Idaho, each time keeping just one step ahead of his tenacious, trouser-togged tracker. Finally at the latter location, wearied and dispirited by the chase, he simply gave up, got a divorce from his wife, and married the woman who had for some time now pursued him back and forth across the northern Rockies.[66]

But the marriage proved unhappy, as they tend to be in such cases. According to this version of the preposterous tale, after she wed, Bronco Liz became a "tigress" with a newfound "power of holding her victim in her clutches." Should he disobey her, she frequently warned, she would kill him, which is of course what happened in Spokane.[67] This latter version of the story, told more from the perspective of a wronged male, does not specify why Bronco Liz ultimately shot Charles. That her sensational trial ended in her acquittal suggests, however, which of the two stories is the more accurate.[68]

Considering the above cases, the logical and practical reasons a woman might change to male attire seem to make sense of female-to-male cross-dressers. This was especially so in the nineteenth-century West, where men predominated, where better-paying work was male centered, where prostitution was seemingly all that was available to a woman, where traveling alone imperiled a woman, where love could be requited (or love gone wrong could be escaped), and where excitement lay for the adventurous female. With such reasons, typically reported by the press with western-flavored plot twists, it is no wonder that the progress narrative might easily be invoked to explain female-to-male cross-dressing in the West. But digging deeper than these widely scattered surface deposits, one strikes a bonanza of evidence revealing that female-to-male cross-dressers undertook a change of wardrobe to help them better express feelings of sexual and gender difference.

As the case of the colorful Bronco Liz attests, the accuracy of newspaper reports about cross-dressers is highly suspect. Oftentimes at the turn of the twentieth century, American journalism proved less a science than an entertainment. Reports on cross-dressers were typically written and edited by male journalists who worked with tidbits of alternately priggish and racy information. Sometimes they fabricated entire stories. Seldom did they objectively report their subject's own feelings. They also interviewed people who likely hid the truth given the circumstances. Their articles, produced with the intent to sell more newspapers, were typically, at least in the West, deeply imbued with regional flavor. Thus newspapers make poor sources for discovering the truth about female-to-male cross-dressers (if such a thing can be said to exist). This is especially so when it comes to issues related to sexuality and gender feelings and identities.

Not surprisingly, historians of female sexuality and of the evolution of a modern lesbian identity have been particularly critical of what turn-of-the-twentieth-century American newspapers can really tell us about these matters. The mass-circulation press typically portrayed women with "queer" (a term often used at the time)[69] sexual interests as mentally unstable, dangerous, and even violent, as the historian Lisa Duggan has shown in the influential 1890s case of Alice Mitchell. Furthermore, Duggan maintains, the newspaper depoliticized, trivialized, and marginalized these women's aspirations "for political equality, economic autonomy, and alternative domesticities." Duggan has also shown that newspapers of the day profoundly influenced period medical experts, the so-called sexologists, who focused their scientific energies on studying sexuality and discovering the etiology of perversions such as homosexuality, or what was more typically at the time called sexual inversion. From some of the most biased items gleaned from the mass-circulation press, and never having examined the subjects themselves, sexologists sometimes created entire case studies, analyses that invariably pathologized female sexual inverts and subsequently influenced modern psychology.[70]

Sexologists aside, journalists and news editors of the day did realize that women could dress as men for all sorts of reasons not linked necessarily to either their sexuality or to their gender feelings. They also did not always trivialize or marginalize these women's economic and political aspirations— one need only recall the *Idaho Statesman*'s sympathetic editorial about Montana's Sammy Williams. Moreover, newspapers, so ubiquitous in America at this time, undoubtedly had a substantially more profound influence on popular views about cross-dressing than did sexological reports. With all this said, it is true that by the closing years of the nineteenth century, newspapers increasingly linked women's cross-dressing to matters of sexuality. Earlier, from the 1850s into the 1880s, cross-dressers' sexuality, unless related to matters of prostitution, concerned the mass-circulation press much less so, if at all. This is hardly surprising, considering what we know about the late nineteenth century. It was then that, thanks to a host of reasons, including the influence of the new field of sexology, western society really began developing its binary sexual system, one that divided people into and assigned to them the categorical identities of homosexuality and heterosexuality. Along with this development came the acceptance (still with us today, but eroded over time) that people's gendered behaviors might very well indicate their sexuality— thus, if one wanted to dress as a man, it was because she (or he) also had "male" sexual feelings, that is, desires for a woman.

This is not to say that earlier in the era society entirely escaped from sexual anxieties that cross-dressing raised. Consider what happened in 1851 when the "lady correspondent" for Massachusetts's *Lowell Courier* meditated on the four Springer girls, each clad in male attire and making their way west on an Ohio River steamer. The journalist described the young women, despite their clothing, as entirely ladylike and said that the other passengers on board, except one, found nothing disconcerting about either their choice of garb or their conduct. This called to the reporter's mind the potentially problematic proposed visit to the United States by Helene Marie Weber, a European women's rights reformer who donned male attire and sought to abolish distinctions in clothing between the sexes. The newspaper correspondent's pleasant interaction with the Springer girls and other passengers assured her that Weber might visit the country without causing undue alarm. She cautioned readers, however, "not to keep your eyes so intently upon her person, or you will be sure to fall in love with her. She is the beau ideal of a handsome gentleman, and I could never desire to see her in female dress."[71]

These concerns prove relatively innocent when compared with anxieties expressed in the popular press later in the century. Sometime by the 1880s the shift began to occur. Thus, we could have the following 1889 story from

Aspen, Colorado, about a relationship between two women, one of whom proposed cross-dressing. A seventeen-year-old girl, referred to in the press as Belle, protested to her father about the unwanted attentions of her twenty-eight-year-old cousin, Blanche. The younger woman complained that Blanche "hugs and kisses and squeezes me nearly to death. She won't let me out of her arms after we go to bed, and presses me so close to her I can hardly breathe. She says if I don't marry her she will kill me, and talks so strange I have grown afraid of her." When questioned by her uncle, Blanche responded calmly that she indeed loved Belle and "just as strong as the love of man ever was for woman . . . and I am ready to prove it with my heart's blood." Although Blanche was not a cross-dresser in the same way as others in this chapter, the newspaper did inform, in the process masculinizing Blanche, that she tried to convince Belle that they could marry, reportedly claiming, "I will dress as a man and as I am somewhat masculine in appearance and figure, I think we can carry out the plan to perfection." The local paper described Blanche's "mad infatuation" for Belle as beyond even that of a man for a woman. It was, in short, "monstrous" and an "unnatural affection."[72]

But in earlier years, and even at times beyond 1889, showing that the transition occurred unevenly and over a space of time, when the mass-circulation press discovered women who dressed as men, it typically feminized them, often by focusing on their womanly bodies and appearances once their disguises failed them. For example, in the 1878 Waco case when officials came upon the boy walking along the Brazos River, they soon spied a more rounded contour "especially about the bust." Suspicious, they took the boy in for questioning. In jail, the individual transformed into a remarkable beauty. "He, or rather she," the officers discovered, possessed a "fine figure, a graceful waist, voluptuous form and . . . medium height; a swelling bust, beautiful, expressive blue eyes, handsome features, and teeth of pearly whiteness."[73]

A year later, various newspapers circulated the story of Annie Harris M'Keene. Years before, she had joined William Quantrill's raiders, marrying one of the men who belonged to this band of Confederate guerillas that roamed the Missouri countryside killing Union sympathizers and burning the towns they inhabited. She involved herself in many of the gang's bloody activities, all the while disguised as a man. Nevertheless, "she was rather pretty." While dressed as a man, she one day literally displayed her feminine wiles in order to escape the law. At the very time authorities shot Annie's husband and closed in on her, she removed her hat and exhibited her long, flowing hair, stopping her pursuers dead in their tracks.[74] Likewise, Nellie Pickett, who donned male attire and terrorized New Mexico Territory in concert with Billy the Kid, was nevertheless "beautiful," and thus a newspaper headline in 1882 would refer to her as "A Pretty Female Bandit."[75] And Geneva Sadler, whom Texas authorities brought in for horse stealing in 1891 and who wore male clothes for some time, became "tall and graceful with deep blue eyes and short fair hair" when the sheriff uncovered her true identity.[76]

Such reports clearly reveal that in earlier years a woman's cross-dressing did not automatically indicate some hidden masculine identity or sexuality. Too, partly these tales of the cross-dresser's feminine beauty related to the fact, or rather to the belief, that such individuals truly did not purport to *be* men or dally with other women's affections. The "boy" authorities picked up along the Brazos River turned out to have donned male attire to protect herself and her husband from a disapproving family. Annie M'Keene married one of Quantrill's gang members. Nellie Pickett was married to Tom Pickett, one of Billy the Kid's cronies. After authorities killed Tom, Nellie became the mistress of Charles Bowdre. After he bit the dust at the hands of a posse, Nellie became the Kid's lover, or at least this is how newspapers depicted her romantic trajectory.[77]

The much deeper cultural implication to this feminization and heterosexualization of western women who dressed as men is examined in considerable detail in Chapter 3.[78] But here let us say that, in part, a cross-dresser's depiction in the press as truly feminine had at least something to do with historical timing. As the nineteenth century waned, society attached increasing sexualized and gendered meaning to female-to-male cross-dressing, and while descriptions of the cross-dresser's feminine beauty continued to appear through the end of the era, more and more news items zeroed in on, as they did in the case of Aspen's Blanche, the "masculine" qualities of the cross-dressers' bodies, appearance, activities, and, in time, sexuality.

In this light, Helen Forslund is something of a transitional figure. Known as the "Montana Terror," Forslund early fell in with highwaymen and gamblers and reportedly went on a bloody crime spree across not just Montana, but Washington, Idaho, Wyoming, Utah, and Colorado as well.[79] She wore men's clothes and variously called herself Charles and Bert Miller. She committed most of her crimes, however, alongside Henry Clark, sometimes described as her lover and at other times as her husband (not that they were mutually exclusive). When the Helena city marshal arrested Helen in 1891, he required her to put on women's clothing. Upon doing so, "she presented a stunning appearance" with petite figure and blond hair.[80]

While these descriptions of Forslund's appearance and romantic associations are in keeping with earlier news accounts that secured the cross-dresser's true womanhood, others concomitantly anticipated what became more common by the later 1890s. These alternate reports claimed that Forslund's "walk was that of a man; in fact her every appearance was of a masculine nature. Not coarse or loud, but she, when in male attire, with her short-cropped hair, would easily be taken for a young man." Furthermore, newspapers also found it necessary, whether true or not, to report that as a child Forslund supposedly disliked the company of girls and only associated with boys. "In fact," one claimed, "she was regarded as a 'Tomboy,' and there were but few about who could climb a tree, ride an unruly horse or play marbles better than she." One day she put on a set of her brother's clothes, looked in the mirror, and decided she made "a better-looking boy than . . . girl," and that was that.[81]

By the 1910s, newspapers' efforts to increasingly masculinize western cross-dressers had become clear. In 1912 when juvenile court officers apprehended Lucille Murphy near Los Angeles for posing as a man and working as a field hand, a news item explained she easily passed as a boy on account of her "muscular build."[82] In 1927, authorities in Butte, Montana, learned that Jack Moret, whom they had jailed several times for refusing to give up men's clothing, was working on a cement crew in Lewistown. The press explained that Moret's employer's ignorance of "her" true sex could be accounted for by the fact that "she" made "a husky young man."[83] In Portland, the troublesome Carmen Fells occasionally did resort to wearing women's clothing, but when she did so in Montana in about 1910, authorities picked her up because they thought she was really a boy masquerading as a girl. In 1911, Portland police officer Lola Baldwin confirmed how such a mistake might be made, declaring that "Carmen makes a much better looking boy than girl."[84] Similarly, a couple years before, papers reported in Council Bluffs, Iowa, that Freddie Adams looked ill at ease when putting on female clothing. "She makes a better appearance in male attire," the newspaper said, "than in the reverse and makes a jaunty appearance in trousers."[85]

In addition to addressing outward appearance, newspapers also more and more focused on the masculine behaviors of cross-dressers as the twentieth century began. Harry Allen's and Sammy Williams's chewing of tobacco, smoking, drinking, swearing, and the like made for particular note, and one of the reports on Helen Forslund, which described her remarkably manly appearance, further divulged that she too engaged in these typically male activities.[86] Jack Moret supposedly had a "predilection for 'whacking' man's sized cigars."[87] And Chicago's Ruth Myer, whom Denver authorities picked up in 1914, reportedly "appeared as the ordinary boy. She frequented pool rooms and bars and smoked cigars."[88]

To be clear, newspapers early on reported such masculine activities of women who dressed as men. For example, when California's stagecoach-driving Charley Parkhurst, who had lived as a man since the 1850s, died in late 1879, newspapers both near and far covered the sensational deathbed discovery of his female body. They explained that for years Parkhurst "smoked, chewed tobacco, drank moderately, played a social game of cards or dice, and was 'one of the boys.'" But lacking in the Parkhurst account was something more common in later reports: smoking, gambling, and tobacco chewing typically accompanied a cross-dresser's dalliances with other women.[89] Seattle's Harry Allen made the *Washington (D.C.) Post* and other papers across the country for the combination of such activities. But there were others, including in 1893 Mary Lease (not the same as the famed Mary Ellen Lease) of Atchison, Kansas, "who drinks beer, smokes cigarettes and runs around with the boys... often dons male attire and flirts with the girls on the streets, and captures their hearts by her dashing manner."[90] San Francisco's Gypsy Harwood, asserted a paper in 1914, "smoked cigarettes [and] flirted with other girls on the street."[91] When Butte, Montana, police arrested cigar-smoking and cross-dressing Jack Moret in a hotel room, he was rather salaciously reported to be wearing nothing more than BVDs (culturally known as men's underwear) while a young woman, a "performer at cheap cabarets," reclined in bed.[92]

Reports that included anxieties over the same-sex sexual activities of female-to-male cross-dressers, even if they did not also reference tobacco smoking, booze imbibing, and card playing, appeared increasingly in the press during these later years. Lake City, Iowa's Shirley Martin, whom papers interestingly reported also to have had a feminine appearance, nevertheless dated women, having taken them to picture shows and other amusements as well as having treated them to ice cream. Although in a 1912 news article Martin claimed never to have received a proposal of marriage, she all the same asserted that "I might have won a wife if I had tried very hard though."[93] The next year, Florence Leisher disguised herself as a sailor in

Oakland, California, and took to the streets, reportedly flirting with several girls who "fell for the soldier suit right away." Arrested for masquerading as such, Leisher was not allowed by the jail matron into the women's quarters. "She told me," Leisher reported to the papers, "I was too good-looking a soldier boy to trust in there until I changed my clothes."[94]

This account, of how Leisher's manly clothing and appearance could have a consequential effect on incarcerated women, serves as a particularly good example of one, if not the greatest, fear of men (and the largely male-produced press) of the period: the loss of male privilege to the "New Woman"—the turn-of-the-century female who pressed for reform, whether it be in sartorial custom, employment, or political rights. The New Woman's assault, in the eyes of the press and even sexological science, was manifold. Two of the more dangerous elements of this attack were, one, she might very well sexually transform into a man, casting her spell on other women, such as it was feared the cross-dressing Florence Leisher might do in the Oakland jail. Sexological science at the time dubbed such women viragints, a term often used specifically to equate feminism with female-to-male sexual inversion and thus to undermine the former.[95]

A second threat the New Woman posed was the complete disruption of the male and female relationship by becoming unnaturally ascendant in it. Thus, the *New York Times* in 1885 expressed concern over a "queer project" in which a group of women planned to create an all-female colony in Colorado's San Luis Valley. The colonists had considered neither putting up barbed wire nor placing "Amazons" on watch to keep men out. But the paper concluded that men would likely avoid the place in any case, as there they would no doubt be permitted only understeward duties and would have to resign themselves to being overshadowed from the beginning.[96] On a more personal level came a San Francisco man's divorce petition in 1912. He claimed that his wife's "mania to pose as a man" inflicted cruelty on him. Or, as the newspaper explained it, the wife's wearing of her husband's coat, pants, and hard hat in the end served to demonstrate clearly that she "wore [the] trousers" in the relationship, something entirely unacceptable, as it usurped the (reputedly natural) male role.[97]

By the 1890s, the mass-circulation press clearly raised sexual and gender questions about female-to-male cross-dressers. Such reports, however problematic, provide the most abundant sources and evidence we have for deciphering their sexual and gender identity. When these reports are treated carefully and compared with non-news sources (when they exist), we can perhaps learn something about the truth (if there is such a thing) of these issues. Papers said that Harry Allen, for example, confessed to having "always played with the boys and wanted to be one of them" and how "she did not feel like a girl."[98] Direct quotations (supposedly) from Allen included the revelation that "I have been posing as a man for . . . years. I can't wear women's clothes. I have worn these so long and walked and talked like a man for so many years it would be impossible for me to make another change of sex."[99] All this evinces that Allen likely had, to use our more modern parlance, a transgender identity.

This longtime Seattleite was among the more unusual cross-dressers of the era in that he drew a great deal of press attention over several years precisely because of his persistent transgendered behaviors and appearance. But newspapers also reported on others along similar lines. For example, the Oakland press carried a story in 1912 of the arrest of four young women for masquerading as men on Halloween. While three of these adolescent females gave "demure replies" as to why they did what they did, one sixteen-year-old among them boldly asserted that "ever since I remember I have wanted to be a boy, and this was my first chance." She defiantly stated, furthermore, that not just on Halloween, but every day of the year she planned to continue to wear male attire.[100]

Another who received ample news coverage was Milton Matson, whose given name the press in 1895 related with a flourish as Louise Elizabeth Myrtle Blaxland Matson.[101] Arresting him for attempting to obtain money under false pretenses, only after he ended up in the San Jose jail did authorities discover that they had a woman rather than a man on their hands. Officers were not exactly sure for some time, however; Matson's voice and smooth face suggested his femininity, but on the other hand his air of swagger and pipe smoking helped to cloud suspicions for a while.[102]

Over several weeks, Milton's story evolved. In extensive newspaper interviews, he divulged that he had dressed as a male for upward of twenty-six years, traveled the world from England, his birthplace, to India and then Australia, always as a man, and finally to the West Coast of the United States in roughly 1893. He explained that his parents had dressed him as a boy when he was very young, after his twin brother's death and supposedly for inheritance purposes. Whatever the reason, and the truth, Matson reportedly told journalists that wearing boys' clothes "seemed natural to

FIGURE 2. Milton Matson, 1895. Alternatively known as Louise Elizabeth Myrtle Blaxton Matson, Milton was arrested in San Jose, California, on a charge related to a mix-up over his gender. Only after he ended up in jail did local authorities find out he had the body of a woman. In a jailhouse interview, Matson divulged to a shocked public that he enjoyed carrying on flirtations with women and found it "a real joy to make love to them." Image from the *San Francisco Examiner*, 10 February 1895.

me from the first."[103] Like other female-to-male cross-dressers mentioned above, Matson asserted that he always felt like more of a boy than a girl, detested playing with girls' toys, enjoyed hunting and outdoor amusements, and, in short, always had masculine tastes and the appearance to match.[104]

Part of the sensation of his arrest revolved about the story of his engagement to Miss Helen Fairweather, a local schoolteacher who claimed she never thought Matson was anything other than a man. "I was loved," said Fairweather, defending herself to the press, "and that it was not a man is no fault of mine."[105] Matson's dalliances with Fairweather led newspapers to quiz him about his past relationships with other women. "Yes, I like the ladies," Matson responded. "It was lots of fun carrying on flirtations . . . and a real joy to make love to them."[106]

Newspaper reports on Matson, apparently influenced by Matson himself, are remarkably suggestive on the issue of his gender and sexual identity. Precisely twenty years later, the California press and its then subject of inquiry had both become more exact in decoding the gender identity of the cross-dresser. By then the role of sexological science, moreover, had become unequivocal. In late August 1915, after a lengthy undercover investigation, the Los Angeles police arrested Eugene De Forest, a local professor of dramatic arts, for masquerading as a man. He claimed to have dressed that way for the previous twenty-five years. News items referred to him, as they did Nell Pickerell at about the same time, as a "man-woman." One noted that science was trying to solve the mystery of someone like De Forest.[107] Another mentioned that De Forest's stepmother, Alida C. Avery, was a medical doctor and a prominent western suffragist. In calling attention to this relational fact, the report alluded to the period claim made by sexological science that the spread of viraginity could in part be traced to feminist mothers' influence on their daughters.[108]

Even De Forest utilized one of the era's classic sexological renderings for the female-to-male sexual invert by describing himself as "a woman with the soul of a man."[109] In explaining his history, De Forest believed his condition partly derived from his biological mother, who, when pregnant with him, hoped and hoped for a boy to replace her young son, who had just died. Then born with the instincts of a boy but the body of a female, De Forest claimed he had always wanted to be entirely masculine. De Forest did marry a man at age nineteen, but only for companionship, consenting to marriage if his intended understood their relationship would remain entirely platonic. It did and the two had no children. When the husband died, De Forest took on male clothes and subsequently lived as a man, eventually marrying a woman. That relationship ended in divorce, but by the time of his 1915 arrest, he had become engaged to yet another woman.[110]

The determination of some female-to-male cross-dressers to persist in the wearing of men's attire even after being revealed, despite unwanted celebrity, police harassment, and incarceration, also suggests that some truly saw themselves as male. Harry Allen falls into this category, as do Eugene De Forest, Milton Matson, and Jack Moret.[111] Another notable example is California's Jack Garland. Born Elvira Virginia Mugarrieta in San Francisco in 1869, daughter of the Mexican consul in San Francisco and granddaughter of a Louisiana Supreme Court justice, Garland first came to public attention as

BABE BEAN.

FIGURE 3. Jack Garland, 1897. Born Elvira Virginia Mugarietta in San Francisco in 1869, Jack (at times affectionately called Babe Bean) was a well-known figure in the Bay Area until his death in 1936. So as not to be arrested as a woman trying to disguise her sex, Garland freely admitted he was a woman who chose to wear men's clothing without the intention of deceiving. In fact, he usually did; for example, he served as a male nurse in the Philippines during the Spanish-American War. Image from *Stockton (California) Evening Mail*, 8 October 1897.

a man in Stockton, California, in 1897. Perhaps due to his rather advanced education and family background, Garland knew a thing or two about dressing as a man and how such an act related to the law. Cleverly, so as not to be annoyed by authorities for hiding his true sex in clothes otherwise considered masculine (which was against local law), Garland told them straight out that "she was not disguising her sex" at all, fully admitting that "she was a girl."[112] Not purporting to be other than a female, Garland was left alone, at least by the law. Affectionately called Babe Bean and Beebe Beam by the locals, Garland became quite the Stockton celebrity, eventually hired by the *Stockton Evening Mail* to write a lengthy series of social and political articles. One of these even told the story of Garland's visit and interview with the California governor.[113] In December 1897 a visit occurred from Garland's mother, important for its revelations about his identity. From her the *Stockton Evening Mail* learned that its employee had been a "tomboy" from early in life, "never caring anything at all for the many little trifles which usually interest and delight youthful femininity," and preferred the company of boys over other girls.[114]

Garland's story continued well beyond his days in Stockton. In 1899 during the Spanish-American War, he stowed away as a pantry-boy on a steamer bound for the Philippines. His sex accidentally discovered on board, he was arrested but escaped and found his way into the armed forces near Manila as a male nurse. Upon returning stateside, Garland told his remarkable story in the 21 October 1900 edition of San Francisco's *Sunday Examiner Magazine*.[115] For the next three decades, Garland continued to live as a man in the San Francisco Bay area. Although he died as a man on 19 September 1936, Garland apparently did not go to his grave dressed as one, reports suggesting that his interfering sister from Los Angeles made sure of that.[116]

The persistence and fortitude of Garland and several others discussed here once again call to mind Oregon's Alan Hart. But it is not only their tenacity in wearing men's vestments that parallels Hart's, it is also their childhood's boyish pursuits, their various masculine activities and behaviors as adults, their view of themselves as men, and for some of them their sexual relationships with women. Hart might be easier to see as transsexual (or to use the period's terminology, sexually inverted); his own words about himself appeared apparently unaltered in the press, and his treatment by a remarkably progressive physician who helped transform him into a man eventually saw print. Judged against Hart, it might be difficult to see others of these individuals as transsexuals. But keep in mind that Hart had certain financial and educational advantages and medical care not necessarily available to others, particularly those who, like Pickerell and Moret, hailed from the working-class. This is not to suggest that Hart found himself on easy street; the heart-wrenching difficulties he endured throughout his life speak otherwise. Still, we know so much more of the details of his story because of his class and other advantages. Had Harry Allen, for example, had access to the same resources, we might have incontrovertible evidence about him. Instead, what we do have are occasional interviews and a number of news stories, mostly filtered through biased social-science researchers and sensational journalists.

Another way to gauge the gender and sexual identity of cross-dressers is by examining what their communities thought about them. Sammy Williams lived, worked, and was accepted as a man in the West for some fifty years, the last eighteen of which he spent among the people in and about Manhattan, Montana. Charley Parkhurst, born about 1815 in New England, lived with an uncle's family on a farm until an altercation drove him away. He put on boys' clothes to make his own way and never took them off. As such he worked as a coachman in Providence, Rhode Island, and then drove wagons in Georgia. He arrived in Santa Cruz, California, in about 1856. For the next fifteen years he drove a stagecoach with routes that took him to Oakland, San Juan, Mariposa, Stockton, and San Jose. Then for a short time he operated a stage station and saloon near Watsonville and, in the last years of his otherwise solitary life, took up farming and wood-chopping. Always considering him "one of the boys," no one ever seems to have suspected he was other than a man. His friends and neighbors found out only when he died in late December 1879.[117]

While Charley Parkhurst and Sammy Williams may have had the bodies of women, they were known as men in their communities. Even when men were revealed to be women, sometimes communities seemed to continue to see such individuals as male, or at least not entirely female. This is perhaps best seen in Jack Garland's story, but evidence for it can be found elsewhere as well. Struck with pneumonia in 1905, octogenarian Charles Vosbaugh had little choice but to seek treatment at the San Raphael hospital in Trinidad, Colorado, a town in and around which he had lived for decades. The attending physician discovered his physical sex, with the news soon leaking and causing quite the excitement. Due to his advanced age and enfeebled condition, Vosbaugh remained at the hospital for the next two years, which proved to be his last, doing light work and receiving regular visits from a family who had recently employed him as a sheepherder, suggesting they had no problems with Vosbaugh's "masquerade." More to the point, the nuns at the hospital where Vosbaugh lived out his remaining days affectionately dubbed him "Grandpa," indicating their continued acceptance, at least to some degree, of Vosbaugh's masculinity.[118]

Vosbaugh lived in the Trinidad area for years. He operated a restaurant there with his wife and then worked alongside other locals in the livestock industry. His continued kindly treatment after the discovery of his female anatomy suggests that some communities might respond positively to revealed cross-dressers who were deeply enmeshed in them. Vosbaugh's experience contrasts markedly with someone like the considerably more peripatetic Harry Allen, who became something of a pariah. There were other differences between Vosbaugh and Allen, however. The latter toyed with women's affections and, at least reportedly, inhabited the netherworld where crime was part of everyday life. Vosbaugh, on the other hand, was well known and liked, and found respectable employment, and his relationship with another woman reportedly found its origins in the most honorable of reasons: he felt compelled to save the woman's reputation, which had become imperiled by a pregnancy.[119]

In fact, Vosbaugh may have been something of an anomaly. Once the news got out in 1911 about Ray Leonard, a shoe repairman in Lebanon, Oregon, who was approximately sixty-two at the time and had lived in his community for decades, the men who had previously befriended him and made his cobbler's shop something of their social headquarters refused to gather there anymore. Some in town even crossed the street to avoid meeting or speaking with him. When a local woman, now somewhat elderly and over whose hand Leonard had once wrangled with another, learned of her old beau's secret, she supposedly remarked, "Why the old !@#*!"[120]

Such responses raise the issue that sometimes revealed cross-dressers who were embedded in their communities might also become the butt of jokes specifically related to sex and sexuality. For example, one newspaper reported during the sensational days following Charley Parkhurst's death that in earlier years he had worked and spent considerable time with a certain Hank Monk. "When Hank heard the report that Charley had turned out to be a woman," as the paper told it, "he gasped for breath, and drawled out: 'Je—hosaphat! I camped out with Parkie once for over a week, and we slept on the same buffalo robe right along; wonder if Curly Bill's been playin' me the same way.'"[121]

Tuscarora, Nevada's Samuel M. Pollard endured particular ridicule, both from his community and from those who learned of his story from some distance. Pollard first came to public attention in May 1878 after his wife of six months, a local woman named Marancy Hughes, came forth with the news that Pollard was actually Sarah Maud Pollard. The press then circulated stories that endlessly debated and poked fun at Pollard's sex, referring to him as "Samrah," combining both his reported male and female names.[122] For example, Silver City, Idaho's *Owyhee Avalanche* asserted that Marancy had given birth to a ten-pound baby boy and "Samrah can now exclaim: 'Whoosh been here since I'sh been gone.'"[123] A week later the paper claimed that the child had died.[124]

The *Owyhee Avalanche* kept up the greatest campaign against Pollard, even carrying in 1878 a doggerel about him, the first part of which appeared in the *Carson (Nevada) Appeal* and the second added by the *Bodie (California) Standard*.

Oh, Samuel Pollard, alias Sarah M. Pollard,
    How came you to dress in pants.
And humbug the fancy of poor Miss Marancy
    With love and all that at first glance?
What good did it do to her or to you,
    That you courted and married Miss Hughes?
You ought to be collar'd, you Sarah M. Pollard.
And spanked with a pair of cloth shoes.

The *Standard*'s addition reads:

Alas! poor Marancy
    To take such a fancy
To Sallie because she wore pants.
    You ought to have known her
    By the shape of her shoulder.
And prevented her playing you pranks.
    Beware, in the future,
    Of any sweet creature
Who sues for your heart's choicest riches—
    Make him swear that his love
    Can your gentle heart move
Far more than could Sarah's old breeches.[125]

S. M. Pollard was also reported to have taken to the eastern Nevada mining camp lecture circuit, "the first half of the lecture is in female and the rest in male attire."[126]

In 1879 the press, both near to and far from Tuscarora, also derisively dubbed Pollard "the Tuscarora What-Is-It" and referred to him as a "man-woman."[127] These terms, like the myriad jokes told about him, had a certain sexual connotation, just as had the joke about Parkhurst sleeping on a buffalo robe with an unsuspecting Hank Monk. If we accept press reports as, at least in degree, indications of community sentiment, then we might draw two more conclusions about the jokes and derision that sometimes circulated about the revealed female-to-male cross-dresser. One is that s/he severely disrupted community gender and sexual standards. The other is that whereas in some cases a community might accept a female-to-male cross-dresser as a man (when that is all it knew about him), on the other hand it might also never be entirely certain.

Years later, the press would invoke terminology more specific and scientifically engineered than "What-Is-It" in an attempt to categorize the cross-dresser, as we have seen in the cases of De Forest and Allen, for example. Another instance appears in the story of John Hill/Helen Hilsher of Denver, Colorado, of whom the question "What is it?" also was asked.[128] Hill first came to light in 1911 near Fort Morgan, Colorado, where for two years he had been "doing the work of a man and never shirking when it was grinding and heavy; wearing the clothes of a man; bearing the name of a man; making love to a young woman with true masculine ardor," all the while finding the time (and energy) to develop his homestead. In the fall of that year he went to Denver in the company of four other men from the neighborhood who would serve as witnesses when Hill proved up on his claim. Since he had taken out the claim under his female name, however, upon arrival at the station in Denver, he had to do a quick switch in the restroom, resuming his female alter ego to finalize the paperwork. When he did, it caused his comrades considerable shock, as one might imagine. Later, the local newspaper, alerted to the alarming intelligence, caught up with the now Helen at her Denver home. "It was the only thing to do," she told the press. "A woman would not have felt safe out there alone, and I just had to do it. Now that it is all over I feel awful about it—but, I am glad I won."[129]

Perhaps, but such words, reported over and over by other cross-dressers across western history for cover, should be taken with a grain of salt. Early the next summer, in 1912, Hilsher, again in the guise of John, arrived in the western Colorado town of Meeker. He found employment in a local roadhouse and began courting Anna Slifka, a waitress and, according to reports, "a comely young German girl of quiet disposition and good name."[130] The two married that November.[131] The following September, Anna's brother Victor filed a complaint accusing John of being a woman. Soon Hill stood before a local justice for the crime of impersonating a man. The hearing revealed his original name, that one witness knew he had been "masquerading as a man" for years, and that wife Anna "did not know that 'Jack' was a woman until recently when the case was brought and then only through hearsay."[132] The entire story caused quite the sensation, though neither Victor nor even Anna claimed to have any ill feelings toward Hill, and others from both near and far spoke sympathetically on his behalf. But the local news editor's response differed markedly. He crudely questioned of Hill, "What is it?" and then retorted with the era's negative medicalized language, "A moral pervert, a degenerate . . . ?"[133]

Women who dressed as men appeared in the American West in large numbers throughout the period 1850 to 1920. And yet regardless of their commonness, they constantly made the news. Some, such as Nell Pickerell/ Harry Allen/Harry Livingstone, became the subject of journalistic interest over a period of years, even decades. Others made the news only fleetingly, some only when they died and were discovered to have female bodies. The great number of these individuals provided (or the press presumed for them) rational reasons to garb themselves as men, reasons in keeping with what scholars later identify in cross-dressing history as the progress narrative. In reporting these reasons, the press typically invoked the specific social context of the American West, providing it as cause for women in the region to don the apparel of men. This has created a historical record that has reinforced the efficacy of the progress narrative for historians who examine female-to-male cross-dressing in the West.

As the nineteenth century advanced, however, popular sources evince an increasing suspicion that sexuality and gender identity might also have contributed to cross-dressing. By the turn of the twentieth century some female-to-male cross-dressers became associated with sexual inversion, a term inclusive of a broad range of sexualities and gender identities not in keeping with what was considered "normal," "acceptable," and heterosexual. At that point local communities increasingly turned to newly available terms, categories, and concepts to accede to these individuals' ambiguous gender and sexuality. Sometimes they created their own that did the same, such as "What-Is-It?" or the hyphenated "man-woman," or the more gender-imbalanced "man-girl." Whether in the earlier or later period, it is also clear that any number of these female-to-male cross-dressers saw themselves not as women, but really as men. Clearly over the years the press became more and more suspect of deep-seated reasons for female-to-male cross-dressing, thus in a way helping to produce the female-to-male sexual invert. And yet still, such individuals had a role in their own creation. A more objective appraisal of the evidence provides clues to the reality of what we would later call transgenderism and transsexuality among any number of these "cross-dressed" people.

Strong evidence, much of it very public and popular, demonstrates that sexuality and gender identity played a fundamental role in the history of female-to-male western cross-dressing. One of this book's central questions is how such a history and tradition have been eliminated from popular memory about the West, as well as from the vision of historians who have studied the region's cross-dressers. The short answer, taken up in greater detail later, is that, when coupled with the myth of the West, the progress narrative has proven a firm bulwark against the notion that sexual and gender transgressiveness is part of, perhaps even central to, American frontier and western history.

CHAPTER 2

"I Have Done My Part in the Winning of the West"

Unveiling the Male-to-Female Cross-Dresser

In the spring of 1867, a fifteen-year-old youth we know only as "M" "kissed his mother a fond goodbye" and headed West to Grand Island, Nebraska.[1] The reason M had for departing from his childhood home traced to his predilection for dressing up in girls' clothing and a row he had with his father as a result. M explained that he had successfully kept his "sinful (?) habit" under wraps from his father for years until a visiting uncle, who was also a preacher, accidentally discovered it. After the uncle "roared his head off," M's father ordered his son "to gather up and burn every article of girls' clothing" he had accumulated. He also threatened M with bodily injury should he ever discover him wearing such adornments again. M could tolerate this authoritarian atmosphere only for so long, yearning to satisfy his "uncontrollable passion for female attire." So M decided to head West. At first glance, this choice of destination might seem somewhat odd for a male-to-female cross-dresser, given what we know or think we know about the manliness of the American West in 1867. On the other hand, heading West could be a very logical alternative. After all, the West at that time represented freedom to so many; why not for a man who wished to dress as a woman?

Although we do not know where M lived as a child, we do know some other details about his early years, thanks to Bernard S. Talmey, a New York physician who presented M's case in his 1914 medical article "Transvestism: A Contribution to the Study of the Psychology of Sex." In his autobiography for Talmey, M described his parents during his youth as energetic, active, and temperate, and his three older brothers and five younger sisters as

FIGURE 4. Bert Martin, 1900. Born Bertha Martin in 1879, in later life Bert determined himself to be a male. His fascinating story came to light when he was lodged in the Nebraska State Penitentiary on conviction of horse stealing. Martin's cell mate grew suspicious of his sex and reported to prison guards his theory that Martin was a woman. An examination followed that determined, to the satisfaction of Nebraska officials anyway, that Martin had the body of a female. In fact, he likely had ambiguous genitalia as other evidence shows that he fathered at least three children. Image courtesy Nebraska State Historical Society, Inmate #3656 Bert Martin.

healthy and robust. Some sixty-two years old when he related this informa-tion to Talmey, M fondly recollected that as a child he preferred girls as play-mates and favored dolls, ribbons, and miniature house furniture as playthings. He also proudly announced that he had excelled in making doll dresses, often doing so for his younger sisters and other girls in the neighborhood. By age ten, M had also perfected the ability to cook a full-course meal. At night he often dreamed he was a girl, only to awaken disappointed when he discovered it was not so. One might imagine that M would have endured a great deal of torment from other boys. He did. But, as he later explained it, he never lacked courage and never shunned a fight, "always" giving his nemeses "the licking coming to them." Despite this show of gruffness, M easily blushed, could never countenance vulgarity, developed large breasts, had no trace of an Adam's apple, and had a high voice.

Known early on as something of a mama's boy, M further recollected that as early as he could remember, his mother would dress him in girls' clothing and then would tutor him in the female arts of knitting, crocheting, and sewing. Throughout his life M believed that his mother guided him in these directions because "she knew that nothing else would appeal to my feelings stronger as being dressed like a girl."

Perhaps this is so, but another report from the era and emanating from the American West describes a situation not unlike that of M's mother, providing a thought-provoking comparison. Similar to M's mother, a certain Irene Moynihan of Victor, Colorado, had given birth first to two sons. She desperately hoped her next child would be a daughter. Overwhelmed with disappointment when, in about 1895, she had yet another boy, Irene withheld the truth from her husband and secretly dressed and raised the child as a girl. No one in the historical record seems to have suspected this switch— that is, until January 1913. At that time, then eighteen years old, the Moynihan son-turned-daughter was making his way from his mother's home in Victor to visit his father in Bisbee, Arizona. During a layover in La Junta, Colorado, authorities became suspicious of the traveler's "masculine appearance" despite his female garb. To the officials' shock, if not surprise, they soon determined that Moynihan was indeed a boy. Even more outrageous was the story they learned from Irene when they hunted her down in Victor to ascertain the reason for this colossal fraud.[2]

The stories of Moynihan in Colorado and M in Nebraska parallel each other in uncanny ways, but whatever the exact facts in the case of M, he asserted that his "almost uncontrollable desire to wear woman's attire" was really his own rather than his mother's, and that when "so dressed, I can always think more logically, feel less encumbered, solve difficult problems in a manner next to impossible under any other conditions." Tellingly, M understood and explained his sartorial habits, the emotional effects they had on him, and their relationship to his manhood, his life, and his accomplishments in the

West in a way that undermines connections to manliness and the West that broader America held at the time and has largely held since. First, M claimed that he could systematically perform just about any women's task. Then he asserted that his ability to do men's work exceeded that of 70 percent of other males. In support, he offered that when he arrived in Nebraska in 1867, he immediately found work, driving teams for railroad construction and hunting buffalo. He next found remunerative service as a detective for a U.S. marshal's office, became a sheriff and justice of the peace for a short time, and then served a stint as publisher of a local newspaper. "I never failed to make good in any of my ventures," M boldly claimed, being always "hale and hearty and dare say that I have been able to conquer most everything" that he ever set his mind to. The one great exception to all this was M's persistent inability to overcome his insatiable desire for donning women's attire.

M's wholly western life between 1867 and 1872 remained the most memorable, exciting, and personally significant to him. Perhaps ironically alluding to Theodore Roosevelt's famed *The Winning of the West* book series in which the author prominently touted connections between the American frontier and virile masculinity, M casually explained that "I have done my part in the winning of the west, with the result that I carry two Indian bullets in my legs to this hour." And yet demonstrating how frills and furbelows could subdue even the most memorably violent, manly aspects of western life, M added with some measure of satisfaction that he covered up his bullet holes "with petticoats as often as opportunity permits. Then I forget all about them, as well as all other troubles." It seems that male-to-female cross-dressing could outflank even the most celebrated aspects of frontier life, on which cherished myths of the Old West so prominently rest.

Bernard S. Talmey utilized M's case history, along with four others he had collected, to put forth one of the earliest scientific arguments that transvestism did not necessarily indicate homosexuality. The conflation of the two had been accepted in medical literature since at least the 1880s. Despite the pioneering work of individuals like Talmey, the association of cross-dressing and same-sex sexuality would of course continue for many years beyond the 1910s, both in the minds of mainstream medical professionals and the broader public. But back in 1914, Talmey supported his argument by using as evidence M's insistence, no matter its truth, that he "never had any homosexual inclinations." Since some medical scientists began to argue that transvestism was separate from homosexuality only in 1910, Talmey explained in his 1914 article that records of "pure transvestism . . . are still scarce."[3]

Regardless as to whether incidences of male-to-female cross-dressing were of pure transvestism or were linked somehow to same-sex sexuality or sexual inversion, some news purveyors in the American West at the time maintained that male-to-female cross-dressing of the everyday sort was rather anomalous in the region. In July 1883, for example, a Denver newspaper affirmed this, albeit for the local level. After police there arrested a man for wearing women's clothing on the street, the reporting journalist declared that "it is a very uncommon thing for men to be caught in Denver masquerading in the clothes of a woman."[4]

Whether familiar with the details of nineteenth-century North American frontier history, when presented with information about male-to-female cross-dressing in the Old West we might initially respond with similar skepticism. Those who are a bit more familiar with the field might recall that many western Native American men's lives mixed female and male gender behaviors; they also typically wore women's clothing or a combination of those and male attire and sometimes had sexual relations with men. People with a bit more knowledge about frontier and western regional history might also recollect that early resident white men, here and there, occasionally dressed as women strictly to entertain and only under prescribed conditions, namely during early days of western settlement when the balance between the sexes tipped considerably in their favor. Such men include those who temporarily dressed and took the role of women at soirees on the gold-rush frontier or on the dusty cattle trail, where women were in short supply but the men wished to have a dance anyway. Also, those who are familiar with the history of professional entertainment in the nineteenth-century West might be aware of female impersonators who worked in and traveled across the region appearing in vaudeville and minstrel acts with billboard regularity.

Even if we confine ourselves to these examples, then men who dressed as women in the nineteenth-century West were not as atypical as either we or the 1883 Denver newspaper might initially think. Unusual or not, we nevertheless *rationally* understand and thus accept the occasional cross-dressing of miners, cowboys, and entertainers. And we likely consent, under the guise of multiculturalism, to male-bodied Native Americans who clothed themselves as women. In fact, with a little more effort, we can uncover many other males who dressed as females, some who even lived as such, and who called the American West their home in the late nineteenth and early twentieth centuries. The reasons they changed into women's clothing were as varied as those provided in the stories of women who chose to attire themselves as men. Such males as females have been all but forgotten in the telling of western history. But they were there throughout, and acknowledging and accounting for their presence provides us with a remarkably different view of the region. I begin this chapter with a brief recounting of the men and male-bodied people we have long known to have occasionally dressed as women in the West. I then consider some of the accepted reasons they did what they did. Then I scour the region, turning up a multitude of other male-to-female cross-dressers and the varied reasons they had for garbing themselves as, and sometimes becoming, women. Among these reasons, I meditate at length on the role that sexual and gender identity played, at least in the eyes of those who reported at the time. Particularly striking in all this, I would point out, is how the local press refused to contextualize male-to-female cross-dressers within a "western" framework. This contrasted markedly with how it responded to female-to-males. This different pattern holds a clue to the forgetting of male-to-female cross-dressers in America's western past, a subject I turn to later in this book.

Western historians have long been aware of the men in the region who took to women's clothing, but did so (purportedly) only occasionally and under prescribed conditions. This has made them acceptable to understandings of western history. For example, typically at dances held on the region's various gold-rush frontiers, where women were scarce (at least those not disguised as men), some men volunteered to become "women" so that couples dancing might take place. In 1849, for example, a "Fancy Dress Ball" made up part of the 4th of July celebration that George Dornin and fellow Americans participated in aboard the *Panama* en route to San Francisco via Cape Horn. Of the 220 passengers and crew, only four were women and only one of these had, according to Dornin, "the taste or inclination to dance." The men had a ball anyway—the younger ones with smooth faces dressing up in calico gowns. Dornin counted himself among these youths. With the help of Mrs. M. E. Longley, a widow who was likewise on her way to California to strike it rich, he became "presentable as a young lady." Though he could not dance particularly well, he could follow the basic patterns and therefore found himself "in active demand."[5] Dornin did not explain just how so many calico gowns could be found on board a ship with a human cargo of 216 men and only four women.

Another dance, this one held by landlubbers in 1868 in Idaho's Boise Basin gold-mining district, also leaves one to wonder. This time St. Patrick's Day events provided the opportunity for the large number of Irishmen in the diggings to celebrate patriotism and collect aid for those back home struggling against British control. The festivities included a ball where the "scarcity of ladies made it necessary," an area newspaper reported, "to uniform several gents in female attire, when the dance went merrily on until the *wee* hour of the morning."[6] Although held at the Minnehaha ranch operated by a Mr. *and* Mrs. Cooper, it is doubtful that the latter had enough gowns to clothe all the miners who dressed as women.[7]

Less ubiquitous than miners' dances, but still somewhat known in western history, were the at times elaborate masquerade balls held in gold-rush-era San Francisco. Although women attended, men made up the bulk of the participants, likely because of their preponderance in the overall population. Hikozo Hamada, a Japanese sailor cast adrift by a powerful typhoon, inadvertently ended up in San Francisco in 1851. Astonished generally by what he saw there, he found the "*masukiri*" (masquerade) particularly noteworthy. "Those who dance wear masks and hide their faces," Hamada explained, "Men dress as women and women dress as men."[8]

Men dressing as women for entertainment purposes has a long history, particularly when for years law and custom prevented women from acting on a public stage, and then in the nineteenth century when female impersonation evolved into something of an art form. In America, female impersonation began in blackface minstrelsy and later spread to vaudeville.[9] Both these forms of entertainment regularly appeared on stages across the American West. Blackface minstrels showed up in San Francisco in 1848, and in 1851, for example, the accomplished blackface Billy Birch and his company opened there for a six-year stint. When Birch closed, Tom Maguire, who produced the show and at the time operated Maguire's Opera House, then brought in the famed George Christy's Minstrels, a troupe that also featured a female impersonator.[10]

Through the end of the century, as it grew in size and importance, San Francisco remained a must-stop on the national and world tours of major minstrel and vaudeville acts. But from there, performers and companies spread to other venues in the far reaches of the West. In 1857, Tom Maguire's San Francisco Minstrels, with W. D. Corrister in the role of an Ethiopian female, appeared at Sacramento's Forrest Theater.[11] New York's Charles Fostelle, whose long career began as a stock actor in Detroit before he moved into blackface, worked for a number of minstrel companies before he launched his own, starring in it as a female impersonator and opening in Denver on 4 March 1872.[12] Just four years later, female impersonator Alf Wyman appeared with the Peak Family comedy troupe in Pueblo, Colorado.[13] By 1881, patrons of Tombstone, Arizona's Birdcage Saloon might witness what was likely local talent when "three men clad in tights with women's under garments" danced the cancan onstage, vying "with each other in the obscenity of their actions."[14] In 1886, Renfrow's Jolly Pathfinders appeared in Bismarck, North Dakota, with a "juvenile female impersonator" nearly stealing the show.[15]

Owners of the West's Chinese theaters produced attractions with their own actors in the role of female characters. San Francisco's Lee Hoo was so successful as a woman that when Portland theater proprietor Lee Ping wished to secure his visit in 1889, he had to shell out $500 just for Lee Hoo to make an appearance. But Lee Hoo proved worth it, at least at first—he became an instant drawing card, according to one report, packing the house nightly. But then, shortly after he began his run, he ran off to San Francisco, taking with him a wide variety of Lee Ping's costumes that were warehoused at his theater (only a successful lawsuit brought Lee Hoo and the missing wardrobe back to Portland).[16] Yet another female impersonator, known for his improbable one-and-a-half-inch feet, also graced the early Chinese stages in Portland, earning $3,000 a year; his physical and fiscal figures reportedly caused considerable jealousy among the other male-to-female performers at Ju Cluey's theater. They, not so diminutively endowed as their rival, brought in a considerably more modest $400 to $1,800 a year, or so a local paper explained in 1891.[17]

Into the early twentieth century, female impersonators remained favorites among audiences. And over the years many performers, including African Americans, Chinese, and whites (in and out of blackface), regularly appeared in cross-dress on western American stages. Some traveled from city to city, in and out of the region, as solo acts or with minstrel and vaudeville troupes. A few, such as Julian Eltinge, who by the early years of the twentieth century had appeared in venues in just about every state west of the Mississippi, gained national and even international fame. Many others, however, remained entirely local, living for lengthy periods of time in the towns where they performed.

Female impersonators on the theatrical stage, men who temporarily dressed as women at gold-rush dances, and San Francisco's masquerade party-goers are the men-as-women whom we typically accept as part of nineteenth-century western American society and culture. As such, they tend not to offend later-day sensibilities. And yet many more male-to-female cross-dressers, almost as numerous as their female-to-male sartorial counterparts, resided in and traveled through the region, especially during the second half of the nineteenth century. Their uncommonly common numbers, in fact, led some early western sources (in contrast to those with which this chapter began) occasionally to warn of them just as they had of female-to-male counterfeits. For example, in June 1871 a newspaper avowed that the lower portion of Georgetown, located in one of Colorado's gold-mining districts, provided a favorite haunt not only for "females in male attire" but also for "males in petticoats."[18] And a Reno, Nevada, paper advertised in 1882 that "it is contrary to the Nevada statute for men to walk the public streets dressed in women's clothes, and the officers want it distinctly understood that all men, young and old, seen after this dressed in female attire, will be immediately arrested and dealt with according to the law."[19] Perhaps stated in a somewhat sarcastic way, nevertheless the adoption and popularizing of a law prohibiting men from donning female attire on the streets suggests that the practice had become noticeable, at least in Reno.

But it was so elsewhere in the West as well: any number of the most casual references to men and boys who dressed as women or girls in western towns and cities can be found in local newspapers from about 1850 onward. A sense of their number and variety can be gained from an otherwise monotonous recapitulation of just a handful. Not surprisingly, San Francisco, the trans-Missouri West's largest and most diverse city through the last half of the nineteenth century, provided the most and the earliest news reports of men arrested for dressing as women. On 6 May 1852, for example, a "gentleman" appeared in the city's streets in his womanly costume. Immediately arrested, he paid a fine of $25.[20] Some years later, on one March day in 1870, Samuel Coleman came before San Francisco's Police Court charged with a misdemeanor: he "appeared on a public street in gorgeous female attire."[21] In September 1874, police apprehended William Thomas on Fourth Street for wearing the clothes of the opposite sex; he had drawn particular attention to himself by badly playing an accordion.[22] Later that same year police nabbed John Roberts for cross-dressing, but instead of disturbing the peace with a musical instrument, he went about the streets boisterously drunk.[23] The next year, authorities collared Davis Graves on Third Street for wearing women's clothing.[24] Subsequently, in August 1879, police picked up John Doyle for masquerading in female attire.[25] On the evening of 19 February 1882, authorities found Paul and John de Martina, likely the unmarried Demartini brothers who worked as San Francisco bootblacks, parading the streets dressed as women.[26] Somewhat later, in December 1907, San Francisco police arrested Robert Nelson for female impersonation.[27]

San Francisco was hardly unique. Other western American cities also had their complement of streetwalking male-to-female cross-dressers. In 1881, authorities discovered a man in women's clothing prowling about Jacksonville, Texas.[28] Three years later, in December 1884, reports came in of a young man in Atchison, Kansas, seen masquerading in female attire and disappearing into a "notorious den near the corner of Eighth and Commercial streets."[29] In 1891, another young man shocked sensibilities yet again in Atchison for also appearing in the street dressed as a woman.[30] That same year J. B. Winslow, who masqueraded as a woman and went by the moniker "Blonde Wilson," came to light in Denver.[31] The following year, Willie Loveland, a fourteen-year-old boy, came to light in Portland roaming about in a "Mother Hubbard gown." He explained that he had worn nothing else for some time.[32]

The list does not stop here. Police in Wichita, Kansas, for example, arrested two men the evening of 2 December 1895 for attending the theater in women's clothing; they accompanied two young women who were dressed as men.[33] A year later, Henry Thomas Cook got drunk in Fargo, North Dakota, and paraded through the streets in female attire.[34] In Houston, forty-two-year-old Louis Pellett was garbed in women's clothing, including underskirts and corsets, when police arrested him in October 1903.[35] Two years earlier and at the other end of the American West in Anaconda, Montana, police collared Nicholas Ashton for disturbing the peace; he was masquerading in women's clothing on Galena Street.[36] A few years later in the same town, Mose Willard donned women's apparel and, in the company of several young women, visited various saloons.[37]

The great majority of the incidents related in the three previous paragraphs appeared in newspapers as otherwise laconic tidbits, remarkable for their lack of descriptive quality given their apparent sensational nature and particularly when compared to such stories about women. It may very well be that such individuals were relatively common and thus not that newsworthy. But it is also true that when arrested, a number of such men and youths

tended to be reticent about their motives, which might explain the media's lack
of juicy tidbits to report. A typical case involved twenty-one-year-old Edgar
Edwards, apprehended at the Union Depot in Austin, Texas, during the evening of 11 December 1901. He was wearing a lady's suit consisting "of a black
skirt, colored shirt waist, straw hat with heavy black veil and light shoes." With
lips fastened as tightly as those on a soldier captured by enemy forces, Edwards
would only admit his name and that he lived in Mason, Texas. He otherwise
said nothing.[38]

But in many other cases newspapers provided considerably more information about the motives and circumstances of male-to-female cross-dressers,
helping us to probe more deeply into why some men and boys might dress as
females in the American West. For example, on 5 May 1859, a "delicate 'lady'"
arrived by carriage at the San Francisco docks. Wearing hoops, a bustle,
plenty of crinoline, and a "love of a bonnet," the individual daintily made her
way through the parting and admiring crowd toward the steamship *Orizaba*.
But when going up the gangway to board the vessel, she unfortunately "lifted
her drapery rather higher than decorum would seem to warrant, which revealed a pair of gaiter shoes of such large proportions" that it spoiled the
whole effect and the assembled crowd began to wonder. Talk among the witnesses, some reportedly in the know, declared that the woman was a man
from an interior town who had toyed with the affections of the wife of some
other man and that he was eluding the disgruntled husband.[39]

Far more typical and numerous in the press are cases in which a male offered the rather simple reason for his change of apparel, whether true or not,
that he intended it only as a joke or because he was out on a lark. For example,
on the evening of 16 January 1877, Oakland, California, authorities inter-
cepted yet another femininely clad young man preparing to board a vessel, in
this case the somewhat more mundane ferry to San Francisco. The captive
explained that he was "only going on a lark."[40] When nearby San Francisco
police apprehended John Doyle in 1879 for cross-dressing—in his daughter's clothing, no less—he explained he did only to pass himself off as a servant girl to fool an unwitting neighbor.[41] In 1893, an Omaha, Nebraska, pa-
trolman arrested a man and woman for drunk and disorderly conduct on
Farnam Street. At the station, the police discovered the woman to be John
Hamilton, who wore a blond wig, corset, and skirt. "His face was powdered
and he talked in a tone which even misled the ever alert Sergeant Ormsby,"
the local paper added. Regardless of the couple's excuse that "they were out

for a lark with some friends and only wanted to fool somebody," the authorities locked them up—Hamilton nearly making it into the women's cell before Ormsby's noted watchfulness kicked in.[42]

Sometimes, in lieu of better evidence for why a man might dress as a woman, people supposed the answer lay in crime. This is exactly what Austin authorities thought when Edgar Edwards refused under examination to divulge his purposes in donning female attire. "The police believe," a local paper reported in 1901, "that he may be wanted for some offence and adopted the disguise to avoid arrest."[43]

In fact, perhaps more stories gleaned from newspapers purport something related to crime as the most common reason men took to women's clothing. In 1877, Joe Hughes brutally assaulted a woman in St. Joseph, Missouri. Disguised in female attire, he made his escape on a train bound for Denver.[44] In that city in 1886, two burglars attempted a job at the residence of a certain E. J. Copeland. Awakened by a crashing noise on a lower level of his abode, the homeowner met the intruders with gunfire and they quickly fled, but not before Copeland could clearly see that the burglars were disguised in female attire.[45] In 1923, Otto Cole, a lifer at the Nebraska State Penitentiary, donned a woman's costume he had made in an attempt to fool guards and escape from prison. He worked in the prison upholstery shop, creatively engineered a corset from steel ribs used in making chairs, fashioned stockings from the sleeves of a discarded jersey, constructed a wig from hair used to stuff furniture, and likewise gathered up other materials from the upholstery shop to complete his hat and gown. At the end of one visitors' day, he fell in line with the civilians waiting to leave and nearly made it through the institution's gate before a wary officer saw through the disguise.[46]

Stage-performing cross-dressers who appeared on the streets or in some other venue than the confines of the theater also supply a large number of incidents reported in the press where a male done up like a woman came to broader public attention in the nineteenth- and early twentieth-century West. Lost in the region's history is the number of the West's theatrical female impersonators, neither famed nor blessed with fortune, who actually lived as locals in the communities where they found employment. In some of the most out-of-the-way saloons and back-of-beyond dance halls, they nightly retrieved their pay as a few coins collected in the bottom of a hat that the few souls in the audience passed around. In many cases, simply because of who they were, what they did, and where they lived, their stage lives blended with their street lives. Thus, when a local comedian appeared on the streets of Bismarck, Dakota Territory, garbed in a long, flowing dress with a pink sash and sun bonnet tied with a bow knot around his chin in 1885, police had no choice but to haul him off to jail.[47] Robert Evans, a female impersonator who sang songs for nickels in various Denver saloons, but especially at the Castle Garden, likewise found himself before the local courts in January 1898. Having arrived in the Mile High City the previous April and often appearing in the streets, he was hauled in for perpetual drunkenness and often causing an annoyance among the patrons of places where he hung out.[48]

A few years later, Percy Yarick, an Anaconda, Montana, impersonator who usually performed at the Casino Concert Hall, came to broader public awareness. One night during his act, Mazie Hopps, another employee of the Casino, made some wisecrack about his character and suffered the consequences. With swollen and blackened eyes, Hopps filed a complaint with the police and Yarick found himself performing in front of a local judge and the press.[49] A year later, in 1906, down the road in Missoula, police arrested Harry Campbell, a local female impersonator who performed in a variety theater; he had appeared in women's clothing carousing, but well beyond the footlights, in a nearby wooded grove with a bunch of men who claimed to be unaware of his true sex.[50]

In addition to the common tales of men who dressed as women for a joke, to commit a crime or escape its consequences, or because it was associated with their work are a variety of unusual stories. One of these concerned Omaha's Henry Snell, who first donned women's clothing in 1887. Previously he had been overtaken by heatstroke five times while suffering from rheumatism and Bright's disease. The constricting nature of men's trousers and vests, he claimed, made his condition unbearable. So, he decided that he might as well try women's clothing, finding dresses considerably more comfortable, a reason that flies in the face of many women's dress reformers of the era, though it appears that Snell did not bother with corsets. Described as a hard worker and respected member of the community, Snell went unmolested by authorities, though admittedly if he needed to take a trip downtown, he did so after switching back to male garments just to be safe. So well-known and accepted had he become that even the *Omaha World Herald* ran a sympathetic feature about him in its 9 July 1899 edition, right during a particularly warm part of the summer.[51]

Also among the more unusual was San Francisco's Ferdinand Haisch, a middle-age carpenter and frustrated inventor, who for several years in the

1890s went about the streets in women's clothing, usually at night when the workday had ended. He took great pleasure in fooling even his most intimate friends, he said, while dressed in female attire and sitting next to them on cable cars, entirely unrecognized. But Haisch's ability to disguise himself seems somewhat debatable, as one report claimed that he appeared rather ludicrous, robed in a "gaudy costume" but walking "with the stride of a man."

While at times Haisch's manly physical attributes made it difficult for him to entirely carry off his disguise, no one could deny his nimbleness with the needle and skill at the sewing machine: in using such tools with the assistance of a wire-framed mannequin, Haisch fashioned all his own gowns, reportedly "of different colors and textures" and filling an entire wardrobe. So well-known had he become that by the summer of 1895, reportedly hundreds of curiosity seekers nightly attempted to catch glimpses of him at his home. Sometimes the crowd turned unruly, which in one case actually led to one of Haisch's more sensational arrests. In July 1895 when a group of nocturnal callers became somewhat ugly just outside his door, Haisch ran upstairs, poured water over the rabble, and then resorted to his roof, where he pitched pieces of wood at them (he was a carpenter, after all, and likely had all manner of scrap on hand). The young men in the crowd responded with a salvo of stones, smashing several of the cross-dresser's windows. When it came to apprehension and prosecution, however, the police locked up Haisch for the disturbance rather than the goons on the street.[52]

Even more extraordinary, if that could be, came a story from Livingston, Montana, in 1912. In May of that year the "whole city," as a newspaper asserted, "was terrified by a person," believed to be "wild" and often seen dressed in women's clothing, bathing in the Yellowstone River. The person turned out to be a man, a local hotel employee. To baffled police he simply explained that he "had a craze for dressing in woman's clothes and getting into the water." Although as a boy his mother whipped him countless times for such activities, such punishment curbed neither his "fever" nor what he called his "queer actions." The police released him only when he promised them he would harm no one. But a couple years later his story was revived in the local press when police heard reports of women's clothing missing from local laundry lines, discovered a suitcase of partly worn feminine garments soaked in water, and then learned from a rancher that on a recent evening's trip to town he had witnessed what he took to be a woman taking a dip in the Yellowstone River (notwithstanding that it was late December) and disappearing into the shrubbery. All suspicions naturally pointed to the hotel employee arrested only months before. But without better evidence, the police could only promise to keep an eye on him.[53]

The local newspaper characterized the Yellowstone bather as a "monomaniac"—the mental diagnosis of what might broadly be termed madness was not uncommonly applied to male-to-female cross-dressers of the period.[54] For example, when the San Francisco police locked up Ferdinand Haisch in the city jail, local journalists caught up with him there. They asked him why he loved women's clothing so much, both making and wearing it. He provided no answer, which left others to speculate "that a young woman to whom he was engaged to be married died, and the loss affected his brain in this direction." And a newspaper simply dubbed him "crazy."[55] Also, when Bernard S. Talmey reported on M from Grand Island, Nebraska, he explained that his subject's habit was "pathological" and that M's considering himself to be "a normal man is quite natural, but his belief does not make him so."[56]

Earlier in the nineteenth century cross-dressers might on occasion be described as having a "mania." As the nineteenth turned into the twentieth, westerners and others increasingly suspected mental defect as just one of the possible root causes of cross-dressing, at least among some everyday males who garbed themselves in female attire.[57] In October 1906 in Reno, Nevada, for example, when Thomas Span dressed in women's clothing and walked hurriedly past a city park, frightened nurses and the children they tended believed him "an escaped lunatic." Local reporters, however, provided a somewhat less damning diagnosis, declaring him only "temporarily demented" from sunstroke.[58] For years Frank Butcher, as a woman, worked as a domestic in a private Los Angeles home. One day in 1913, at her hairstylist, the woman who "marcelled" her mane noticed, apparently for the first time, that her client had "down on his chin." She quickly made a few calls. Arresting authorities forced Butcher to resume male attire, something she reportedly did with great reluctance. They then sat her before a proper barber for the first time in years. Butcher's problems did not end there. She had to appear before the lunacy commission, which declared her insane.[59]

Between the time of the California gold rush and the opening years of the twentieth century, male-to-female cross-dressers appeared with ubiquity in the West. Some, both in contemporary and present-day eyes, had a good and defensible reason to do what they did. But a surprising number of others dressed as women for reasons that went well beyond the occasional, the temporary, and the begrudgingly "understandable." In this context, that someone like M might run off to the West becomes entirely understandable—the West at this time obviously countenanced such individuals, as many found a home there. It might also be that certain traditionally female-oriented tasks and services that such people could perform—as in the case of M, who grew up learning to cook and sew—and that were in fierce demand in a region dominated by the male sex might further make it possible for them to find a niche there. Phil Poland appeared as "her" alter ego, Eva Lind, in Colfax, Washington Territory, in the 1880s, for example. So successful were her talents in such a disguise that she found employment for a considerable time as a waitress, all the while not raising suspicions.[60] Just after the turn of the twentieth century in Los Angeles, Frank Butcher so succeeded as a female cook that she was able to work as a domestic for years entirely undetected.[61] Most notably, the very fact that so many local female-to-male impersonators (many of whose lives offstage indicate that their gender and even sexual transgressiveness were part of their everyday identity) could be found in the nineteenth-century West recommends that a demand for them in the region did in fact exist. Female impersonator Robert Evans, arrested for vagrancy and drunkenness in Denver in 1898, even explained to curious reporters that an invitation for work in the West initially brought him out from Virginia; he found that employment impersonating women and singing in local saloons.[62]

But as the 1870s slipped into the 1880s and the 1880s faded into the 1890s, everyday men who donned women's clothing in the West did in fact come under increased scrutiny for their gender ambiguity and what it implied about their sexuality. We can see this in news coverage of the activities engaged in by stage-performing female impersonators when they were not strictly on the boards. We can also find it in accounts of cross-dressing men not connected to theater employment at all, but who appeared regularly on city streets and done up in ways that evinced great care and practice. These and other reports raised suspicion of mental defect and, therefore, sexual deviance. This paralleled developments in the public perception of women who dressed as men; it also resulted from the same broad historical processes whereby at least some female-to-male cross-dressers became understood as deviants, perverts, sexual inverts, and lesbians by the turn of the twentieth century. While the broader public came to see the male-to-female cross-dresser as a sexual invert, at least some of the male-to-female cross-dressers who came to light in the West (and probably many who never made it into the historical record) also understood their sexual and gender identities to in some ways comply with the era's concept of sexual inversion.

For male-to-female cross-dressers, compared to their female-to-male counterparts, there existed additional ingredients in the historical recipe that by the early twentieth century newly created them as homosexuals: everyday men who donned female clothing also had to contend with a perception of them very much influenced by a changing public reaction to onstage female impersonators and these performers' lives and behaviors beyond the footlights. The historian Sharon R. Ullman has examined this issue, finding that the largely male-produced press at the time increasingly focused specifically on (homo)sexuality when reviewing, critiquing, and considering the character of men who performed theatrically as women.[63] Ullman has shown that because both media and, in turn, popular audiences increasingly wondered about the private sexual activities of men who impersonated females so well onstage, these performers had to more consciously cultivate an unquestionably masculine and transparently heterosexual identity offstage. "This created," in Ullman's words, "problems for most, and their careers often rose or fell on their capacity to successfully negotiate this contested terrain, which was unstable and constantly shifting." The career of Bothwell Browne, a well-known western regional female impersonator, Ullman explained, floundered in the 1910s as a result of these very issues.[64]

Ullman places these developments at the national level in the early years of the twentieth century by examining the career vagaries of well-known female impersonators, namely Julian Eltinge and Bothwell Browne. My research on the American West supports Ullman's findings; however, it also suggests that the development of public suspicion of female-impersonators' sexuality, in particular as a result of their offstage actions, began several years earlier. Moreover, in the American West it was the *local* female impersonator who played the key role in raising public suspicion about the relationship between transgressive sexuality and theatrical female impersonation.

But before we explore this, let us consider these more general reports from Atchison, Kansas, in the 1880s. On 3 November 1880 a minstrel troupe appeared in town. "When the female impersonator began his solo," noted a local paper in its gossip column the next day, "we heard a young man lean over and whisper to his friend: 'A Nance.'"[65] At that time, "Nance" and its variations "Nancy" and "Miss Nancy" generally meant a finicky and effeminate young man. The term derived from the historical figure Nancy Dawson (whose full name was also occasionally used at the time to label such people), a well-known eighteenth-century English prostitute and dancer who became the subject of a popular sailors' song.[66] By 1884, the Atchison press used "Nance" as a generic way to refer to a theatrical female impersonator. For example, in December of that year it called Frank Howard of Thatcher, Prinsrose & West's minstrels, who appeared on the local stage as the blackface character Bettina, the "Nance of the company."[67]

Popularly understood to have become in the early twentieth century a disparaging term for a sissified homosexual man, nevertheless "Nancy" had a sexual connotation early on, as its derivation from the real-life Nancy Dawson suggests. Its early sexual connotations might also be discerned in the words of President Andrew Jackson. He supposedly once referred to William Rufus King, Franklin Pierce's vice president and a lifelong bachelor, as "little Miss Nancy" after he became roommates (and remained so for twenty years) with future president James Buchanan, another lifelong bachelor.[68]

An 1885 news report from Atchison demonstrates that when the term was used there a year after Frank Howard appeared on the local stage, press editors intended to cast doubt on the sexuality of yet another female impersonator, W. Henry Rice. The nationally known Billy Rice was in town performing with the McNish, Johnson & Slavin minstrel company. After witnessing his act, the *Daily Globe* intimated that Rice was a "Nance." A day later, Rice marched down to the newspaper office to defend his reputation. To journalists gathered there he exhibited photographs of his *ten* children as "evidence that he is not a Nance." Rice also told the *Daily Globe* reporters, however, that the newspaper was not entirely incorrect in its association of female impersonation with the Nance: he explained that "most of the female impersonators are Nances, but that he happened to be an exception."[69] The Atchison newspaper seems to have accepted Rice's view that a Nance and a female impersonator might not necessarily be one and the same, opining about the same time that the "most disgusting part of cheap minstrel show is the introduction of a Nance to do the female impersonator."[70]

While it appeared somewhat flexible in its views of the Nance in this 1885 episode with Billy Rice, by the end of the decade the Atchison press had hardened on the issue. On 12 December 1890, the local Young Men's Christian Association arranged an appearance by the Harvard Quartet at a local theater. The day after the performance, a *Daily Globe* reporter declared the public presentation "fine, with the exception of a falsetto singer," a Mr. Paine, "who should be a female impersonator in a minstrel show." The manager of the quartet wrote an indignant response denying that Paine had a falsetto voice. He explained, rather, that the performer had a woman's larynx, further evincing that the man's condition was one of only two known cases in the world. Moreover, the manager exclaimed, Paine "is a gentleman." As if repetition might make it so, the paper shot back that, call it what you will, the vocalist had the same voice of a female impersonator as could be found in a minstrel show. Moreover, such a voice "always makes people laugh except when used in female impersonations."[71] The newspaper also subtly questioned the singer's character, calling him inappropriate entertainment for young Christian men. But the quick and outraged response of the quartet's director, insisting that Mr. Paine "is a gentleman," further suggests that the vocalist's reputation had been deeply impugned.

Somewhat more innocent, but still raising the specter of inappropriate sexuality, was the *Omaha Daily Bee*'s response to the onstage actors in Madame Stanley's Female Mastodons, who appeared locally in 1884. The best-looking woman in the company, at least in the opinion of the *Bee*, was a female impersonator. A good many of the "'boys,'" as the paper referred to them using quotation marks, "got badly mashed upon him before they discovered that he was not a her."[72]

Also relatively benign and yet pregnant with sexual innuendo was a scene that blended stage performance with audience misapprehension in Mandan, North Dakota, in October 1899. A female impersonator in a "negro show" at the local opera house came onstage, happened to point in the general direction of a certain George Owens, a cowboy in the audience, and exclaimed, "Oh! there is my lost lover Georgie! How could you be so cruel and heartless as to desert me after you fondly promised to love and cherish me—your own darling!" Perhaps a bit quick on the trigger, but certainly hoping to defend his manhood, Owens drew his Colt 45. While shouting "here's a wild heifer trying to take advantage of me," he got off two rounds. Both missed their mark. One entered the backside of another audience member, and a woman sitting nearby received powder burns to her face.[73]

From 1880 on, stage-performing female impersonators' daily lives outside of the theater also caused the western news-reading public to wonder about sex and gender. Yet another Atchison source carried a piece in 1889, though neither local nor western, that dealt exactly with this issue. It concerned

George Goodwin, a theatrical female impersonator in St. Albans, Maine, who made his own gowns of black silk, with lace sleeves and low-cut necks. He also "wears a beautiful blonde wig, frizzled a la mode, and the way he handles a fan is described as simply charming." Goodwin's problem, in the eyes of the Atchison paper, was that he "is not content with his triumphs on the stage." But in continuing to don his costumes beyond the footlights, he "is guilty of the reprehensible practice of flirting with the susceptible married men he encounters while on his starring tours." Apparently he had caused several most public scenes doing so.[74]

More at the local level was the less-than-innocent take on Charles Harrington, a resident female impersonator arrested in a San Francisco resort in 1907. Police were offended when Harrington, in costume and in character but not officially performing, sat on a table at the saloon where "she" worked and flirted with two reportedly unsuspecting sailors. "I'll let you go this time," the judge who heard the case sternly admonished, "but I warn you that in the future you must confine yourself strictly to the footlights and if you step down but for the brief space of a moment . . . I will go hard on you," which is probably what the sailors had promised, too. For, as a newspaper vividly detailed, Harrington had "a woman's voice and extremely effeminate appearance, and it was doubtless easy for him to beguile the hardy mariners who frequent the Barbary Coast into thinking he was indeed the pretty young woman that he seemed."[75]

As performers and as everyday citizens, female impersonators toyed with the affections of men on- and offstage even in some of the most remote western locations. From the summer of 1906 into the winter of 1907, several South Dakota towns dotting the Black Hills enjoyed the piano recitals of the recently arrived and curiously named Helen Manley. Her tour was such a triumph that in Lead she reportedly received several marriage proposals and in Belle Fourche she made an untold number of conquests. But Manley held out for the hand of Spearfish's Roscoe Billman. Regrettably, the day before their planned wedding, Manley met with a slight accident that revealed that she was a he. Knocked from her pedestal, Manley quickly lit out, leaving Billman at the altar.[76]

As the nineteenth century came to a conclusion, public suspicion increased about the gender identity and sexuality of theatrical female impersonators or other men who passed as women, regardless of whether they provided entertainment. As several of the above stories reveal, the line that separated western stage-performing female impersonators from male-to-female cross-dressers in the workaday world could easily become confused: the two were often one and the same in various western locales. But whether reporting about those on- or offstage, as the nineteenth century advanced newspapers increasingly suspected a corollary between a fellow's (homo)sexuality and his effeminate behaviors, actions, and appearance.[77] For example, in the summer of 1883, Denver police picked up Edward Martino, who "made a very handsome woman," wearing the "most ravishing and fascinating style." Using descriptions that mirrored some of the reviews of theatrical female impersonators, a local paper explained that Martino also carried "a fan in the most approved fashion." Particularly problematic, Martino made "innumerable 'mashes' on the hearts of the tender young men who hang around in the shade of the Windsor hotel of summer evenings." On the night that authorities tailed him, they claimed that he had "flirted in a manner that nearly drove two or three young men of the dude order into hysterics."[78]

Alternately, for some years in the 1880s, Phil Poland posed as Eva Lind and worked as a waitress in a Colfax, Washington Territory, hotel. She reportedly perfected a recipe to stop the growth of her beard, something that caused comment, to be sure. But more troubling was that she had also received several offers of marriage and she even committed to one man.[79] In another case, this one in Omaha in 1891, police apprehended George Todd promenading in female attire one evening about Twenty-First and Farnam Streets, where he was attempting to "make a mash on one of his own sex."[80] And in yet another instance, also in 1891, Topeka, Kansas, authorities arrested a local photographer who had reportedly been wearing women's clothing and walking the streets, usually during the evening hours, for at least a year. Once down at the station, he claimed he only wanted "to have some fun with the men."[81]

A particularly curious case comes from Altman, Colorado, in the thriving Cripple Creek gold-mining district. There, in 1901, Douglass McPherson, a twenty-seven-year-old Scottish immigrant and ore sorter who donned "long flowing curls," occasionally cross-dressed.[82] Soon dubbing him the Countess McPherson, the local newspaper in its "Altman Briefs" carried episodic tidbits about him, including what he wore to the theater, a dinner party he and his roommate hosted, his appearance once he shorn his locks, and the injury he sustained when a large rock rolled onto his foot while he separated stones at the Pinto mine.[83] A news item in early June 1901 reported that McPherson planned to leave shortly for New York City to attend acting school. It appears that he never in fact did this. Probably dreamt up by an editor on a slow day, the item intentionally poked fun at McPherson for his transgender habits. The tidbit also indicates a Rocky Mountain mining town's views on the relationship between cross-dressing, stage performance, and even New York City. More to the point about conflating female impersonation, workaday world cross-dressing, sexuality, and the theater is an "Altman Brief" from later the same summer musing on McPherson. On 20 July 1901, the paper explained that during a theater show held a couple nights before, "Countess McPherson fell dead in love with the female impersonator . . . and wanted to stay . . . [to] escort her home."[84]

The local newspaper wrote in either neutral or positive terms about McPherson, but that it wrote about him suggests how he stood out in his community. The press's constant focus on McPherson might have been related to the news editor's middle-class sensibilities and anxieties, for it also seems that McPherson met with some degree of acceptance among the working-class men in his western community. He was a member of the Western Federation of Miners' Free Coinage Union Number 19, for example. When he fell for the theatrical female impersonator and wanted to "escort her home," his fellow workers actually intervened and "dragged him away by force." This reveals, as the historian Elizabeth Jameson has pointed out, that the bonds of working-class camaraderie were strong between McPherson and his coworkers, who needed to make sure that one of their own got to work on time the next morning.[85]

The relative acceptance and tolerance of other male-to-female cross-dressers, in particular those who worked locally as female impersonators, is also suggested in other documentation to come out of the American West. One need only think back to San Francisco's Charles Harrington, Omaha's George Todd, Colfax's Phil Poland, and Topeka's local photographer. They apparently carried on their cross-dressing lives and same-sex sexual dalliances for extended periods of time in their communities, suggesting that not only were they tolerated, but they were needed, likely for purposes of sex. We know that at this time in American history, working-class men found little problem having sexual relations with other male-bodied persons, as long as they themselves performed what they viewed as the traditionally male role and their sex partner the female. Typically the latter in these relationships also evinced other feminine gender characteristics, such as those displayed in the cases of Harrington, Todd, Poland, and the Topeka photographer.[86]

There is also evidence of less-than-positive responses from the working classes in this vein. George Owens, as noted above, took up arms against a Mandan, North Dakota, female impersonator who placed him in something of an awkward position. Earl Lind, who sometimes went by the alter ego Jennie June, found "the adolescent cowboys and miners of the Rockies the most prejudiced against effeminate males" he had ever come across. A self-described homosexual from New York City who also took great satisfaction in dressing as a woman, Lind explained that sometime around the turn of the twentieth century, his news-business employers dispatched him to the Rockies "to write up an unusual affair transpiring" there. He traveled "in a caravan with fifty men of the roughest type, cowboys, miners, etc." Although he went entirely dressed as a man, he could not altogether hide his effeminate nature. Soon his fellow travelers "began to heap up insults, particularly taking pains to refer to me within my hearing by the obscene term most often used by roughs for a girl-boy."[87] After flashing his national journalistic credentials, Lind was treated more kindly. He eventually befriended one Wyoming cowboy, who claimed to have traveled with the Buffalo Bill show, and who confided all manner of personal information in him. Lind finally felt comfortable enough to confess his sexuality and gender proclivities. Much to his "surprise and almost to my death," Lind explained, his friend "jilted me with an unparalleled display of horror."[88]

The cases of George Owens and Earl Lind refer to negative western working-class reactions to effeminacy, cross-dressing, and same-sex sexual innuendo. These transpired when working-class men were confronted by effeminate men in fairly public settings. And yet the relatively positive and supportive reactions that working-class men had to Altman, Colorado's Countess McPherson also came in public.[89] If anything, both working-class and middle-class reactions to the West's male-to-female cross-dressers varied as greatly as they did in the case of female-to-male cross-dressers. A more unequivocal point here is that the press's 1901 considerations of McPherson's love interests in the guise of a stage-performing female impersonator and the jokes about him preparing to leave the western mines for acting school in New York City demonstrate that however much McPherson might have been locally liked and accepted, nevertheless his occasional female gender representation was associated with the interrelationship of homosexuality, female impersonation, and the theater.

In 1912 and in 1914 two separate major male homosexual sex scandals rocked Portland, Oregon, and Long Beach/Los Angeles, California, respectively.[90] In both these cases it came to light that men who had sex with other men occasionally dressed in women's clothing and in such garb attended drag balls or parties, some of which ended in sexual activities among those who participated. Both these scandals received extensive news coverage, carried well beyond the cities in which they occurred. They served to crystallize in the public mind the connection between males' effeminate gender activities, cross-dressing, and their homosexuality. But it is clear that before 1912 and 1914, some in the American West had already made these connections, as evidenced in the various stories related above about theatrical female impersonators and their sexual dalliances offstage and other males who dressed as females and their flirtations with men in public.

But before leaving this subject entirely, consider this clear case that came to light in Denver in 1895. The press headlined it "A Queer Case, This." Though it did not revolve about a stage-performing female impersonator, it nevertheless involved a male-to-female cross-dresser, his reported affairs with men, and his effeminacy. Joseph Gilligan was the subject of consideration. Authorities ran him and his accomplice, Elmer Brown, in on charges of burglary and forgery. Only after Gilligan's arrest did police learn of his "real character," as a paper put it. During their initial investigations, authorities first went to the hotel where Gilligan and Brown shared a room. Thinking the landlady had mistakenly sent them into a woman's apartment, they found there a wardrobe full of dresses, corsets, a yachting cap, a blue veil, and two complete changes of ladies' underwear. On a nearby bureau, they discovered powder, a hair curler, makeup, a lady's size-five shoes, gloves, and dainty handkerchiefs, among other objects that might complete a woman's boudoir. Further searching the room, the police uncovered a booklet kept by Gilligan containing the names of prominent Denver men and tell-all letters of a sexual nature. The press quoted from the letters, specifically pointing out the "endearing terms" contained therein and that were exchanged between men. After apprehending the two, Gilligan supposedly "wept and sobbed and his actions were not very manly." "Gilligan is very girlish in his actions and his talk," a local newspaper reported in further shocking detail, "but does not appear to worry over the publicity of his life and seems to gather sympathy from the fact, as he tells it, that Denver has others like himself." Brown admitted to the police that what they suspected of his accomplice was true. He also disclosed that his companion had supported him and several other men. The newspaper described Gilligan as "peculiar" and it likened the entire affair to London's recent Cleveland Street scandal and to "Oscar Wildism." In fact, a newspaper called Gilligan "a real Oscar Wilde."[91] Invoking the attention-grabbing story of Oscar Wilde, a sensation evolving in the press at the very time Gilligan came to light, and a story in which the press liberally spoke of same-sex sexual acts and male effeminacy, attests to the fact that western Americans could conclude that local male-to-female cross-dressers like Gilligan were inverts.

On occasion in reports such as those recounted above, news and other sources from the West might employ the term "hermaphrodite" to describe a subject. The term had at least two meanings at the end of the nineteenth century. The older one used in both medical discourse and at the vernacular level meant someone who had both male and female sex organs or someone who had ambiguous genitalia.[92] Somewhat later in the sexological literature, "hermaphrodite" came to mean a sexual invert—a person with the body of one sex, but who behaved in ways and had the mind, soul, and desires of the opposite sex. Such an individual was thought to be an amalgam of male and female (without regard specifically to sex organs) and thus a hermaphrodite.[93] This is how Rocky Mountain traveler Earl Lind employed the term when he used it to describe himself, for example.[94]

What definition police in Omaha employed in 1890 when they described Henry Brockman is not entirely clear. On March 3 of that year, they apprehended Brockman as a "suspicious character" at Eleventh and Farnam Streets. At first they thought him to be a young man, especially when he gave his name. When they more closely searched, authorities changed their opinion and for a time considered their prisoner to be a woman. "He has a feminine countenance and form," they told a newspaper, "his voice is soft like a woman's, his hands and feet small." Circumstantial evidence also suggested Brockman to be a woman: his valise contained "a box of face powder, three dresses, a pair of ladies's hose and several articles of female adornment, such as cheap jewelry, etc." In this case, it seems that the police could not figure out exactly what they had on their hands, in the end submitting only that their captive "is at any rate a hermaphrodite."[95] In using that term, police likely meant by it the more current meaning akin to sexual inversion, although the newspaper headline for the story read CAUGHT A FREAK. There is no evidence that they eyeballed Brockman's genitals, though clearly they performed some sort of pat-down.

The "hermaphrodite," or what might later be known as someone who is intersex or has ambiguous genitalia, complicated the nineteenth-century's public response to cross-dressers. Such individuals may be a man or a woman, but with genitals indicative of both or, in some cases, neither. Should such an individual (who would be following her/his gender feelings and dress as s/he saw fit), in lieu of external bodily signs to indicate proper comportment, be considered a cross-dresser simply because broader society could not decide how to define the individual's sex? Complicated or not, in one sense this is really the same question that all cross-dressers faced. As the story of Henry Brockman demonstrates, such an individual, however his or her hermaphroditism was defined, might leave a wondering public with questions entirely unanswered.

Such uncertainty, debate, individual choice, and social incredulity appears in varied degrees in just about all male-to-female cross-dressing stories, but it is well captured in the relatively lengthier accounts of James Arthur Baker and Bert Martin (pictured at the beginning of this chapter), who are examined here in turn. Baker's case developed in the western press between 1910 and 1913, tracing from Oklahoma to Japan and then finally to Kansas. The story began in Harrah, Oklahoma, when James Arthur Baker or Arthur J. Baker, in the guise of a woman, taught at a local school. Still in female attire, she then left for Oklahoma City. There a man fell in love with her, but upon discovering that she was a he, the shocked lover reported Baker to the police. He also shared with the authorities his supposition that his former girlfriend was "insane." Soon arrested for masquerading in women's attire, Baker nevertheless quickly found his freedom and left for parts unknown—at least unknown to Oklahomans.[96]

The following year, as a man, Arthur J. Baker secured a teaching position in Segundo, Colorado. Several schoolboys suspected their teacher really to be a woman disguised as a man and brought their concerns to authorities, who arrested Baker. Convinced "he" was in camouflage, they lodged "him" in the women's quarters at the local jail. Baker refused to reveal his sex, but during the hearing that followed ten days later, the truth apparently came out. In a packed courtroom, the prosecutor supplied evidence that Baker had also gone by the names Madeline Baker, Mabel Baker, and, somewhat out of character, Irene Pardee, and had kept up a correspondence with both men and women acting as both a man and a woman. The prosecutor also showed that Baker was the mother of two children and had deserted them and her husband in Oklahoma. He also displayed various items of women's wear taken from Baker's trunk. Despite this considerable evidence, it proved insufficient in the face of expert testimony from three physicians who examined Baker and pronounced him a man. The judge dismissed the case.[97]

A year or so later, Baker appeared in Portland, Oregon, begging for assistance from the Woman's Peniel Mission. He showed up at the door in men's attire but explained to the wife of the institution's superintendent that he was really Alice Baker from Idaho. After having a disagreement with her parents back home, Baker explained, she had to don men's clothing to make her way to the West Coast. To complete her manly disguise, Baker said, she ingeniously used paraffin wax to fill in the bridge of her nose and grafted a fake moustache onto her lip. She now wished to resume wearing women's clothing and hoped locals would take pity on her, given her dire circumstances, and help her as she prepared to take a position at a country school. A number of people showed compassion, responding in part by furnishing a "transformation" wig to replace the hair she had lost when she had to cut it. While resident at the mission, Baker also told how in the past she had at one time married a man and at another time a woman. Her romantic endeavors were hardly a thing of the past, however: when in Portland she pursued the hand of a local evangelical minister and received an offer of marriage. Unfortunately for Baker, some malady overtook her and she ended up in the hospital. A physician who operated on her discovered her to be a man and reported his findings both to the Peniel Mission and to local authorities. Not long after leaving the hospital, Baker, now a man again, took a steamer for California. He was last seen at the Portland docks leaving in the company of another man. Whether that was the evangelical preacher went unrecorded.[98]

Baker's departure from Portland terminated neither her brush with history nor acquaintance with the western press. She next landed in the Kansas City, Kansas, jail, this time in 1913, for dressing as a woman. At the time of this arrest, Baker explained that she was on her way to an art school in Illinois where she planned to study drawing and painting. It also came out that she had traveled and taught in various western and midwestern states as a woman, including Iowa, but had recently traveled from California with her lawyer husband (whom she had met one night at a dance sometime in the past). The two had worked as counterfeiters on the West Coast forging and passing gold certificates. They even traveled to Japan, as Baker revealed to dumbfounded police, where they succeeded in exchanging their imitation bills for gold. On returning to California, Baker stole a bunch of blank money orders from a post office in Summerfield, where her sister happened to be postmistress. Police surmised from all this that Baker was heading to art school in Illinois to further perfect his/her skills at counterfeiting.[99]

From there, the remarkable Arthur, James, Madeline, Mabel, and Alice Baker and Irene Pardee slip from the historical record. But during the few years when they made history, they left a great deal of uncertainty wherever they traveled as to whether they were male or female, showing the degree to which the true gender identity of both the man who dressed as a woman and the woman who dressed as a man had become difficult to pin down by the early years of the twentieth century. It also reveals how hard society tried to do just that. Pardee and the various Bakers took on both female and male personas, interchanging them convincingly and not so convincingly in rapid succession. In Oklahoma City, police recalled that when s/he was incarcerated, Baker's voice altered markedly, at times a deep basso and at other times a shrill falsetto. Schoolboys in Segundo thought Baker a woman masquerading as a man and local authorities believed them. Oklahoma City and Kansas City police picked Baker up, as they thought him/her to be a man dressing in women's clothing. Peniel Mission operators in Portland believed Baker's explanation that s/he was a woman, an explanation s/he offered while dressed as a man. On two separate occasions, one in Colorado and the other in Oregon, attending physicians declared Baker to be a man. But such physical evidence never entirely laid suspicions to rest. During Baker's last known incarceration, in Kansas City, the newspaper declared that its subject had a "dual nature" and referred to Baker as both "mentally and physically a phenomenon."[100] Finally, throughout the Pardee-Bakers' three- or four-year history in the headlines from the eastern plains to the West Coast, they were a husband, a mother, and more often than not a girlfriend or a wife, or at the very least seen in the company of men. Baker received marriage proposals from evangelical ministers and lawyers and even reportedly married the latter.

One fall day in 1900, a few years before the Bakers began making the press, authorities in Keya Paha County, Nebraska, arrested Bert Martin for the crime of horse stealing. He was convicted and sent to the state penitentiary in Lincoln on a two-year sentence. Soon his crime became less serious a matter than other aspects of Martin's life when an inquisitive cell mate whispered to a guard his suspicion that Martin was a woman. An investigation followed, and officials reported that Bert Martin was indeed a female. They re-dressed him accordingly and shipped him to the women's side of the jail. Wardens and watchmen, public pickets and prison peepers seemed satisfied with the sartorial switch, at least at first, though many questions lingered. A bemused and somewhat incredulous public wondered how something seemingly as obvious as someone's sex might escape watchful guards, as upon entering the prison all convicts had to disrobe, bathe, and then have their bodies examined for distinguishing marks (or lack thereof). In fact, the physician who examined Martin upon his prison debut became the butt of all sorts of jokes. The volume of criticism decreased, however, when journalists turned up the information that authorities regularly allowed newly arrived and naked prisoners a towel for modesty's sake.[101]

Yet still fascinated with the perplexing story, newspapers discussed at length Martin's body, searching it for signs of maleness and femaleness. On the one hand they explained that the prisoner had an ungainly appearance and a coarse voice, as well as the chest of a young man, and rather narrow hips. Dressed in men's attire, Martin looked strikingly like a man.[102] And yet, the prisoner also had the anatomical curves, however slight, indicative of a woman. Not to mention (though papers did), Martin had small hands and feet, a smooth face, was five feet eight inches in height, weighed around 140 pounds, and had a delicate constitution, which reportedly accounted for his work assignment in the prison's broom factory rather than at something more physically demanding.[103]

As journalists dug deeper into Martin's story, they discovered he had a wife named Lena and a child. In fact, newspapers told something of a romantic story about how one day while working for a cattle-dealing firm, Martin showed up in Ashland, Nebraska, and decided to stay on, finding a position as a farmhand at Lena's parents' place. One thing led to another and, before long, Bert and Lena found themselves involved in a shotgun wedding.[104] With this added dimension to the story, journalists speculated that on a recent penitentiary visitors' day, when Lena came to call on Bert, she traded places with him and that was how it came to be that the Martin in prison turned out to be a woman.[105]

All this evidence-grappling, tale-spinning, and body re-dressing demonstrates the ways in which broader society desperately needed to pin down Martin's precise sex and how remarkably elusive that endeavor proved to be. The major foil in all this was the fact of Martin's genitals. In 1901, prison physicians who examined Martin declared he had "all the characteristics of a woman, but for reasons of certain imperfections, could never become a mother."[106] Early the following year the Nebraska governor gave a somewhat different, graphic, and mean-spirited accounting. He called the prisoner "a sexual monstrosity, unfit for association with men or women ... and that prison morals imperatively demanded its removal." (He then commuted Martin's sentence to eighteen months and released him immediately.)[107] Though not so derisively, but just as descriptively as the governor, officials who maintained the inmate files similarly noted in Martin's case that he was first "found to be a woman," but a later investigation revealed him be "'alf & 'alf."[108]

Other evidence from Martin's life rendered him a female, though with uncertainty undergirding that conclusion. He was born in September 1879 in Nodaway County, Missouri, the first child of Samuel and Dony Martin. A few months later, in 1880, the U.S. federal census enumerator paid the Martins a visit. They gave the sex of "Bertha" as female.[109] The 1890 manuscript census no longer exists, so we do not know if Samuel and Dony had changed their minds about Bertha by then. But in a 1901 interview, during the height of the Martin sensation, Nancy Martin, a cousin living in Long Pine, Nebraska, explained that Bert's given name was Bertha (independently verifying the information contained in the 1880 census) and that since childhood "she had many attributes of a male person and other peculiar characteristics." Nancy also related, invoking both popularized Lamarckian science and folk medicine, that her aunt and uncle always thought that Bertha's strangeness was "owing to her mother having been badly frightened by a bear while hunting berries in Missouri a few months before the child was born."[110] And a journalist who spoke directly with Martin when in prison reported that as a growing youngster "she" found herself to be "not more than half a woman."[111]

In the nineteenth century, medical experts realized that sometimes people with ambiguous genitalia might be raised as a girl or a boy by unsuspecting parents, though later in life find themselves with feelings and a changing body that led them to then lead lives of the sex just opposite of the one by which they had been raised.[112] A case of this sort came to light in Nebraska's neighboring state of Iowa in 1868. Ellen Burnham of Broadhead, Wisconsin, married a man by the name of Powell at age nineteen and then, two years later, her voice changed, she grew whiskers, and she "gradually changed her sex, developing into a man in all respects." Ellen took the name of Edgar and later married Gerta Everett, also of Broadhead. The two removed to Waterloo, Iowa, where they resided at least up to the time of the

1868 news report. A press release declared the story proof that such "malformations [are] met with occasionally in the practice of the physician. A slight surgical operation removed the difficulty, and restored to nature its function."[113]

The story of Ellen Burnham is paralleled in that of Bert Martin. Despite his brief prison confession to being a female, likely from the stress of the moment, the best evidence purports Martin to have been considered a female during his youth, but during his adulthood he was male. In light of his maleness as an adult, the Nebraska press's 1901 claim that Martin had a wife and child was among its more accurate shreds of reporting. Bert indeed married Lena Dean from Ashland, Nebraska, in 1899. The following February, the two had a child, whom they christened Dewey.[114] For some unknown reason, perhaps the hoopla that occurred in 1901 during Bert's incarceration, his marriage to Lena ended, after which Lena drops from the record. Her parents, on the other hand, moved from Ashland to Liberty Township, Iowa. They took Dewey with them. Although their last name was Dean, they eventually changed their grandson's to Dayton.[115] Bert remarried in about 1907 and had at least two more children by his second wife.[116]

All the time, then, Bert was apparently a male. When dressed as a such, he fully abided by his social duty. And yet his cell mate, the prison guard, the penitentiary's physician and warden, and the public residing beyond the reformatory's walls refused to accept it. To suit their own definitions of gender, sex, and the body, they seemed satisfied only when they did the dressing. In a way, Bert Martin's tale reverses the typical cross-dressing story. Rather than the individual choosing to cross-dress to suit whatever design s/he may have in mind, including to fulfill emotional and psychological need, in Martin's case society did the cross-dressing to suit its own notions, ideas, and identities. When one thinks about it, this was no reversal at all.

Like their female-to-male counterparts, male-to-female cross-dressers abounded in the nineteenth-century American West. Many male-bodied persons in Native American cultures worked and lived as women (as Chapter 4 addresses in more detail). Many men of other ancestral backgrounds dressed as women to pull off jokes or to disguise themselves in the commission of a crime. Some worked as female impersonators onstage while others ended up in female attire for reasons of health, or because unwitting and witting parents garbed them as such, or because they wished to attend a masquerade or a dance. While many of these reasons might seem understandable, many a nineteenth-century observer remained puzzled by men who dressed as women, and in particular in the case of those who did so for extended periods of time. In 1878, for example, upon learning the male identity of an individual who had passed himself off as a woman and who had worked for years as a laundress for the Seventh Cavalry, a Chicago news editor thoughtfully pointed to the many understandable reasons a woman might switch her clothing and live as a man. But "why did this man," asked the editor reasonably (at least from an 1878 perspective), "leave the wider field of action vouchsafed to man, and take upon himself the drudgery incident to a poor woman's life on the frontier[?]"[117]

In the face of general bafflement raised by such a question, one is left only to suspect answers more discomfiting to those who hold to the mythic manly nature of the Old West, answers that the broader public and the medical profession slowly began to supply in the years following. As the nineteenth century ebbed, the sartorial habits of male-to-female cross-dressers, arguably much more than those of their female-to-male counterparts, could be explained only through gender and sexual inversion. Among the most interesting aspects of this process was the role performed by the local western cross-dresser, in particular female impersonators who lived and worked in towns and cities throughout the region. In blending their stage performances with their street lives in very public ways, local female impersonators helped to produce what their audiences feared the most. And what they feared the most they quickly applied to male-to-female cross-dressers more generally and rather assertively.

With all this said, it should be kept in mind that this was not purely a story of the broader public coming to conflate cross-dressing with gender inversion and same-sex sexuality. Many of the individuals considered in this chapter, like Joseph Gilligan, James Arthur Baker, Charles Harrington, George Todd, and Earl Lind, undoubtedly understood themselves to be sexual inverts, whether that was what we might call in a later era homosexual, transsexual, or transgender people.

After considering the evidence presented in this chapter, the reader might be struck by the differences in how the press reported on western male-to-female as compared to female-to-male cross-dressers. In the latter case, the press and a few other odd sources typically explained sartorial switches using elements of popularly understood western culture and life. In the former instance, the press rarely, if ever, tried to find purpose and meaning in male-to-female cross-dressing by casting it against a western backdrop. This is not to say that western male-to-female cross-dressing cannot be understood in regionally specific ways. This chapter exposes, for example, the local role that female impersonators in the West had in shaping and altering public understanding of sexuality there. It also discloses that male-to-female cross-dressers might have come to the West precisely because of who they were and because the region demanded them, or at least their skills. Too, some male-to-female cross-dressers connected their lives and sartorial endeavors to the cultural meaning of the West. The transvestite M, with whom this chapter began, clearly did so when explaining that he had done his part in the winning of the West. Earl Lind likewise integrated his turn-of-the-twentieth-century experiences into western motifs. He alternately described his fellow travelers as the "roughest type" of men but also portrayed one as a "Nature's nobleman." He feared that in the "wilds of the Rockies," those who tormented him "could easily push me over a precipice." When the one cowboy friend he made on his trip recoiled from his confession about his gender and sexuality, Lind described his feelings of abandonment as leaving him in a "desolate stroll in the bear-infested wilderness."[118]

But the popular press—the most public of representations of cross-dressing males in the West—remained reticent on connecting male–male sexuality and male effeminacy to the exigencies of the region. Though western women's cross-dressing would be accounted for, rationalized, regendered, and resexualized within the context of the American West and frontier, this would not be so for male-to-female cross-dressers, which is why the richness of their numbers and stories remains obliterated from our collective and popular memories about the American West and the frontier.

PART TWO

"The Story of the Perverted Life Is Not Attractive"

Making the American West and the Frontier Heteronormative

"And Love Is a Vision and Life Is a Lie"

The Daughters of Calamity Jane

Most sources suggest that Joe Monahan turned fifty-three in 1903. By then he had made his home for almost four decades in and about the Owyhee Mountains of extreme southwestern Idaho. The last twenty or so of those years he resided on Succor Creek, a small stream that tumbles westward, down from the Owyhees, before it meanders out into the deserts of neighboring southeastern Oregon. In the last days of 1903, just as late autumn turned to early winter, Monahan contracted some unspecified malady. As he led an otherwise solitary existence, his enfeebled condition led him to seek refuge at the home of Barney and Kate Malloy, who lived just down a spot, on the Oregon side of the state line. The Malloys were friends to Monahan as much as anyone in the area. The couple and their children had for some years provided their neighbor with a stopping-off place when, every fall, he drove his small band of buckskin horses and growing herd of cattle down to winter feeding grounds. This year, Monahan had again turned out his twenty or so horses to pasture on the nearby Roswell Bench, but due to not feeling well he had someone else trail his cattle to the Boise Valley, north of the Owyhees, where he had secured winter range for them. Unfortunately, as the new year arrived at the Malloy ranch, Monahan's sickness only worsened. A virulent coughing fit overcame him during the evening of 5 January 1904. Sometime later that night, Monahan's otherwise obscure life slipped away.[1]

Similar stories—the sad passing of a weakened and relatively aged pioneer—were stuff of the everyday in the West by the turn of the twentieth century. But this tale turned out to be among the more newsworthy: when

FIGURE 5. Joe Monahan, 1904. One of the best-known female-to-male cross-dressers of the Old West, Monahan migrated from Buffalo, New York, to the gold-rush district of Idaho's Owyhee Mountains by 1870. Long after the rush subsided, Monahan continued to live and work as a man in the area. He died there in 1904. When they prepared him for burial, locals discovered he had a female body, though they had suspected for years that he was not the man he purported to be. The mass-circulation press, most notably the *American Journal Examiner*, fictionalized his womanhood, femininity, and heterosexuality. Later storytellers, playwrights, and filmmakers have uncritically accepted what period newspapers reported. Image courtesy of Denver Public Library, Western History Collection, Z-8995.

Monahan's neighbors began to prepare his remains for burial, they discovered that their pioneer friend had the body of a woman. Troubled by exactly what to do, they administered a rather perfunctory funeral. A local from nearby Rockville, Idaho, who had for some time known Monahan, later wrote in dismay to a Boise newspaper when he learned about how Monahan had been treated in death. "Not a word was spoken, not a word read, not a prayer offered," the concerned man lamented. And yet, in his mind, "'Little Joe' never did anyone harm . . . so far as is known her life was pure, although disguised as a man. . . . And who can say they never sinned more than 'Little Joe,' and who knows the cause that made her do as she did? A cause that might have made [any] one of us a vagabond, a drunkard or a criminal. So let us pray that 'Little Joe's' soul has been received at the 'Pearly Gates' as we would wish our's to be received."[2]

As this Rockville correspondent's words evince, despite the fact that Joe Monahan had resided for many years in this remote corner of the Idaho-Oregon borderlands, few there knew a great deal about him. What seems certain about this Idaho pioneer, in fact, composes a rather short list. Monahan shows up in southwestern Idaho as early as the 1870 federal census. He was born about 1850; the census over the years varies somewhat on the exact year. Most sources identify his birthplace as New York. He was also somewhat complacent about picking up his mail at the Silver City, Idaho, post office; the local newspaper regularly ran advertisements listing those who had mail waiting for them, and Joe's name often appeared among the remiss. We also know that Monahan voted in the Republican primary on 28 August 1880, some sixteen years before women in Idaho received suffrage rights. When he died, his estate included about one hundred head of cattle, some thirty-five of these being steers of no more than three years old.[3]

But the further we move from these verifiable facts, the less certain the story becomes. Upon Monahan's death, William Schnabel, an old-time cowboy who had recently returned to the area from the Klondike gold rush and whose mother, Frederica, had formed something of an attachment to Joe years before, took it upon himself to try to track down Monahan's kin. Wracking his brain for what little he could recall, Schnabel vaguely remembered some years back when he and Monahan worked the local range together, the latter had occasionally entrusted him with letters to post. These letters, Schnabel harkened back, were addressed to either a Mrs. J. Waters or Walters who lived in Buffalo, New York. At the time, Monahan had told Schnabel that the woman he wrote to was his sister, of whom he was very fond. Spurred on by these fragmentary recollections, this resourceful western detective next penned a letter to the chief of police in Buffalo, seeking his help in tracking down Monahan's family, hoping its members might benefit from the modest estate Joe had left behind. Upon receipt of Schnabel's extraordinary missive, the Buffalo police turned it over to the local paper, which eagerly printed it on page one of the next edition.[4]

The advertisement had its desired effect: within the day, Mrs. Katherine Walter, who coincidentally happened to be the mother of Anna Walter, matron at the police station, came forward claiming knowledge of "Johanna Monohan." The Buffalo paper carried the bittersweet news. Walter explained that she had served for about six years as Monahan's foster mother, taking Monahan in when the girl was eight years old, because the child's stepfather was "an habitual drunkard." Not long after Monahan turned fourteen, Walter further recounted, "she" decided to head West, hoping to strike it rich in mining. Over the years, Katherine and her daughter Anna kept up their correspondence with Monahan, receiving the last letter from Idaho a few days prior to Christmas 1903.[5] That Monahan's neighbors reportedly discovered a stash of correspondence from "her mother and sister in New York" buried in an old trunk in Joe's cabin just days after his death lends credence to the account in the Buffalo paper.[6]

Such details, however, serve only to further becloud Monahan's life and origins. A search of Buffalo's 1860 census uncovers no Johanna Monahan at about the time Walter would have taken him in. There does appear an eight-year-old Mary Manumon, born in New York and living with a younger sister, Anne, her mother, Bridget, and, importantly, a *stepfather* named Peter Reily. That Reily also worked as a saloon keeper might provide support for Katherine's characterization of Johanna's stepfather's relationship with alcohol. Too, perhaps "Manumon" was how the census enumerator heard the name Monahan. Or over the years Manumon might have transmogrified into Monahan. Of even more interest, living with the Reily-Manumon family was a thirteen-year-old servant girl named Johanna Burke. Perhaps Johanna took Mary's surname to become Johanna Monahan or Mary took Johanna's first name and headed West a few years later as the alter ego who soon turned up in Idaho and lived there until early 1904.[7] In any case, local stories purport that Joe Monahan first appeared in Silver City in 1867, which, should this have been Mary Manumon, would have made "her" roughly fifteen at the time, about the age that Katherine said Johanna was when she headed to the gold-rush frontier.[8]

Further complicating the story that Walter provided the Buffalo press in January 1904 was another she later furnished by letter to Fred Palmer, a

RUBY CITY, OWYHEE DISTRICT, IDAHO.

FIGURE 6. Idaho's Owyhee Mountains gold-rush district, 1869. Joe Monahan arrived in the Owyhees at about the time an artist rendered this view of a portion of the area. Image from Albert D. Richardson, *Beyond the Mississippi: Life and Adventure on the Prairies, Mountains, and Pacific Coast* (Hartford, CT: American Publishing Co., 1869), 505.

merchant in Jordan Valley, Oregon, who had taken charge of Monahan's estate. In that missive, its contents relayed by Palmer to Idaho newspapers, we get additional as well as somewhat different information about Monahan and his life in Buffalo. Walter explained to Palmer, for instance, that Johanna's mother "always dressed her in boy's clothes and let her earn her own living by running errands and selling newspapers." Fully aware of the young Johanna's masquerade, Walter nevertheless took the girl in with her mother's consent and sent her to school. In this version, Monahan supposedly left for the West in 1869, first heading to California before making her way to Idaho.[9]

Over the days following the deathbed mystery of Monahan, locals in the Idaho-Oregon border country began to relate to the press additional bits of information that they claimed to have learned over the years about their secretive neighbor whose national celebrity was now growing. These stories pretty much held to 1867 as the year that Monahan originally showed up in Silver City. They explain that he began working there first in a livery, followed by a stint in a sawmill. He struck it big in mining, accumulating upward of $3,000, but he had the misjudgment of entrusting the sum to a shady mining superintendent to invest in the business's stock. Instead, the rascal departed the country, absconding with Monahan's life savings. Doggedly starting anew, Monahan began selling milk from a cow and eggs from a few chickens he still retained and worked odd jobs here and there until he had accumulated somewhere between $800 and $1,000. He held on to his money this time, taking it with him when he left Silver City and moved across the divide to Succor Creek in about 1883. There he built a rather mean cabin, which some described as little more than a chicken coop while others likened the shack to a dugout. He fenced in forty acres and hired, at least for a short time, a Chinese laborer to help cut grass to feed the one cow and one horse he had brought with him to his new homestead. Over the years Monahan saw his stock increase, tending it about as carefully as he did his earnings. He became known as something of a miser, living sparingly in his cabin, dressing poorly, and often denying himself food, though availing himself of the hospitality that neighbors gladly and often provided. During these years, Monahan also took his civil duties seriously, reportedly voting in every election and serving several times on a jury. Locals also recalled that he could well handle a revolver and a Winchester rifle and that he had become an accomplished horseman.[10]

As the news related these bits and pieces of Monahan's life, papers farther afield described the revelation of his successful masquerade as causing a local sensation. An Olympia, Washington, publication, for example, explained with the certainty of an eyewitness that "when friendly neighbors were preparing the body for burial the community was given a decided shock when it was announced that 'Joe' Monahan was a woman."[11] In reality, that Monahan turned out to be physically female caught hardly anyone in and about the Owyhees off-guard. When William Schnabel wrote to the Buffalo police, he explained rather sensitively that "it was always surmised that Joe was a woman. . . . He was a small, beardless, little man with the hands, feet, stature and voice of a woman."[12]

The 1880 census lends credence to Schnabel's story. That year, a local farmer and father of six by the name of Ezra Mills served as the census enumerator for District 29, Owyhee County, Idaho Territory, the very census tract in which both he and Monahan resided. In fact, Mills counted his family's dwelling house as the 221st and "Joseph" Monahan's as the 218th that he visited, revealing that he and Monahan lived in close proximity and were likely more than casual acquaintances. For Monahan's sex, Mills recorded "M" (male) in the appropriate column but took the time to pencil in next to it the editorial comment "Doubtful Sex."[13] Clearly, for years locals had suspected that Monahan was a woman. But, as Schnabel explained, "no one could vouch for the truth of it. . . . He never would reveal his identity and all cowboys respected him. . . . He never told a word to his best friends who he was and what he was."[14]

Furthermore, residents in and about Silver City had become fully acquainted over the years with any number of local women and those farther afield who dressed as men. In March and then again in August 1875, for example, the Silver City newspaper the *Owyhee Avalanche* related accounts of several young resident women who donned male attire to have some fun. In the former case, the paper explained in explicit detail, while awkwardly straining against propriety, that one of the young ladies had ripped the seams of her pantaloons as a result of her womanly hips while another in the little party of jokesters wore "a vest entirely too small to shield properly the region from which sustenance for young children emanates."[15] A few years later the newspaper took a vigorous role in the debates and discussion about "Samrah" Pollard of Tuscarora, Nevada. Then, in 1891, commenting on revelations from another paper about a young woman in the not too distant Boise City "who dons male attire and goes into the country gunning," the *Owyhee Avalanche* told of Silver City's own "charming young lady who does the same thing, and the town is full of young men who have been 'shot.'"[16]

This awareness of the ubiquity of female-to-male cross-dressers might have served to further harden Succor Creek and Silver City residents when they learned of Monahan's biological sex. As an aside that takes us back to Chapter 1 and its consideration of the various ways in which western communities responded to their revealed female-to-male cross-dressers, it is clear that residents of the Owyhees, although they might have wondered for years and maybe even "surmised" that Joe was a woman, nevertheless had long accepted Monahan as a man, one who was deeply enmeshed in their community. Moreover, the cowboys of the area, to use Schnabel's words, "treated him with the greatest respect, and he was always welcome to eat and sleep at their camp." Tellingly, throughout his letter that he sent to the Buffalo police, even now that the mystery was cleared up, Schnabel used "he," "him," and "his" to refer to Joe. Schnabel even began his letter with the compassionate sentence, "Dear Sir, there died near here a little man, who has been known by all fron- tiersmen, such as miners and cowboys, as 'Joe Manahan.'"[17] Such persistent sentiment shows that to his community, despite both certainty and uncer- tainty, Monahan was a man.

Given what little is truly verifiable about Monahan's life, it would seem ironic, then, that of all the female-to-male cross-dressers who appeared in the American West in the second half of the nineteenth century, Monahan is also among the best "known" to us in the present day. Beginning in the 1950s, Old West enthusiasts regularly revived his story in book print and sensational newspaper columns.[18] In 1981, dramatist Barbara Lebow produced a play about Little Joe; directors and performers soon staged it in playhouses across the country.[19] And then in 1993 Hollywood released director Maggie Greenwald's full-length feature film about this cross-dressing Idahoan, *The Ballad of Little Jo*.[20] Because so little is known with any degree of certainty about Monahan, it is not surprising that these iterations of his life are filled less with fact than with fancy—the things writers either believe about him or would like to envis- age; they thereby remain mute on the possibility of sexual inversion in his life. Rather, wherever they can and with invented information, they transform Monahan into a heterosexual woman and claim that it was "her" troubles with men in earlier life that drove her to sartorial alterations and refuge in the West.

This rendering of Monahan's life is not without historical if still fictional foundation: it traces directly back to 1904 when, in lieu of more truthful in- formation about Monahan and during a time when cross-dressing caused increased sensation and raised pronounced sexual suspicion, those near to and far from southwestern Idaho did their best to reclaim Monahan as the most feminine of women. Already in March 1904 the *American Journal Ex- aminer* produced an apocryphally heterosexualized wire release of Monah- an's life and gave it authenticity by providing a few accurate facts as well as a dateline of Boise City.[21] In it, the *Examiner* changed Monahan's name from Joe to Jo, dropping the "e" to feminize him, produced a photograph of a hoopskirt-clad debutante purported to be Jo, and told a remarkable tale about "her," quoted here in part:

> This is the closing chapter in the life story of a beautiful girl who loved not wisely but too well a villain by whom she was deserted in her darkest hour, who was driven from her home into a pitiless world, having left to her only the constant

love of a sister, whose testimony now is all that reveals the identity of "Little Jo," the cowboy of Succor Creek.

Shortly after the close of the War of the Rebellion exclusive society in Buffalo, N.Y., received a severe shock in the announcement that the house of one of its leading members was closed permanently. Rumor had linked the name of its fairest daughter with that of a well-known society man of dissolute habits. The girl was still in her 'teens and had but recently made her debut in the social world. The young man was some years her senior. Their intimacy dated from the first hour of their meeting. The association was obnoxious to her parents, who essayed to dampen the ardor of her devotion, but to no purpose. Clandestine meetings were arranged by the lovers. For months this order of affairs prevailed, followed by the distressing announcement that the young girl had been driven from home by the unyielding parents.

At this serious juncture of her life the outcast besought her lover to right the wrong he had done. Fair promises were easily made, and on assurance of an early marriage the girl accompanied her betrayer to New York City. The promises were never fulfilled. Nor did the advent of a baby boy serve to spur his lagging conscience. He deserted both the baby and its mother.

Left in almost destitute circumstances, the girl-mother cast about for means of existence. Her efforts met with no success in attempting to secure a position in keeping with her education. Driven to it, she was compelled to accept a place in an eating house on Broadway, New York City, where she labored through a trying period of seven months. Her recent poverty had taught her the value of money, and by dint of much care she accumulated a small sum. From her meagre wages she had to care for herself and pay the board of her child, which she had placed in an asylum in that city.

Throughout all her trials and vicissitudes her sister, younger than she, had been her one true friend. They had exchanged letters regularly, and from her came the news of the death of the unrelenting parents, who died broken hearted. Had she desired it, her old home was now open to her, and her sister besought her return. Disgraced, she had been expelled from it, and, dishonored still, she would not return. But she did not hesitate in agreeing to her sister's proposition to part with her boy. Mother love prompted this act, for at the old home the child would receive the care and attention that it could not secure at the asylum.

The child's future secure, she determined to begin life anew in the West, that was then offering homes for the outcasts of all lands. In those days a journey across the continent was an undertaking attended by many hardships and not a few dangers. This was the more so in the case of a woman traveling alone. It was on this account that the brave little woman decided to don the more conventional attire of the male sex, discarding her own dress with her past. Assuming the disguise of a man, she joined a party of homesteaders and prospectors and started for the West.[22]

Almost entirely fabricated, the *American Journal Examiner*'s version of Joe Monahan's life no doubt served immediately to assuage contemporary anxieties about Monahan's sex and gender (after all, a very reliable source reported that Monahan had dressed in boys' clothing since girlhood). It also provided later writers, dramatists, and filmmakers the basic outlines for the rather fantastic heterosexualized stories they told about this Idahoan. The *American Journal Examiner*'s reimagining of Monahan—she was a feminine woman, she was a debutante, she had a male lover, she was a mother—was part of a broader turn-of-the-twentieth-century national undertaking Americans engaged in: the heteronormalizing of the fictive frontier and the mythical Old West.

In this chapter I explore this phenomenon at the popular-cultural level in America and the West, analyzing the invented tales that circulated in the press in the late nineteenth and early twentieth centuries of both real-life and entirely fictionalized western American female-to-male cross-dressers. I show that as the local and national press reimagined western cross-dressers' gender and sexuality, it drew directly and purposely on western tropes and myths as well as on contemporary and long-circulating literary devices to explain why a woman might dress and live as a man at a specific place and moment in history. The contemporary and traditional literary formulas the press invoked included period dime novels, older sentimental seduction tales, and the superannuated female-warrior ballad.

For the most part, this heterosexualizing of the cross-dresser was accomplished before the frontier closed—that is, the frontier West as it was popularly understood: a place of great sexual imbalance and social fluidity, a place of violence and lawlessness, and a place not generally welcoming to women. On the other hand, the transformation of the cross-dresser into a respectable woman usually occurred after the frontier era had ended, or else when the subject moved out of the West to a more settled (and thus post-frontier) part of America, or when the figurative frontier era of her own life concluded— for example, when she gave up her questionable attire and behaviors and entered into marriage. The entire project of resexualizing and regendering the West's female-to-male cross-dressers was completed precisely when the western region entered the modern era and integrated into the rest of the nation. As such, myths of the West and of the frontier worked hand-in-hand with period anxieties about cross-dressing and about strong and independent women to produce a heterosexualized and gender normalized regional history and a heterosexualized and gender normalized version of the birth of the modern American nation.

In the winter of 1884, John McCafferty made his way along a thirty-three-mile snow-covered trail that wound through the Rocky Mountains from the Trout Creek station of the Northern Pacific Railroad in Montana Territory to Eagle City in the newly opened Coeur d'Alene, Idaho Territory, mining district. "Anticipating the roughness of the trip," McCafferty packed nothing more than a sturdy walking stick that, he later explained, saved him "from many an ugly fall." Others with whom he traveled pulled sleds, each packed with some 125 pounds of supplies. Making the hike even "more memorable" than the conditions in which he performed it was "one woman in the party, dressed in male attire." McCafferty took pity on her, assisting her over the more "rough and dangerous" places. He also offered only a few words about the woman's background and the reasons for her perilous journey. But in these few words McCafferty actually said quite a bit. "Poor girl!" he described in a way later echoed in the *American Journal Examiner's* rendition of Joe Monahan's life, "the only daughter and sister of a worthy family, led astray, then abandoned, not more than twenty years of age, with female paraphernalia strapped upon a toboggan, tramping over snow-clad mountains to an asylum of sin. What a subject for contemplation! She could truly exclaim 'And love is a vision and life is a lie.'"[23]

This western woman likely dressed herself in male attire not so much because she wished to disguise her sex, but rather because such clothing seemed more reasonable for one who planned on towing a toboggan through two- to eight-foot drifts of snow and over a mountain pass in the dead of winter. That she hauled along all sorts of "female paraphernalia" perhaps confirms that she had no intention of living as a man. So, too, the innuendo that, as a fallen woman, she headed West for a life of prostitution. Wronged in a relationship and then forced to take up the prevarication of masculine attire, in her case truly love had been but a vision and life had become a lie. It was also the same, at least in popular telling, of the lives of myriad other western female-to-male cross-dressers around the turn of the twentieth century. Led astray and then dumped by the worst sort of lover, or wronged or thwarted in love under some other unfortunate circumstance, and then fleeing to the West in men's clothing, is a trope that many—both westerners and easterners—resorted to in order to explain, in lieu of more definitive information and instead of a more sexually suspect account, why females in the region might be discovered wearing men's attire.

In part, this story line had its roots in the late eighteenth- and early nineteenth-century sentimental seduction novel. Structured as a morality tale, the seduction novel typically concludes with the death of the unfortunate girl who became pregnant and then was abandoned by a dastardly male lover after he lured her away from her family's protection. The later accounts of female-to-male cross-dressers in the American West, however, have the young woman fleeing from her shame in the East and finding anonymity on the socially fluid frontier, further abetted by the camouflage that male clothing provides her. The differences here between the seduction novels and the western tales can be accounted for by the fact that many of the cross-dresser stories like Joe Monahan's revolve around real "women" who obviously did not die in shame, but ended up in the West and often lived there for many years.[24]

Another in this vein is California's Charley Parkhurst, who died at the very end of 1879 (and whose long-term western fame rivals that of Monahan; over the years many publications that normalize him as a woman have hit the bookshelves of local historical societies).[25] Unlike in Monahan's case, no one in California seems to have seriously suspected Parkhurst to be a woman during his twenty-some years among them. In fact, upon his death many refused to believe it until doctors who examined the body announced that sometime earlier in life Parkhurst had given birth.[26] From this medical finding, stories then began to circulate about both a love affair having gone wrong and "her" having been forsaken sometime before "her" sartorial switch. One paper explained a few days after the Californian's death, for instance, that "a mother she is represented to have been, and it may date back to that proud eminence from which virtuous women alone can fall, fall by the deception of some man monster."[27] Another reported the numerous rumors spreading through the neighborhood "that in early years 'she loved not wisely, but too well,'" anticipating the very words later employed in the fanciful account of Joe Monahan.[28]

In the few weeks following Parkhurst's discovered mystery, stories about a love gone wrong never developed beyond the terse anecdotes related above. Several years later, however, they had. Interest in Parkhurst's life renewed at that time, as by then the press, particularly in the West, confronted increasing numbers of women who dressed as males. In 1885, Denver's *Rocky Mountain*

News, for example, carried a story that recapitulated several such individuals, among them prominently profiling Parkhurst. The item, however, made no claims about a romance in "her" past. The following year, the *Surf*, a newspaper in Santa Cruz, California, seems to have become the first in this later period to offer more details of Parkhurst's supposed earlier love affair, details that other newspapers picked up and embellished. By the time the story ran its course, Parkhurst had become "Charlotte" Parkhurst, or "Lotte . . . as she was known," of Sandusky, Ohio, where she had once lived a secure life with her parents. In 1848, when she was but twenty years old, however, a dashing young westerner came to town to take the position of postmaster. The acquaintance between him and the "prepossessing" Lotte "ripened quickly into love." The two quietly eloped and disappeared. Lotte's "distracted father searched for the girl for months, without success, and finally concluded that she had destroyed herself." According to the story anyway, she later turned up in gold-rush California as a stagecoach driver. What happened to Parkhurst's lover went unexplained, but earlier reports about the interference of "some man monster" and later claims that her father believed she had "destroyed herself" suggest that her love had indeed gone awry.[29]

While Monahan's and Parkhurst's fictional stories differ from the seduction novel in that the protagonists became pregnant, gave birth, and lived rather than died forsaken, fleeing to the West instead, they nevertheless keep to the essential trajectory of this literary form: the fabricated western stories of real cross-dressers reveal their subjects' early falls from grace only after the protagonists actually die. The *American Journal Examiner*, after all, introduced its rendition of Monahan's early life with the sobering line, "This is the closing chapter of the life story of a beautiful girl who loved not wisely but too well a villain by whom she was deserted in her darkest hour."[30]

These words about being "the closing chapter of the life story" hint at how fabricated cross-dressing accounts traced their origins to popular fiction, whether in the tradition of the seduction tale or in the contemporary dime novel.[31] In the 1870s—well before the popularly understood closing of the frontier—dime novels turned women's cross-dressing into an art form, normalizing the act by relating it to her love affairs and sexual relationships with men. Among the earliest and most famous of such dime novels is Edward Wheeler's *Deadwood Dick on Deck; or, Calamity Jane, The Heroine of Whoop-Up*. It appeared in 1878, a year after the cross-dressing Calamity Jane first debuted as a dime-novel heroine.[32] Based on the real-life Martha Jane Canary, who evidence suggests seldom dressed as a man and actually identified as a woman, the Calamity Jane of *Deadwood Dick on Deck* does not choose men's clothing because she wishes to *disguise* herself as a man.[33] In addition, she falls in love with the story's male protagonist, though Calamity is also eventually thwarted in that love. In the tale, furthermore, she is never really understood to be a man, though some at times do wonder about her sex. For example, one minor character proffers, "At least they say she's o' the feminine sex, fer w'ich I can't sw'ar, purtic'lar."[34] And Calamity herself confirms in the story that she is a woman, though she concomitantly fudges the truth, suggesting the ways in which social uncertainty over such an issue has even influenced dime novels of the era. "Well, yes," Calamity Jane thus responds when asked if she was a woman, "I reckon I am in flesh, but not in spirit o' late years. Ye see, they kind o' got matters discomfuddled w'en I was created, an' I turned out to be a gal instead of a man, which I ought to hev been."[35] But even with these questions about her true sex, we learn that the Calamity of dime-novel manufacture took to male dress and her spirit changed toward the masculine only in the later years of her life, as she herself explains. More to the point is the actual cause for her cross-dressing: "a man's defiling touch," a "villain . . . who foully robbed Jane Forrest of her maiden name, but *never* her honor." Calamity then dons male clothing and "tuk ter the rovin' life ter hunt down her false lover; [or] thet she hed bin married ter a Nevada brute, an' kim over inter thes deestrict ter escape him."[36]

Other dime-novel heroines cross-dress to escape a brutish husband. Such is the case of Dusty Dick, also a character in *Deadwood Dick on Deck*, whose real name is Edna Sutton. At the behest of a guardian uncle, Edna marries Cecil Grosvenor in Richmond, Virginia, thinking him to be a gentleman. She only later learns that he was already married and entered into a sham relationship with her to gain access to her inheritance. Grosvenor then tries to murder her. Edna's father, who provided his daughter's fortune and might also have protected her, is dead, and so, "To save my life I fled," Edna later explains, "and came West, preferring that he should have the money rather than my life. But he pursued me, and hoping to escape him, I donned this male attire and entered the mountains."[37] At the end of the novel, Dusty Dick is transformed back into Edna and marries the story's male protagonist, Sandy.

Similarly, Gentleman Sam's Sister or Dauntless Jerry, who in truth is the more prosaic Iola in Philip S. Warne's *Hard Crowd; or, Gentleman Sam's*

Sister, takes to male attire only temporarily while on the way to finding heterosexual love. Like *Deadwood Dick on Deck, Hard Crowd* appeared in 1878. It revolves around three women who dressed as men in and about Omaha, which was then "at the meridian of her glory as the 'hardest place' east of Denver City." Iola chooses to impersonate her nonexistent brother to help the aunt who raised her (the only mother she has ever known) find her own long-lost son. Iola eventually succeeds in her task and she and her cousin fall in love as the denouement to the story.[38]

Dime novels such as these also on occasion have women cross-dress to make it easier for them to track down and exact vengeance on a man who wronged them—one of the suppositions offered for Calamity Jane's sartorial alterations. It is also the case with Nebraska Larry, who in truth is Countess Pepita, another cross-dresser in *Hard Crowd*. In men's clothing, Pepita hunts down the story's main antagonist, Red Hand, who had "been her hard master" for some dozen years. Near the end of the novel, and after being mortally wounded, Pepita briefly revives just in time to gleefully see Red Hand hanged. "Die, you devil! die!" cries Pepita as Nebraska Larry during her last breath before sinking "back dead."[39]

By 1878, then, popular fiction might explain a western woman's cross-dressing as related somehow to an opposite-sex relationship having gone bad. Cross-dressing might also simply serve as a way station toward consummating heterosexual love. These explanations for sartorial switches normalized the western female-to-male cross-dresser and made her a heterosexual woman well before the very end of the nineteenth century, just when notions of hetero- and homosexuality crystallized in broader society. Whereas in real life during this era cross-dressing became increasingly associated with sexual inversion, in western frontier fiction, and thus popular myth, a woman who turned to men's dress remained above such sexual suspicion; cross-dressing had become coded in the region as an act related to heterosexual love and sex (whether good or bad). Cleansed of social anxieties, this theme worked its way into how westerners as well as easterners imbued with western myth would explain many of the real-life female-to-male cross-dressers they encountered in the West at the turn of the twentieth century. Joe Monahan and Charley Parkhurst represent just two examples.

Another is Sammy Williams of Manhattan, Montana. Tales of Williams's past love having gone wrong also developed over a space of time, though within a few days rather than a few weeks or even years. The first

report of Williams's death and the concomitant discovery that he had the
body of a woman appeared in the *Anaconda (Montana) Standard* but two
days after his demise. In that dispatch, the reporter claimed that the "reason
is mystery" for Williams's cross-dressing.[40] There is no mention of a past
love, though the paper did offer some details about Williams's biography,
including that he had hailed from Oshkosh, Wisconsin, and worked for a
time in the Dakotas before arriving in Montana.

Only four days later, the *Grand Forks (North Dakota) Herald* carried an
article with a dateline of Eau Claire, Wisconsin, offering a more romantic
tale, though in this one Sammy has been renamed Billy Williams, who earlier had been Ingeborge Wekan. Reportedly born in Hallingdale, Norway,
Ingeborge fell in love there with the neighbor boy, named Sven Norem. The
Wekans and Norems migrated to America together, settling in Waukon,
Iowa. But after arriving, Sven's parents objected to their son's interest in Ingeborge, "declaring the girl's parents were of a lower station in life." Devastated, Ingeborge apparently did the only sensible thing: she dressed in male
attire and headed to Eau Claire. There, as a man, she cooked in a lumber
camp for about ten years and did such a fine job that she earned more than
any other similar employees in the camps. She attended dances "with the
girls, drank and in every way acted like her male companions." Still, she could
not "overcome the longing to behold those who were near and dear to her."
So, she slipped back to Waukon in the disguise of a tramp. As such, "she
called at her old home as a beggar. From there she went to the home of her
old lover . . . who had married another woman by this time and settled down.
Here she was given some food." All the while undetected, Williams re-
treated yet again disappointed in love, returning briefly to Eau Claire before
drifting westward still in male clothing.[41] Versions of this more fanciful tale
appeared in other western newspapers.[42]

The literary motif of cross-dressing as a temporary stage on the way to
achieving heterosexual love made its way especially into stories that circulated in the press about western women who were likely fictional but were
passed off as real. This is the case in the recollections of "W.B.S." of Santa
Rosa, California, which he recounted for an area newspaper in 1875 of a certain Lizzie Clark from the Deep South. W.B.S.'s story climaxes on a Mississippi steamboat in 1856 where, disguised as a male, Clark defeats a seasoned
gambler to win back the fortune lost, just moments before, by a youthful

planter's son with whom she has instantly fallen in love. Among the passengers, Clark recognizes W.B.S. as an old family friend and reveals herself to him after she has won back the planter son's lost wealth. Explaining how she came to her present circumstances, she tells W.B.S. that when she was nineteen she had planned on becoming engaged to a certain Charley Hart, who, as a mechanic, was considerably below her social rank. Her father objected, intending her for Thomas Clendening, scion of a wealthy family. Due to her father's protests, Hart left town and Lizzie never heard from him again. Brokenhearted, she refused to marry Clendening. Instead, she stole a suit of her brother's clothing and ran away. She found work as a cabin boy on Mississippi steamers for some three years. Because she instantly fell in love with the young man she encountered at the poker table, however, she now wishes to change back to a woman and she enlists her old friend W.B.S. to help unite her with her new obsession. W.B.S. obliges, and as of the 1875 telling of the story, "Lizzie is living as happy as a queen in the Southern States."[43]

The dime-novel motivation of seeking vengeance against a man as reason for female-to-male cross-dressing appeared in various versions of the (supposedly real-life) story of Mountain Charley. Accounts of Mountain Charley began surfacing in Colorado in 1859 with different traditions appearing in 1861, 1874, 1879, and 1885.[44] The apparent significance to western history of these fantastic tales, each one normalizing the cross-dresser, led the University of Oklahoma Press to collect them in a compendium it issued in 1968.[45]

The first extensive version of Mountain Charley is the one published in 1861. It is actually the autobiography of Mrs. E.J. Guerin. In it she cites revenge as the motivation for her to become Mountain Charley. Guerin explained that, bereft of parents, and while at a New Orleans boarding school, she met and married a Mississippi riverboat pilot. Although only twelve years old at the time, she appeared sixteen. The couple moved up to St. Louis, where E.J. gave birth to two children over the next three years. Meanwhile, her husband operated steamers on the Mississippi and the Ohio. One day, while they were plying the waters above Cairo, Illinois, a difficult deck mate named Jamieson shot and killed E.J.'s husband. Left destitute and with two children, Guerin became obsessed with exacting revenge on her husband's murderer. She took to male clothing to support herself and her children and because disguised as a man it would be easier to track down her nemesis. After three years, she finally found him at a St. Louis gambling resort. A gun battle ensued in which both were wounded. Jamieson recovered and fled. Guerin took longer to convalesce. Prior to their encounter and then subsequent to her recovery, Guerin, masquerading as a male, worked as a cabin boy on riverboats and then as a brakeman on the railroad, squirreling away money to support her children. Caught up in the California gold fever, Guerin, still as a man, headed across the plains in 1855. On the Pacific Coast she made a small fortune in the mule-packing business. She then returned to the East twice—in 1857 driving a herd of cattle back to California, and then setting out the last time from Missouri as a trapper with the American Fur Company. The latter occupation took her into the upper Platte River region just when the Pike's Peak gold rush commenced. She turned to prospecting for a short time, gaining the sobriquet Mountain Charley, but then retired to Denver, where she opened a bakery and a saloon, all the while disguised as a man. One day above Denver, Guerin chanced upon her old nemesis, Jamieson. She shot him several times, but with the help of traveling companions he escaped once again. He recovered just enough to journey to New Orleans, where he finally succumbed, done in by yellow fever.[46]

George West, publisher of the *Golden (Colorado) Transcript*, told, to rave reviews, the definitive version of Mountain Charley's life in serialized form in his newspaper in 1885. He offered her real name as Charlotte and claimed that he first encountered her in the region during the summer of 1859. In keeping with the theme of vengeance, West subtitled his account "A Colorado Story of Love, Lunacy and Revenge." In his version, Charlotte grew up in Iowa and there her stern stepfather wished her to stay at home where he treated her as little more than a servant. Tiring of this life, at age nineteen Charlotte "ran away with a dandified looking young man who was almost a total stranger in the neighborhood." They married in Des Moines and though her husband professed to love her and she "loved him with all my heart of hearts," Charlotte soon learned that "he was nothing but a gambler and a villain of the deepest cast." After giving birth to a stillborn child, Charlotte could not be consoled. Tiring of her carrying on, her "brute of a husband" struck her, left her destitute, and ran off to the Colorado gold rush in the company of a "low-down wench." Charlotte pulled herself together and determined to dress as a man to track her husband and his brazen consort. Following them up and down the Platte River, Charlotte eventually made contact with them in Colorado, where she finally exacted her revenge.[47]

FIGURE 7. Pearl Hart, 1899. Known as the "girl bandit" who "fought like a tigress," Hart led a sensational life, mirroring those of other Southwest borderland female-to-male brigands whose stories became fiercely heterosexualized. She reportedly led a colorful life as a prostitute, but not "satisfied with the large degree of social and individual freedom of Arizona life," she changed her clothes for the convenience that a man's suit afforded and became an outlaw. In concert with her male lover, Hart held up a stage and then the two made out for Mexico. Authorities nabbed Hart while her paramour, whose identity forever remained a mystery, escaped. Her story is told in the *San Francisco Call*, 11 June 1899, and the *Kansas City (Missouri) American Citizen*, 12 August 1899, from which this feminized image comes.

Revenge also played the central role in the story a writer for the Denver newspaper *Field and Farm* related as true in 1912. He explained that some years before, while he traveled by stagecoach to Silver City, New Mexico, a desperado struck. "The bandit seemed rather nervous and new at the business," the writer recalled, "but held a[n] ugly looking gun in one hand and that was quite enough to keep us quiet." The robber singled out only one passenger and emptied his pockets of "a roll of greenbacks that wou'd choke a cow." Then he tossed off his "mask and revealing the face of a handsome black-eyed woman. 'This measly hound here,' pointing to the stout chap whose roll she had appropriated, 'was once my husband. I got a divorce from him up at Las Vegas and for a year I never could get a cent out of him for alimony; not even the courts would help me; so here I've taken the law in my own hands as a high spirited woman should.'"[48]

The *Field and Farm*'s highwayman was likely as real as Dauntless Jerry, Dusty Dick, and Nebraska Larry. The same can be said of the Mississippi River's Lizzie Clark and Colorado's various Mountain Charleys, though the number of stories and remarkable evidence about the latter strongly suggest that he may very well have been real. Regardless, Clark, the Charleys, and the Silver City desperado were reported in the press as actual people; they differed from their dime-novel counterparts whom readers knew to be fictional. But of course this is not an entirely accurate statement, as the most renowned female-to-male cross-dresser in the western dime novel, Calamity Jane, was also a real person, however altered in fiction. But the veracity of Lizzie Clark, the Mountain Charleys, and the Silver City bandit is less important than the stories about why they dressed as men—something, sometime, somewhere (usually farther to the east) had gone wrong in their love affairs with men. Those stories were closely mirrored in the concomitant tales spun about verifiable female-to-male cross-dressers, such as Joe Monahan and Charley Parkhurst. In the last years of the nineteenth century and the first few of the twentieth, fiction became fact in the lives and deaths of real cross-dressers, just as they had become woven together to fabricate the biography of Calamity Jane.

In fact, the dime novel itself was at times mentioned in the stories about (reportedly) real-life western cross-dressers. For example, in 1905 after Sheridan, Montana's Ed Donovan passed away and was learned to be Kate Maher, newspapers throughout the country sensationalized his life, summing it up as being of "the dime novel brand."[49] Similarly, in recounting in 1898 the nefarious deeds of the Middle Border's cross-dressing bandit Dora Cox, who "committed almost every crime on the list," one western paper explained that her exploits might very well lay "the foundation for a dime novel."[50] And in Charley Parkhurst's case, a report at the time of his death in 1880 supposed his strange history would supply a source of inspiration to a "novelist."[51]

Through narrative traditions of the seduction tale that were then promoted in dime-novel renditions of cross-dressing women, actual women as well as characters reputedly true to life figuratively became the daughters of Calamity Jane. As such, they were secured in their heterosexuality well before the frontier closed. In some cases these characters did arouse sexual and gender suspicion, but this uncertainty was almost always assuaged by the deus ex machina of a love affair with a man, a love affair that in some way went astray and led the woman to cross-dress. This happened in the dime novel *Deadwood Dick on Deck* when one character could not swear to Calamity Jane's true sex. And even the fictionalized Calamity herself lends confusion to the issue, suggesting that she might have been a man except for some mix-up when she was conceived. But as also shown in *Deadwood Dick on Deck*, she takes to male attire to track down the man who defiled her, or perhaps to escape a brute of a husband. Moreover, she falls in love with the leading male character, and she does so during the socially fluid frontier epoch. Most notably, at the end of the 1899 dime novel *Deadwood Dick's Doom*, significantly subtitled *Calamity Jane's Last Adventure*, Dick and Jane marry, verifying Calamity's sexuality and signaling her return to respectable womanhood just as the nineteenth-century West evaporates. The same plot continued to find its way into subsequent popular renditions of Calamity Jane's life, including the 1953 Hollywood production *Calamity Jane* starring Doris Day in the lead role. By the end of the picture (which won an Academy Award for its song appropriately titled "Secret Love"), the altogether masculine and unkempt Calamity transforms into a beautiful, genteel women who finds female attire, love, and marriage to Wild Bill Hickok.[52]

Marriage and the recovery of genteel womanhood brought down the curtain on western cross-dressers' frontier adventures in any number of the stories spun about them. Stories that followed this plot reflect the basic outlines of the female-warrior tradition which, having reached its zenith in popularity in the eighteenth century, had otherwise vanished from mainstream literature by the mid-nineteenth century. The female-warrior tale revolves about women who were at one time celebrated for masquerading as men and behaving in the most unfeminine of ways. But it typically terminates when the heroine reverts to femininity, marries, and settles down to domestic life.[53]

Accounts of western female-to-male cross-dressers constructed along these lines typically portray their subjects as dressing as men and then heading to the frontier West. There they engage in all sorts of behaviors unbecoming of a woman. These behaviors, moreover, are connected with both the real and imagined exigencies of the region and the frontier: for example, violence, lawlessness, general social turmoil, and the availability of male-only occupations. This is particularly so in the case of female-to-male cross-dressers in the notoriously violent western subregion that stretched from the Middle Border, across the southern plains, and through the Southwest. The cross-dresser in these stories is restored to normal womanhood by returning, either literally or more often figuratively, to the East and thus to the post-frontier.[54] In the East she is married off and perhaps even becomes a mother. Or, if the tale is told only after she dies, we learn at the end of her life that it was in the East that her past marriage or other relationship with a man occurred. Sometimes the transformation into respectable womanhood might take place in the West when a cross-dressing woman gives up her male garb and her frontier carousing to enter into married life there.

Both Joe Monahan and Charley Parkhurst are real-life cross-dressers who originated somewhere back East as women and then changed into male clothing to head West. Another is Sarah Pollard. As a man who took the name Sam, he heads to Tuscarora, Nevada, and in 1878 marries a local girl, Marancy Hughes, for the supposed purpose of completing his camouflage.[55] It took Marancy so long to come forth with this ignominy for a couple reasons. One, "she was ashamed to acknowledge that she had been so imposed upon, and shrank from admitting the truth." Two, Pollard threatened to kill her if Marancy exposed "her."[56] When the truth does get out, Sam becomes Sarah Maud Pollard, who "had trouble with her relatives in the East, had lost her property and assumed the disguise of a man for the reason that avenues for making money would be open to her in that character which would be closed to her as a woman."[57]

It should be said that some stories had the women switching to male attire when actually in the West. An 1881 version of the Sam Pollard sensation explained (somewhat differently from that reported in 1878) that he had actually headed to the West as a woman on his own. En route, his trunk with feminine garb went missing. As a woman, "she tried for many days to find employment, but failed, and became dispirited and discouraged.... Early one morning, seeing a kindly-faced woman in a store, she went in, told her story, and then and there made a trade, exchanging her own garments for a suit of boy's clothes ... she had her hair cut" and moved to another neighborhood. After that, Sarah had all the work she needed.[58] Similarly, Montana's Kate Maher supposedly switched to male clothing in the 1870s when already in the West. His father died, leaving him "an orphan when she was yet in her teens."[59] He took on the persona of a man when he could not earn a satisfactory living in the "approved feminine occupations" in that "hard, rough world ... of Colorado and Nebraska, of Nevada and Arizona and the adjoining states, in the early Seventies—a world of ro[i]stering hard drink, hard-hitting, rough tongued men—a world that had no time for women and made no place for them, that offered them no shelter and grudged them apparently their daily bread."[60]

The accounts of such cross-dressers next had them engage in manly pursuits popularly associated with the romantic West. Upon learning that Portland's Harry Allen was Nell Pickerell, for example, local papers dubbed him Spokane Nell, described his dress as that of a cowpuncher and gunfighter, labeled him a bad man, and claimed that he had been in and out of jails up and down the West Coast for a range of offenses wholly western in nature: horse stealing, saloon brawling, selling bootleg liquor on Indian reservations, and highway robbery.[61] One reporter asked Allen, "And you used to work on ranches and 'bust' broncos?" "Yes indeed," supposedly came the response, "and I'm some bronco buster, too, if I do say it myself.'"[62] (The veracity of the information is highly suspect in light of the more mundane details of Allen's life in urban Seattle and Portland, as well as his own later protest against the press for alleging him to have engaged in these exploits.)[63]

In the case of George West's Mountain Charley, previously known as Charlotte, she prospected in Colorado and New Mexico, drove mules for the federal government across the southern plains, was a remarkably accomplished horseman, followed the "warpath" to avenge her husband's desertion, successfully tracked her estranged husband back and forth between Nebraska and Colorado, and engaged in an astonishing gunfight.[64] The Mountain Charley of E.J. Guerin's autobiography twice crossed the plains all the way to California, one time with sixty gold-seeking men and another time driving cattle. She trapped furs, operated a mule-packing business, prospected, ran a saloon, and "mingled freely in gatherings of men at hotels, saloons or in short in any and all places to which my curiosity led me." She also engaged in two gun battles.[65]

During her thirty years on the range as Edward Donovan, Kate Maher smoked, drank, gambled, and told risqué stories. He also reportedly prospected for gold, drove freight wagons and stagecoaches, successfully dueled with enemies, fended off stage robbers, was shot and dug the bullet out of himself, turned scout during Indian troubles, and saved girls in peril.[66] Similarly, California's Charley Parkhurst "smoked, chewed tobacco, drank moderately, played a social game of cards or dice for the drinks, and was 'one of the boys.'" He also developed a reputation as one of the top stagecoach drivers in gold-rush California. During a torrential downpour on the Tuolumne River, for example, he dared a collapsing bridge, safely making it across with his freight and passengers intact moments before it gave way. Another time his "team ran away so suddenly as to throw Parkhurst from the box. Still re-taining his grasp on the lines he was dragged along until he succeeded in turning the runaways into the chapparal [sic], where they were caught among the bushes and stopped." Parkhurst also fended off highwaymen, even fatally shooting the notorious "Sugarfoot" during one particularly perilous run on the Mariposa–Stockton route.[67]

Of all the cross-dressing women of the West, those who engaged in the most egregious gender-nonconforming activities were those who (dis)graced the particularly violence-prone Middle Border, southern plains, and South-west. From the mid-nineteenth century on, Mexican banditry, Mexican re-bellion, Anglo repression, Indian raids, cattle rustling, stagecoach robbing, and other forms of lawlessness, resistance, and retribution plagued the South-west borderlands from Texas to California. At the same time, the most noto-rious western outlaw gangs—Quantrill's raiders, the Jameses, the Daltons, and the Doolins—all operated on the Middle Border and southern plains between the 1860s and 1896.[68] Not surprisingly, this milieu attracted its fair number of female villains, such as Annie Harris M'Keene, Flora Quick, Dora Cox, Jennie Stephens, Nellie Pickett, and (the likely fictional) Net Bet-tie, to name but a few.

Annie Harris M'Keene, who joined William Quantrill's raiders, is the earliest of this illustrious group to turn bad. Her family lived near Indepen-dence, Missouri, and was a sworn enemy of the anti-slavery Kansas Jayhawk-ers. During the early days of the Civil War, Annie hand-sewed Confederate flags, which she liberally distributed throughout the neighborhood, and boldly wore a red and white dress, driving federal authorities in the area to distraction. The Harrises became natural allies of the Quantrill gang, which visited their farm one day in September 1862 and procured supplies. Among Quantrill's men was John M'Keene, who "was handsome . . . like an athlete, and had a rude manner that was graceful in its way." Likewise Annie, report-edly a pushover for any rebel soldier, "was rather pretty." When John and Annie met, it was something like kismet—"he had said she was the bravest woman in Missouri; she had said he was the bravest man of all the rough rid-ers of the border." The next day, after Quantrill's band departed, a contin-gent of federal soldiers descended on the Harris farm, shot and killed An-nie's father, and then laid waste to the property. Sometime later John returned to find Annie devastated. At that moment, the two "pledged their vows of eternal vengeance" and rode off together. Annie "threw away her

TOM KING.

FIGURE 8. Tom King, 1895. Born somewhere in the Ozark Mountains, Flora Quick made a name for herself as Tom King, stealing horses with her male lover along Oklahoma Territory's South Canadian River. As they did with others of King's ilk, newspapers heterosexualized and racialized her cross-dressing and criminal activities. Image from *Decatur (Illinois) Daily Review*, 31 January 1895.

woman's dress and donned male attire. She put on [a] belt, besides, and two revolvers, and her long hair she tucked up under her hat." Together the lovers went on a rampage across the countryside until sometime in 1863, when a detachment of the Seventh Missouri Militia caught up with them, shot John dead, and wounded Annie in the arm. She survived, revealed herself as a woman to her captors, and begged them to allow her to go to Kansas City, which they did; the "tone of her voice and style of earnestness . . . touched the heart of the rough soldiers."[69]

In another case, Flora Quick became Tom King. She grew up in the Ozark Mountains of southwestern Missouri, apart from civilization, society, schools, and churches. Described as "fearless as a Comanche," Quick supposedly was the daughter of a Cherokee Indian. In her youth she became introduced to a life of crime through manufacturing bootleg hooch. After eloping with a "desperado lover" in the 1890s, she turned her attentions to horse thievery along the South Canadian River in the Oklahoma Territory. Her male disguise always helped her elude deputies and, when jailed, escape from behind bars.[70]

Rivaling Tom King, Dora Cox had become "the most noted woman outlaw that ever lived in Oklahoma." She was reputed to be a friend and companion of Belle Starr, the Dalton Boys, and Bill Doolin.[71] Wearing male attire, she participated in the Pawnee, Oklahoma Territory, bank heist of 1893. She also committed murder, burglary, and highway robbery, as well as bootlegging whiskey and rustling horses and cattle throughout the region. Several times jailed, Cox successively made her escapes, always by mesmerizing her jailers to the point that they fell in love with her and then became complacent. In 1898, after a perilous thirty-six-hour pursuit during which Cox led a posse along the Arkansas River "through swamps and thickets and in and out of timber, over hills and through rivers," the law finally caught up with her.[72]

Also arrested in 1890s Oklahoma Territory was Jennie Stephens, a "'new woman' in a depraved line" who "liked men's clothes better than those of her own sex, especially for her business." Similar to that of Tom King and Dora Cox, her business was bootlegging whiskey and stealing horses. She ran away from her home in Jennings, Oklahoma Territory, when not much more than a girl and married a man (described in the press as a deaf mute) named Midliff. After a quarrel and to spite him, Jennie naturally organized a gang of outlaws "in imitation of the Dalton and Dool[i]n gangs," whom she came to know back in Jennings.[73] After her eventual capture, she was sent to a reform school in Boston, but on returning to Oklahoma Territory in 1897 she swore "to avenge" the killings of Bill Dalton and Bill Doolin. As an aside, these plans came to naught. At the precise moment of Stephens's homecoming, a religious crusade swept the notorious Triangle region of the territory. What the law could not secure, the good book apparently did: "The saloons were turned into Sunday schools and religious meeting houses. Former saloon keepers have been elected Sunday school superintendents." Among the converted was Jennie Stephens (and "a brother-in-law of Bill Dool[i]n, who was really the most noted of all the highway men").[74]

Like many of her already named contemporaries, Nellie Pickett, who died at Fort Sumter, New Mexico Territory, in 1882, had also originated on the Middle Border, having been born in Missouri. There she married Tom Pickett before the two moved on to Texas and then places west. Tom fell in with Billy the Kid during the Lincoln County war while Nellie, "a fearless

JENNIE STEPHENS.

FIGURE 9. Jennie Stephens, 1897. In the guise of a male bandit in the 1890s, Stephens terrorized Oklahoma Territory. Only her arrest, stint in a boarding school back East, and then finally a religious revival secured her return to feminine virtue. Image from Boise's *Idaho Statesman*, 12 August 1897.

horseman, a crack shot, beautiful, and with great strength of mind . . . ruled the band with despotic ways." She dressed in male attire, always riding "astride a horse," and acted as a spy and messenger for the gang. After her husband bit the dust at the hands of authorities, Nellie became the mistress of Charles Bowdre, who reportedly died in a gunfight with Sheriff Pat Garrett. Next Billy the Kid won over her affections. The third time was not the charm for the lovers, however, as Billy also soon ended his career in the grave.[75]

A more detailed story revolves around Net Bettie who was born near Fort Gibson, Indian Territory. Of mixed-blood parentage, Bettie was early on "very pretty, and a pet and favorite with the young officers . . . stationed at the old fort." One handsome soldier won her favor and promised marriage once he received a discharge from the army. But Bettie soon cleverly surmised that he intended to marry another and so "shot him dead." This event transformed Bettie "from an innocent maiden into a devil." Once dispatching her false lover, she slipped into a suit of boys' clothing and sped away on horseback toward the Texas prairies. There she fell in with a company of unsuspecting cowboys as she "knew all about cattle, smoked cigarettes and used terms never heard very often except around the campfires on the plains." With this group of men, Bettie participated in a murderous rampage through Denison, Texas. Having by now earned the sobriquet "Little Cherokee," Bettie went on to work for a ranch where she busted mustangs and herded cattle. Near the Rio Grande she shot and killed the cook of her outfit and so fled to Mexico, where in Santa Rosa she promptly saved the residents from a "Mexican desperado" who had plagued them for some while. This elevated her celebrity as "the citizens were glad to see the villain's career ended."[76]

Bettie next moved on to Chihuahua, where, back in female attire, she won the heart of the elderly "Don Juan Serrano, a wealthy cattle owner, who had a magnificent hacienda in northern Mexico. They were married, and the old 'nightmare,' as she called him, took his little bride to his country home. In less than two months the old don was in his grave and Net was engaged in the pleasant pastime of spending his millions." Serrano's jealous and suspicious heirs began making life difficult for Bettie, so she fled, along the way rustling two thousand head of her late husband's cattle north across the Rio Grande. With the money she secured from their sale, Bettie bought a ranch near Flagstaff, Arizona Territory. Before long, she found herself embroiled in difficulties with a neighboring rancher. Dressed again as a man, she caused her nemesis's wife to fall in love with her and then stole her away to El Paso, where she revealed herself to her shocked consort. (As an aside, the duped woman then tried unsuccessfully to repair her marriage.)[77]

Bettie then headed back to Mexico and retired from her errant ways until one day when she heard of an old cowboy friend who had gotten mixed up in some trouble and ended up in a Texas jail. Bettie crossed the border in men's clothes and executed a daring rescue, but a posse eventually caught up with the fleeing partners in crime, killing the cowboy while Bettie made it to safety, finding her way back south of the border. "Her father's family moved . . . to old Mexico some years ago," came the denouement to her apocryphal story, "and this wayward character enjoyed the satisfaction of spending her last days surrounded by those who knew her best and doubtless loved her in spite of her faults."[78]

The American West and its frontier analogue abounded in violence, rang-
ing from domestic abuse to race war and even imperial hostilities. The larger
southwestern region composed of the Middle Border, southern plains, and
desert Southwest was particularly violent and the stories produced there of
cross-dressers (whether real or semi-fictional) painted their antagonists as
the most lawless, untamed, warlike, and bloodthirsty of the entire West. So
compelling was the connection of this wild and woolly western subregion to
anarchy generally and women's rebellion through cross-dressing specifically,
that stories of even distant Idaho's Joe Monahan could not escape its allure.

After Monahan's death, one set of rumors that started swirling claimed
that he was in reality Kansas's "notorious Kate Bender." In 1873, the entire
Bender family mysteriously disappeared from their Kansas home when authorities there discovered several grisly murders had taken place at their
roadhouse—the Benders apparently fleeced their victims of loot and then
buried their bodies in shallow graves about the place. At the time of Monahan's death, a recent migrant to Idaho imagined a link between him and
Bender, recalling a pair of suspicious "smooth faced" men who some years
before had shown up in Sweethome, Oregon, where the storyteller had lived
at the time. He explained that because of the men's outward appearance,
Sweethome residents believed they really were women. They imagined, furthermore, that they were none other than Mrs. Bender and her daughter
Kate. That the younger "man" had set out for eastern Oregon at about the
time that Joe had turned up in the region led to suspicion that Kate and Joe
were one and the same. "The Bender disappearance," an Idaho paper reported in March 1904, "had been one of the historic mysteries of the west,
and although many have professed knowledge concerning its true solution,
nothing has ever resulted." "The true history will probably never be known,"
the same paper continued in its next issue, "but the belief will always remain
in the minds of many pioneers of the northwest that Joe Monaghan and Kate
Bender were one and the same."[79]

The female-to-male cross-dressers of the southwestern region behaved in
ways that most egregiously transgressed genteel womanhood. So far had
they crossed to the other side that these women seemed beyond redemption.
Other than Joe Monahan, and perhaps somewhat in the case of Jennie Stephens (thanks to a religious revival) and Net Bettie (banished to Mexico and
surrounded by a forgiving family there), neither in reality nor metaphorically

did these women ever reenter respectable femininity. Rather, their lawlessness followed them to the grave or to the jail cell. Nevertheless, they at least
conformed to opposite-sex relationships. Each of the cross-dressers fell in love
with men, eloped with men, carried on affairs with men, married men, or did
some combination of all four. Moreover, their turn for the worse was a result
of their opposite-sex relationships.

The return to respectable womanhood generally did take place in the period stories of cross-dressers who inhabited other areas of the West. Neither
these cross-dressers' redemption nor their return to female identity, however, characteristically took place on the frontier, simply because of its socially bumptious and masculinized nature. Instead, their transformation
had to take place literally or metaphorically in the East, or perhaps in the West
in what might socially be considered a post-frontier milieu. This was the case
for Joe Monahan, Charley Parkhurst, and Sammy Williams.

Various of Colorado's Mountain Charleys also saw their womanhood secured at the conclusion of their stories and farther to the east, beyond the
bounds of what then constituted the West. Sometime in the winter of 1859–
1860, E.J. Guerin married the keeper of her Denver saloon's bar. The two
soon left the territory and took up residence in St. Joseph, Missouri. At the
time she penned her autobiography, Guerin's children from her first marriage were enrolled in school in Georgia.[80] After George West published the
first part of his biography of Mountain Charley in the 14 January 1885 edition
of the *Transcript*, he reportedly received a letter from Charlotte, who had
come into possession of a copy of the newspaper. West had not seen or heard
from her since 1860, so the surprise was a welcome one, in that her letter
filled in the details of her life after she had left the West (including that she
served, disguised as a male, in Union forces in Iowa during the Civil War).
This enabled West to update her story for his readers (not to mention sell
more newspapers). West concluded his sequel by explaining that Charlotte
was now "happily married" in Iowa "with a tenderly loving husband and family of loving children around her . . . passing her declining years in a sphere
suited to her sex, loved and respected by all who know her."[81]

Tuscarora, Nevada's Sam or Sarah Maud Pollard enjoyed a similar fate
back East, at least according to some accounts. Having been discovered to be a
woman in 1878, Pollard then left the West. By 1881 "she" had returned to "her"
mother in Binghamton, New York, where "she" "again donned her womanly

attire."[82] Subsequent reports explain that "she" then married and, by 1884, had given birth to at least two children.[83]

In a few cases, a western cross-dresser need not necessarily leave the West to be restored to womanhood, though she did have to forsake her male clothing and its attendant gender-nonconforming behaviors, typically to enter into marriage. In other words, like Calamity Jane's "last adventure" that concluded in her marriage, a female-to-male cross-dresser had to give up the frontier-like (and thus masculine) era of her own life. This was the case, for example, with Jack Hall as told in turn-of-the-twentieth-century Arizona Territory. Some years before, and overcome with the shame and disgrace caused by her father's horse stealing and hanging, Hall "hid her sex, masqueraded as a cowboy, lassoed cattle, took part in shooting scrapes, leading the wild, free, adventurous life of the Arizona vaquero and in the beating of hoofs and whizzing of bullets sought to down the memory of the disgrace." In 1898, Hall took up work at a ranch whose cowboy crew was headed by a certain Captain Dick Wells, "the bravest and boldest cowboy in Arizona." Considered a bit of a tenderfoot, Hall also refused to carouse with the other men. He remained above suspicion, however, due to performing his duties well. He one time nursed a fellow cowboy back to health following a shooting fracas. "Of course this appealed to the crowd and he grew very popular, being christened 'Nurse Jack.' . . . He ain't a drinker and can't play cards worth a _____, but he was all right taking care of people when sick." Awhile later his nursing services were called on again, this time to care for Captain Dick while he suffered a bout of typhoid fever. As the story goes, "Captain Dick . . . assumed a strong liking for the frail youngster." Then a broach of western etiquette on Hall's part landed him in jail (he rode his horse into a local mercantile and it kicked a female customer in the head). To avoid being placed in the men's ward, only then did Hall reveal his true identity. Captain Dick "came to town and was considerably startled to see his boon companion attired becomingly in woman's garments. He became quickly used to the change and while waiting for the trial, Jack told the story of her life." The victim of the horse kicking refused to take the case further, "but the justice was called in anyhow. . . . 'Captain Dick' and Nurse Jack were made man and wife." "As a fitting finale," the paper reported, "when her sex was discovered, she doffed her adventurous attire and married the man whose life she had saved." Firmly secured now in gentility, her wild days and the associated sartorial choices were now things of the past. As such, Mrs. Wells could accompany her husband "on a wedding trip to see her brothers and sisters, and mother, who reside in Portland, Ore."[84]

Drawing on myths and popular narratives of western American history, the above stories are progress narratives in their own right, providing an acceptable rationale for why a woman would cross-dress. As a collection (and in some cases individually), these stories have a structure that mirrors the frontier's history as told by Frederick Jackson Turner in his classic thesis. Casting the unfolding tale of the revealed cross-dresser against this story of national advancement from a state of savagery to civilization provided a sure way for participants in and observers of the otherwise disturbing events of the historic West and the passing of the frontier to reclaim a sense of normalcy and explain certain aberrant circumstances about the region and its female-to-male inhabitants as momentary. In other words, the specific circumstances of western history and life prior to the so-called closing of the frontier made it possible to normalize cross-dressing gender behaviors, accounting for them as evanescent aberrations tied to the vanishing frontier.

This view is somewhat captured in two period newspaper pieces that equated the existence and (hoped-for) disappearance of female-to-male cross-dressing with the existence and disappearance of the frontier. The first comes from 1903 San Francisco when a newspaper there reported on three women arrested in male attire who told local authorities that they believed that dressing as men was the only way women could see the infamous Chinatown. "Notwithstanding the current Eastern ideas concerning the characteristic wooliness [sic] of the Wild West," the newspaper added with editorial flourish, "the fact that San Francisco is not [any longer] sufficiently of the frontier to permit of ladies walking its streets in male attire was aptly demonstrated" with the apprehension of the women under consideration.[85]

The second and more elaborate example comes from two years later—a *Portland Oregonian* editorial that responded to the deathbed revelation that Montana's Edward Donovan was really Kate Maher. The piece referred to the extinct frontier as "a now vanished era" and depicted it as "that wide border-land upon which civilization and savagery met and engaged in fierce combat." It also recounted the (apparently) well-known relationship between the conditions of that place and "the young woman who, discarding the apparel of her sex, and disclaiming a woman's place in the settler's home, took up life as a man and became a daring, adventurous, lawless 'plainsman.'" The editorial also recounted the typical way in which the cross-dresser's true sex became known. "Now and then," it announced, "one of these actors in the great and stirring drama of human life on the border is eliminated from the fast-dissolving shadow by death, the final event being preceded by a few days, perhaps not at all, by the discovery of a secret that she had concealed through the rough vicissitudes of border life for many years." Asserting the ephemeral nature of the frontier and its cross-dressers (and that "this perverted life is not attractive") the editorial explained that the frontier represented "conditions happily exceptional," while cross-dressers identified with it are in death gratefully "made to conform to [nature's] law through forced acceptance of its final decree."[86] Or, one might add, given the evidence provided in this chapter, the cross-dresser is made to conform to nature's law through the apocryphal stories spun about her as the historic West became the frontier of vernacular imagination.

Scholars who have examined stories similar to those in this chapter have found various meanings in them. Some have argued that such accounts provide welcome evidence for the lives of certain women, in particular those from the lower classes who otherwise left little historical information behind. Others have claimed that such narratives destabilize the cultural construct of gender because the women in these stories dress and behave like men. Some suggest that rather than destabilizing gender, these stories privilege and valorize masculine behaviors and activities while they sideline feminine virtues. Scholars have also determined that such literature is alternately conforming and subversive in other ways. For example, it might warn young women about the hazards of disobeying parents and becoming involved with roguish men. It might also recommend that true and appropriate happiness ultimately comes from a romantic relationship with a man or, more exactingly, marriage. Alternatively, such stories could have provided women in the nineteenth century with a different model by which to pattern their lives. And yet other scholars might see in such tales the various ways in which the protections supposedly offered by domestic law and domesticity generally failed women in the nineteenth century. One might also argue that some of these women were female versions of social bandits, more or less worshipped as folk heroines when law and lawlessness were one and the same.[87]

And then there is Henry Nash Smith, who in his seminal work, *Virgin Land: The American West as Symbol and Myth* (1950), included a short chapter on dime-novel heroines, using their appearance and development in that literary form to demonstrate how the genre had become increasingly sensationalized, and thus less reflective of the reality of the West, in the last couple decades or so of the nineteenth century. Smith explained that "because the genteel female had been the primary source of refinement in the traditional novel," a break from this gentility exhibited even better (than in the case of male characters) the novels' increasingly sensational nature.[88] Smith noted that at the end of the 1870s, "the Amazons and heroines in male attire took a distinct turn for the worse." He focused specifically on the ever-increasing theme of vengeance as a motivation for female characters to dress as males and to come to the region, where they were then permitted, because of clothing and social atmosphere, to undertake violent and other antisocial activities. Notably, in Smith's estimation, vengeance that accompanied a love gone bad provided a justification for violence that was now much easier to account for than had been the older drawn-out form of creating and then staging some elaborate war between Indians and whites. This narrowed "frame of ethical reference" for western violence, Smith concluded, resulted in a "marked loss of social significance in the stories," as they now revolved around individuals rather than societies.[89]

Scholars have thus found varied meanings in western cross-dressing women, whether found in dime novels or in similar tales in other literary forms. But another perspective provides a different reckoning. Late nineteenth- and early twentieth-century stories about cross-dressers, whether real people or fictional fabrications, hold great social significance, despite what Henry Nash Smith might have once thought. They were created as part of a large and forceful national project that heteronormalized America's frontier past and thus its own national origins. This all happened in response to period anxieties over ever-increasing rates of homosexuality, transgenderism, and transsexuality, collectively collapsed into the period's term "sexual inversion" and symbolized by the cross-dresser. As earlier chapters in this book demonstrate, cross-dressing was very much part of daily life in the nineteenth-century West and on the so-called frontier. At the same time, social understanding increasingly linked cross-dressing to sexual inversion—depravity, decadence, and degeneration—the very thing America's frontier past promised the nation it was not. Thus, cross-dressing had to be transformed into something else. This could easily be done (at least) in the case of women, thanks to the imagined and real social exigencies of the West and older themes prevalent in the seduction novel and the female-warrior ballad that continued to lurk in the pages of the popular dime novel.

It is true, as Chapter 1 presents, that Americans in the West and elsewhere did find sexual inversion in the stories of women in the region who cross-dressed. But the stories of people like Milton Matson, Eugene De Forest, John Hill, and Alan Hart where such concerns are readily highlighted are not the women-dressed-as-men we remember in telling our western and frontier past. Instead, we recall Joe Monahan, Charley Parkhurst, the Mountain Charleys, and the many other daughters of Calamity Jane, whose fabricated heterosexualized stories have been told and retold in period press reports, dime novels, pamphlets, magazine articles, newspaper reprints, books, compendiums, plays, and even Hollywood films. Their supposed heterosexuality has become part and parcel of western myth. In fact, it *is* western myth.

CHAPTER 4

"He Was a Mexican"

*Race and the Marginalization of Male-to-Female
Cross-Dressers in Western History*

During the winter of 1868, Captain Louis McLane Hamilton of Troop A of
the U.S. Seventh Cavalry recognized a Mexican woman he had known, though
she was then disguised as a man, driving a bull team through the streets of
Leavenworth, Kansas, and just arriving from Santa Fe. Hamilton had first
become acquainted with the woman, whom we know only by her later married
name of Mrs. Nash, sometime before when stationed in New Mexico Territory and serving as the regimental quartermaster of the U.S. Third Infantry.
When in New Mexico, Hamilton had hired Nash to do his laundry after finding everyone else he had employed for the job something of a disappointment.
Whereas Hamilton's career moved upward, out of New Mexico and into the
cavalry, times became somewhat more difficult for Nash. As she later explained, she had to don men's clothing to find work driving oxen teams across
the southern plains. The reunion in Leavenworth in early 1868 proved propi-
tious for the trail-weary woman: Hamilton rehired her and for the next decade she worked as a laundress with the cavalry while it reconnoitered the
Great Plains. Not that the life of a western army laundress was one of luxury.
But Nash could return to the gendered comforts of female garb, became "an
honored attache of the Seventh Cavalry," and spent much of her time rather
sedentarily stationed at Fort Lincoln, Dakota Territory, just outside Bismarck, rather than traveling about the West.[1]

Nash found plenty of remunerative work in the service, what with all the
enlisted men needing a washwoman. But when the officers' wives "discovered
her artistry in laundering delicate materials," her future seemed secure.[2]

FIGURE 10. Mrs. Nash, 1878. Nash worked as a laundress and domestic arbiter for the U.S. Seventh Cavalry from 1868 until her death ten years later, mostly while stationed at Fort Abraham Lincoln in Dakota Territory. She married three times. When a fellow wash-woman prepared Nash's body for burial, she discovered her male anatomy, and the story became a national news sensation. Image from New York's *National Police Gazette*, 15 February 1879.

Captain Francis M. Gibson's wife, Katherine, dubbed Nash the "superlaun-dress" of the regiment. Elizabeth Custer explained that "when she brought the linen home, it was fluted and frilled so daintily that I considered her a treasure." Such talents proved in short supply on the western frontier, and even more so at Fort Lincoln, to the particular chagrin of Katherine. When the Seventh Cavalry was stationed there, "some indiscreet woman," as Kath-erine described her, "whispered" the cavalry's best-kept wash-day secret to the officers' wives at the nearby infantry post. Nash then received "an ava-lanche of work" and thus had even less time for the somewhat exclusive group who had previously exploited her.[3]

Nash's considerable talent at the tub and washboard extended to other domestic tasks as well. For example, "No party was complete without her culinary assistance," one observer noted, almost in the same breath declaring that Nash's husband grew fat and lazy on her tamales. Those tamales, not to mention pies, cakes, and donuts, provided Nash additional income, raking it

A MEXICAN CART.

FIGURE 11. Mexican cart, 1869. After losing her job as a laundress for the U.S. Infantry in New Mexico, Mrs. Nash explained that she found work driving oxen teams on the Santa Fe Trail while dressed as a man. This period sketch suggests the work Nash performed immediately before taking a new position as a laundress with the U.S. Seventh Cavalry. Image from Albert D. Richardson, *Beyond the Mississippi: Life and Adventure on the Prairies, Mountains, and Pacific Coast* (Hartford, CT: American Publishing Co., 1869), 227.

in from sales to enlisted men and even to civilians living as far away as Bismarck when the Seventh was stationed at Fort Lincoln.[4]

Nash's skills likewise proved indispensable decorating for garrison festivities. During the preparations for a wedding at Fort Lincoln, one observer expressed admiration of her ability at darting "up and down ladders, stringing bright-colored cheesecloth draperies here and there."[5] Not surprisingly, Nash lavished her gifts as an interior decorator on her own otherwise drab and meager quarters. When Elizabeth Custer visited them at Fort Lincoln, she "found the little place shining. The bed was hung with pink cambric . . . bits of carpet on the floor, and the dresser, improvised out of a packing box, shone with polished tins. Outside we were presented with chickens . . . riches indeed out there in that Novaya Zemlyan climate."[6] A journalist later verified, at least in essence if not in particulars, Custer's depiction: "Her house was as clean as could be," the reporter explained, "and the walls were ornamented with some beautiful pictures. In fact everything about the house, both in and outside, was very tastefully arranged."[7]

Nash also knew a thing or two about the needle and thread, possibly having worked at some time as a milliner. She took in a great deal of sewing for the servicemen, made all "kinds of fine shirts," and completely retailored her husband's standard-issue uniform into a suit that, as Elizabeth Custer described it, "displayed to advantage his well-proportioned figure."[8] Perhaps Nash was best known for the northern plains couture that she fashioned for herself. She kept bolts of silk and woolens and pink tarlatan on hand for these creations, variously described as "gauzy, low necked gowns" and as "the finest of the land."[9] Nash typically wore them to garrison dances, gaining a reputation for changing her lavish garments as many as three times during an evening's entertainment.[10]

Although Nash explained to others that she had given birth to two children, who had died in Mexico, she did not particularly like youngsters. This proved one of the major drawbacks of her profession: many army laundresses had them and these women and their broods typically lived together, usually sharing tents out on the range and barracks back at the stockade. One escaped such a sentence if she married, moving into more private quarters, which might partly account for why Nash always seemed to find herself a husband in the Seventh, as discussed below. Speaking of her aversion to children, when in 1868 the cavalry marched from Fort Hays in Kansas to Fort Lincoln, Nash naturally had to ride in the wagons with the other laundresses and their teeming numbers of offspring. She could tolerate it only so long, one day begging the sentry in charge to transfer her to another wagon, even one fully loaded, to be by herself. The "childers," as she called them in her accented English, annoyed her to no end.[11]

And yet oddly, Nash grew famous and added yet more to her coffers for her prowess as a prenatal nurse and baby-care provider. And why not? She had experience giving birth and claimed she had learned midwifery from her mother, a likely story as the *partera* (midwife) tradition typically passed from mother to daughter in northern Mexico.[12] This skill came in handy among the varied women of the garrison, from the more finicky officers' wives who typically expressed dissatisfaction with the inexperienced post surgeon, down to the other laundresses, many of whom regularly gave birth out of wedlock as they earned additional income by selling sex.[13] While stationed at Fort Lincoln, Nash sometimes even traveled as far as twenty-five miles to render her much demanded services to civilians—"allus in demand to chase the rabbit when some woman was expectin' a baby," one acquaintance of Nash crudely put it.[14] "She was a careful midwife," explained Katherine Gibson in somewhat more proper verse, "no less an embryo trained nurse, and she handled those babies not only with efficiency but with marked tenderness as well."[15]

Nash also seemed conversant with witchcraft, something no doubt also rooted in her Mexican-American borderlands background where the practice was tradition.[16] Cavalryman John Burkman, who regularly availed himself of Nash's laundering facilities, recalled that on one visit, when he lamented that his luck with the cards had run dry, Nash took his deck from him, spread it across the table, passed her hands over it, "and spoke some gibberish I couldn't understand." "Thar," Nash said. "Now you'll win." To Burkman's considerable surprise and even greater pleasure, his fortune dramatically improved: reportedly he thenceforth won every game he played. Although he offered to divide his winnings with Nash, she refused the gesture.[17]

But with taking in laundry and sewing, working as a midwife and nurse, and selling pies and tamales, Nash had plenty of income. When she died in 1878, rumors spread that she had socked away upward of $10,000. That likely stretched the truth, but in fact she had succeeded in saving up several hundred dollars at various times during her ten years with the cavalry.[18] It also seems, at least according to some, that Nash's relative good fortune with money led to her occasional reversal of fortune with men: while with the Seventh Cavalry, Nash married soldiers three times, the first two relationships ending when her husbands reportedly stole her money and deserted not only her, but the service as well.[19]

Uncertainty persists about the exact identities of Nash's first two husbands. But it seems clear that one had the surname of Clifton and the other Nash, army people continuing to employ the latter name even after the laundress married for a third time.[20] A woman of unusual fortitude, after each of these first two men took her money and ran, Nash mourned her losses for a time but soon dolled herself up in her frilly dresses and artificial curls and headed off once again to the soldiers' balls. By such means she always seemed to corral herself another husband. And neither the annoyance of law nor the inconvenience of divorce ever stood in Nash's or her newly intended's way.[21]

Her last marriage, in 1873, was to the Seventh's John Noonan.[22] Elizabeth Custer believed that Nash's popularity among the men came not from her looks, but from the simple fact that she was "a woman of means," an assessment that coincides with the report that her first two absconding husbands fleeced her of her considerable savings beforehand. "The trooper thought he had done a very good thing for himself," Custer asserted specifically in the case of Noonan, "for notwithstanding his wife was no longer young, and was undeniably homely, she could cook well and spared him from eating with his company, and she was a good investment, for she earned so much by her industry."[23] But in fact, Noonan proved something of a prize himself: he had an excellent military record, achieved considerable popularity among the other men, and at one time served as George Custer's right-hand man, and Elizabeth Custer described him as "the handsomest soldier in [his] company." His apparent eligibility suggests, then, that Noonan's union with Nash equaled something more than a *"mariage de convenance,"* as Custer belittled it.[24] A newspaper later reported, too, that while Nash's first two husbands apparently "didn't like the combination [with her] . . . Noonan seemed to enjoy it." In fact, on 14 January 1877, more than three years after their nuptials, Noonan's service expired and he was discharged from the cavalry as a sergeant. The next day he reenlisted, though now reduced to the rank of corporal, and his relationship with Nash continued unabated.[25]

But as the saying goes, all good things do come to an end. On 1 October 1878, while Noonan reconnoitered in the Black Hills with others of the Seventh Cavalry, back at Fort Lincoln Nash fell ill with appendicitis. She struggled with the discomfort for much of the rest of the month. During the afternoon of the 29th, feeling her time drawing near, Nash asked friends to summon the Catholic priest from Bismarck; he came at once and heard her confession. She died at five o'clock the next morning. John, whom she had affectionately nicknamed "manny manny," was still out in the field.[26]

A few days beforehand, Nash had remarked to a fellow laundress that when she went, she wished to be interred at once, in whatever clothes she had on at the time.[27] But those she knew felt Nash needed a more dignified burial. One of the post's laundresses volunteered to lay out the body. Soon after commencing her work, she came dashing out of the makeshift mortuary screaming, "Holy Mither of Moses, Holy Mither of Moses." Quickly surrounded by startled and curious laundresses and their children, the ersatz undertaker in an earthy vernacular befitting her station coarsely exclaimed, "She's got balls on her as big as a bull[s], she's a man."[28] A medical exam followed, probably conducted by the post surgeon. "Not the slightest trace of femininity could be found," the exam more delicately revealed. "It was a well developed man."[29]

An eyewitness explained that a few days later when Corporal Noonan was returning from the Black Hills and learned from a messenger of Nash's death, "He didn't say much, but his face went white and kinda jerked."[30] With his return to Fort Lincoln, and after days of wonderment and speculation about Nash, attention now shifted to Noonan. In large part people hoped that he might shed light on how a man could disguise himself as a woman and have three husbands in succession, each keeping his secret. In fact, this turned out to be something of the $10,000 question—some newspapers having supposed that Nash's rumored $10,000 purse had bought the silence of each of them over the years.[31]

Scoffs, ridicule, mean-spirited jokes, and the "cold shake" from his fellow servicemen immediately dogged Noonan upon his return to Fort Lincoln. "We'd say," fellow serviceman John Burkman later recalled, "'Ain't you lonesome without your wife?' . . . 'When I want a girl I'll git Nonan [sic] to pick her out fur me.'" This example from later memory likely had more mean-spirited counterparts at the time. As Burkman also admitted in reference to the barbs sent Noonan's way, "Things like that all the time till we purty nigh drove him crazy."[32]

If taunts from his peers were not enough, Noonan might also have brooded over the Bismarck Tribune's public speculation that he would likely be "kicked out of the army." After all military service had become a life for him, working as George Armstrong Custer's trusted servant for some time and then later reenlisting the day after being mustered out when, on the other hand, so many soldiers routinely deserted the western army due to its grueling life.[33] Because of these attacks and his sense of shame, as sources claimed, over the next several days Noonan kept increasingly to himself, "lonely and forsaken." He lost weight and grew sickish. He also took long walks by himself across the lonesome prairie. He may also have done these things and acted in these ways, as sources seemed unable to countenance, because he deeply mourned the loss of a wife and companion whom he had obviously loved and chosen to stay with for some five years.[34]

Right at the end of November, precisely a month after Nash's death, Noonan disappeared from sight for a couple days. Rumors spread that he had deserted. Rather, he seems purposely to have kept himself out of the way. Then, on Saturday the 30th he shot himself straight "through the heart," taking his own life.[35] Versions of the particulars of Noonan's final earthly act vary. Some maintain that he quietly entered an unoccupied stable and committed the act there. Another claimed that Noonan walked into the black-smith and carpentry shop, where a number of men had gathered. "His face was gaunt and sorta set," John Burkman recalled of that particular moment. "The carpenter looked up. 'Hello, Nonan!' he says. 'Say, you and Mrs. Nonan never had no children, did you?' We all started laughin' and then we stopped sudden. Nonan was standin', lookin' at us . . . and his eyes was wild. . . . He pulled out his gun and shot hisself dead, right thar at our feet."[36]

Mrs. Nash and reactions to her provide rich material for exploring varied aspects of male-to-female cross-dressers in the American West. Take for example the issue of sexuality. Just a few days prior to Noonan's suicide, a *Bismarck Tribune* reporter caught up with the doomed man, hoping the soldier might provide answers to questions about sex that seemingly everyone had. Noonan straightforwardly explained that from the time he married Nash he knew her to be a woman. When the reporter pressed the issue, asking delicately if Noonan was "a husband to her . . . with all that the name implies?" Noonan responded directly that indeed he had been. In fact, during their marriage, the corporal divulged, they longed for children and at one time Nash even told him that they were to have one. "She told me of the coming footsteps pattering on the clouds, but it resulted in nothing but pain and sickness." The mournful couple concluded that the rather heavy burdens Nash had carried through her hard work as a younger woman had relaxed her muscles to the point that she could no longer bear a child.[37] Unless Noonan was completely oblivious to such matters, his answers here clearly indicate that the two had sexual relations.

As the nineteenth century waned, male-to-female cross-dressers, just as had women who dressed as men, increasingly raised suspicion in the press, whether in the West or elsewhere, about questionable sexuality, same-sex sexual activities, and inverted gender identities. The 1878 journalistic fascination with the sex life of Noonan and Nash presaged this development. Other tidbits strewn here and there across the record do as well. One newspaper covering the engrossing story referred to Nash's relationship with her husband as an "unnatural union." The Seventh Cavalry's John Ryan, survivor of the Battle of the Little Bighorn, invoked the alternately popular and medical term "hermaphrodite" in reference to Nash, while another news source preferred the term "man-woman."[38]

Nash's life might also illustrate the myriad men in the American West who took to women's clothing to disguise themselves in the perpetration of a crime or to escape in its aftermath. Or, to put it in a slightly different and more accurate way, one theory offered for why Nash donned women's clothing demonstrates the more traditional belief that male-to-female cross-dressing had something to do with criminal disguise and fleeing from the law. Thus, in December 1878, about a month after Corporal Noonan committed suicide, Madame La Secher, a trance medium, arrived in Bismarck and over the course of the next month or so held a series of séances with the assistance of local spiritualists. During the first of these, Madame channeled the enigmatic Nash. Nash's supposed spirit, appropriately now mired in hell, apparently admitted her true name was Joseph Drummond and said she had changed her sex to escape detection for the murder of the Grosser family in Washington, D.C., some years before. She had drugged the adults and strangled the little ones. Whether anyone believed the sensational tale is impossible to know, but the reporter who observed the séance claimed no chicanery was evident. And in any case, the *Bismarck Tribune* felt the story significant enough to merit the front page.[39]

Nash's story also casts further doubt on the all-encompassing efficacy of the progress narrative in explaining cross-dressing. In this light, consider a reflective editorial about the laundress's life and death that the *Inter Ocean*, a Chicago newspaper, carried upon learning of the unfolding events at Fort Lincoln. "Romantic stories in which girls and women masquerade as men are common in the record of life experiences," the *Inter Ocean* reminded readers, "but it is comparatively easy to find the motive and influencing causes in each case." The *Inter Ocean* editor pointed out, along the lines of the progress narrative, that women sometimes dress as men for love, sometimes for adventure, and sometimes to escape the limits imposed on their sex. "But here is a case that is a mystery," the baffled columnist continued. "Why did this man leave the wider field of action vouchsafed to man, and take upon himself the drudgery incident to a poor woman's life on the frontier[?]"[40]

The *Inter Ocean*'s question goes straight to the heart of the essential problems with the progress narrative—its cross-dressing gender specificity and its blindness to questions of identity. On the one hand, the progress narrative neatly explains that a woman, historically an otherwise second-class citizen in a man's world, might disguise herself as a man to avail herself of male privilege. But this interpretation ignores cross-dressing as a multi-gender exercise. As the *Inter Ocean* intimated way back in 1878, a man who chooses to don female attire and live as such surrenders all the prerogatives that a woman seeks by changing her clothes. On the other hand, the progress narrative's intense focus on "rational reasons" (at least by definition of unsuspecting bystanders) for a woman to dress as a man fails to account for the emotional—the need for some to do so because they feel themselves to be men. Surely the case of Nash, who not only dressed as a woman but also wholly conducted herself as one, provides irrefutable evidence that some nineteenth-century western cross-dressers, whether female or male, did so because they identified with the sex just opposite of what their biology would otherwise recommend to an incredulous public.

Hopefully by now it is clear that the progress narrative is of only limited use as an explanatory tool for cross-dressing in the history of the American West, not to mention elsewhere. Chapter 2 deals with issues of sexuality, crime, and hermaphroditism in western American male-to-female cross-dressing. Although in the remainder of this chapter I continue to explore all the above, I do so more through focusing on something else that Mrs. Nash's story can enlighten us to. Notably, period texts racialized Nash, as they did for certain other cross-dressers of the region. Within this racialization project we can find an answer to why and how male-to-female cross-dressing and, by implication, same-sex sexuality have been eradicated from mainstream America's collective memory about its frontier and western American past.

Shortly following Nash's passing, Davenport, Iowa's *Daily Gazette* carried an item asserting that the laundress's real name was Carlos Marrillo; supposedly letters found in her remaining worldly possessions disclosed such information. "He was a Mexican," the paper declared in a highly prejudicial tone, "and as a Mexican had the usual national characteristics. Was vindictive and treacherous and in consequence was rather feared then [sic] liked by . . . the other laundresses of the regiment." It is true that Nash was Mexican; at least all other reports declared it so (save possibly Madame La Secher's séance, which conjured Nash's identity as Joseph Drummond). But while Nash may have somewhat kept to herself when mixing with the other laundresses, in fact she had a well-regarded reputation for helping and caring for people in need. Though they perhaps considered Nash a bit odd, all reports claim that army personnel and camp followers liked and especially respected her. The Iowa paper's response, written from afar and unique in its claims that Nash's real name was Carlos Marillo, clearly based its characterization of the Seventh's laundress on popular Anglo racial biases.

In its coverage of Nash, the *Davenport Daily Gazette* clearly resorted to overtly racist sentiment. Other sources about Nash also contained racial themes. For example, whether news reports at the time or memories recorded in later years, they almost always noted Nash's nationality or, more precisely for the period, her race, as Mexican. In fact, Sergeant John Ryan explained that in the Seventh Cavalry people simply called Nash "The Mexican."[41]

Along similar lines, period accounts of other cross-dressers also typically highlighted the person's race when the individual was not white. Only one source that I came across referred to a white male-to-female cross-dresser's race. Significantly, the newspaper that divulged this identity did so for the purposes of questioning that individual's character because he otherwise associated with African Americans: in 1897, Topeka, Kansas, police arrested a twenty-six-year-old resident female impersonator known only as "LeCroft," for dressing up in women's clothing to rob men. The paper reporting the incident described LeCroft as "a white man who lives with negroes . . . and had traveled with a minstrel company."[42]

Otherwise, sources characteristically added ethnic and racial identities to nonwhite cross-dressers, whether male-to-female or even female-to-male. Thus, Edward Martino, arrested in 1883 for donning a woman's "rich costume" and flirting with men on the streets of Denver, was a "Spaniard." In Portland in 1911 the notorious Carmen Fells, who made a "much better looking boy than girl," had a "Mexican" mother who, with Carmen, "smoke[s] cigarettes almost constantly."[43] Pearl Mitchell, whom authorities apprehended in Redding, California, in 1908 in male attire was "colored." So too were Henrietta Alexander, who posed as Henry Alexander in Fort Worth, Texas, in 1905, as well as a young runaway girl clad in male attire whom authorities discovered on the wrong side of the tracks in Albuquerque, New Mexico, in 1908.[44]

In Brenham, Texas, "Frank," who had worn women's clothing for some time, was "a negro."[45] In Portland in 1887, police arrested a "Chinaman masquerading in female attire." The same source described in racialized terms the hoopla surrounding this individual's appearance on the street: "From the amount of jabbering that took place among the heathen over the discovery, one would have thought Bedlam had broken loose," peace returning only when two policemen arrived, apprehended the offender, and took him to the city jail.[46]

Also regardless of biological sex, sources likewise read cross-dressers' bodily attributes through the lens of race. Thus Montana's Minnie Ferrell was "supposed to be a fat colored boy." But when authorities pulled off the hat she used in her disguise, it revealed "the kinky locks and full face of a negress."[47] In 1877, a local paper described St. Louis's Alice Hunter, recently arrived from the Black Hills and disguised for some ten years as a man, as variously a "bright young mulatto" and a "darky." When authorities who arrested her for a pawn deal gone awry realized that Hunter was a woman, she became "a buxom wench."[48] Commonly used as a term for a black woman during the era (including in billings for blackface female impersonation), "negro wench" was employed by newspapers to refer to the alter ego of Edward Livenash, whom authorities picked up in San Francisco wearing female attire and having blackened his face with a burnt cork. The same reports also called him a "Dusky Damsel."[49] The infamous James Arthur Baker, whose story is related in some detail in Chapter 2, had long black hair, "somewhat like an Indian's which he explained by saying that he was a half-breed," or so a newspaper reported.[50] In 1893, news sources applied the physically descriptive phrase "the little Chinese" to a theatrical female impersonator from San Francisco who played the part of a prostitute in an elaborate scheme—apparently hatched by a white man—to dupe countrymen who were quite desirous of obtaining a Chinese woman concubine now that the Exclusion Act was in full force.[51]

Race charged almost all sources that described Mrs. Nash's body. Likewise, it infused accounts of her behaviors and speech patterns. "She was half Mexican," John Burkman explained. "Leastways she was funny-lookin'."[52] Nash wore a veil pinned across the lower portion of her face, something she would only remove indoors and in subdued lighting. Everyone seemed to know that she employed it to conceal her quickly growing beard.[53] But this did not prevent Katherine Gibson from racializing her masking habit: she "preserved the Latin coquetry of always wearing a veil," the officer's wife averred.[54] It also seems widely known that Nash shaved daily.[55] To account for this, Elizabeth Custer reasoned that "the woman was a Mexican, and, like the rest of that hairy tribe, she had so coarse and stubborn a beard that her chin had a blue look after shaving, in marked contrast to her swarthy face."[56] And Katherine Gibson remarked that "if one, from time to time, noticed a bit of down on her lips, one reflected that Latin women as they grow older are prone to develop hair on their faces and let it pass at that." In addition to referring to Nash's dexterous digits as "Latin fingers," Gibson also had the habit of mimicking Nash's accented English when later recalling conversations with her or bits and pieces of discussions she otherwise overheard. When recollecting Nash's explanation for her always present veil, for instance, Gibson explained that the laundress once exclaimed, "So bad theese vinds . . . for a jung girl's complexion." Another time, when Gibson's tactless sister Mollie asked Nash the rather personal question of why she had no children, Nash supposedly responded, "Ah, Senora . . . it is not given to us all to be mothers." When Mollie tried to apologize for her rudeness, Gibson reported that Nash simply replied, "Eet ees nozzing Senora."[57]

Sources typically examined the bodies, comportment, and behaviors of cross-dressers, whether black, Chinese, Mexican, Indian, and even (apparently) white. In the case of blacks, Chinese, Mexicans, and Indians, sources racialized their subjects. In the case of whites, but also usually in the instance of racial minorities, when sources examined the body they did so in search of clues not solely pertinent to race but also for what they might reveal about the impersonator's true sex. This was noticeably so in the case of male-to-female cross-dressers. Countless such individuals fooled alternately suspecting and unsuspecting observers with a womanly voice, a feminine appearance, a curly lock dangling just so, and an adequately smooth and powdered face. On the other hand, a hoarse voice, a manly physique, a lumbering gait, an unusually large foot, perhaps some article of men's clothing revealed when the subject hiked "his" dress uncommonly high, or a moustache exposed when a handkerchief covering the face inadvertently swished to the side—these telltale signs exposed any number of male-to-female cross-dressers in the American West.

After the fact, the *Bismarck Tribune* claimed that always the other laundresses in the Seventh Cavalry looked upon Nash as "'something' between a man and a woman."[58] It may have been her bearded chin, her coarse voice, her flat chest, or her overall physical features, bodily elements that sources remarked on time and again. For example, Elizabeth Custer described Nash's body as "tall, angular, awkward," "architectural" and "massive," and even like that of a "great giraffe." And yet, at the time of her death, outright shock prevailed when the reportedly long-suspecting laundresses discovered Nash's male anatomy.[59] That shock reverberated with force from the drab quarters of an otherwise out-of-the-way Fort Lincoln, perched as it was on a cold, windswept, and lonely plain in Dakota Territory, and then onto front pages across the country. This all suggests that the people of the Seventh Cavalry who generated that outrage in the first place had always considered Nash to be a woman, likely chalking up what they thought to be unfeminine physical features to her Mexican race rather than to her maleness.

Some years following Nash's death, the imperious Katherine Gibson recorded in her memoirs about life in the Seventh Cavalry a story that the man who posed for so long as Mrs. Nash had actually been a fugitive who years before had escaped north across the Mexican-American border. The story is entirely apocryphal, not to mention absurd, with many of its points running diametrically counter to historical fact. But the story does depict the common belief of the day that men might dress as women for extralegal reasons; likewise it hints at a popular period association of Mexican banditry and lawlessness with cross-dressing and questions about Mexican manhood.

Exactly what Nash supposedly absconded from is unclear in Gibson's narrative. But the lack of precision on that point is less significant in Gibson's account than the fact that the U.S. Seventh Cavalry's "Sergeant Nash" happened to be stationed in the Southwest when a "swarthy man disguised as a woman approached" him several times at "sundry gambling joints along the border." The cross-dresser eventually succeeded in bribing the sergeant into marriage to complete his escape northward. The marriage, according to Gibson, offered the serviceman long-term benefits in addition to an immediate reward: he would not have to eat the same lackluster fare as the other regulars, he happened to be partial to tamales anyway, and his new "wife" would be permitted to work in the regiment and thereby add to the couple's otherwise limited income. "Goaded by greed and his appetite," Gibson asserted with some measure of authority, Sergeant Nash "introduced his bride to the regiment."[60]

From one perspective, concluding that Nash cross-dressed for reasons of crime or because she was a fugitive from justice or something else, observers like Gibson normalized his otherwise inexplicable (to them) habit. That is, such storytellers established a perfectly logical reason for Nash's sartorial actions, rather than surmising one based in the ethereal realm of emotions, feelings, and perhaps identity. There was considerably more to it than this, however. Gibson's account, purposely (mis)remembered, preposterously constructed around intricate details of Mexican cross-dressing and border crossings, and told many years after both Nash and Noonan had died, was likely influenced by the numerous period stories that combined race, crime, banditry, and the deceptiveness of cross-dressing and that circulated out of the inscrutable Mexican borderlands where Nash and her sartorial choices supposedly originated.

As the last chapter explores, the Southwest supplied a particularly large number of highly romanticized stories of female-to-male cross-dressing bandits. More than those operating in other subregions of the West, these narratives incorporated racial elements. They tended not to focus on racialized Mexican identities, however, so much as they did on Indianness. Strikingly, these tales associated wild cross-dressing women in the Southwest with the long-held and -honed fears that whites in the region had of despised Comanche and Apache raiders. They may also have spun out from older traditions in the American West of warrior women in Indian tribes who crossed gender boundaries and took on the role of men and sometimes even married other women.[61] Net Bettie, for example, born near Fort Gibson in "Indian Territory," turned rogue, dressed as a man, made love to her enemy's wife, and reportedly carried on a reign of terror up and down the Rio Grande and even into Arizona Territory. In fact, she earned the sobriquet "Terror of the Plains" and eventually retired to Mexico, apparently the only haven that could countenance her. To help account for her actions, and no doubt cast aspersions on a southern neighbor, a paper reported that Bettie's parents "had plenty of Indian blood in their veins."[62] Similarly, though not only entirely about behavior, Oklahoma Territory's Tom King, really Flora Quick, who otherwise had a good home, nevertheless took to men's clothing, stole horses, and rode with desperadoes. "It is not believed that Tom King is altogether a white woman," vouchsafed one source, while another remarked that she showed "in her appearance the Indian blood in her veins."[63] The Middle Border's Annie Harris, who rode with Quantrill's raiders and caused and took part in any number of deprivations, had eyes "blacker than an Indian maiden's . . . and her hair was as long and straight."[64]

In addition to marking their subjects with race, the content of these southwestern stories is noticeably violent, lawless, and bloody in nature, especially when compared to romantic stories of women-as-men elsewhere in the West. Considering the history of Indian–white relations in this region, it makes sense. Among the tales from the same region that involved men who dressed as women, these stories often took Mexican men as their subjects and depicted them as treacherous and deceitful, explaining that they might serve as spies and lookouts for accomplices in deadly crimes and armed raids all the while deceptively appareled in female attire. One account from 1886, for example, reported that the entire town of Eagle Pass, Texas, located directly across the Rio Grande from Mexico's Piedras Negras, became consumed with terror, fearing that it would soon be raided by armed Mexican marauders because, among other apparently tell-tale signs, authorities discovered in the streets two Mexican men dressed in female attire they assumed to be spies.[65]

Whereas southern borderland tales of cross-dressing women directly questioned their race, associating them with feared Indians, tales of cross-dressing Mexican men called into question their manliness. Although Anglo Americans' racialized views of borderland Mexicans stretch a considerable distance back into history, thematically the accounts of effeminacy among Mexican men find their roots nurtured in the Mexican-American War.[66] At that time, myriad popular stories written in and circulated throughout the United States typically depicted Mexican men, when compared to Anglo men, as cowardly and weak. They could not successfully defend their nation from northern invaders, as this view would have it. And earlier they had reputedly responded only with the utmost cowardice in the face of Comanche raids.[67] These narratives provided a gendered defense for the U.S. offensive against Mexico. As literary scholar Shelley Streeby notes, a preponderance of cross-dressing Mexican women soldiers, described as "admirably masculine" in tales of the Mexican-American War, served as counterpoints to the lack of manliness among Mexican men and indicated a larger national crisis in Mexico. That crisis the United States would remedy on the national level through actions taken at the local: having its soldiers, who proved particularly manly, conquer its southern neighbor and capture the hearts of Mexican female-to-male cross-dressers, marry them, and return them to their proper domestic sphere (not to mention appropriate sartorial custom).[68]

True, these 1840s depictions of Mexican men did not actually dress them in women's apparel. But that would happen in time. Border troubles, Mexican banditry, and Mexican-American rebellion occurred sporadically across the U.S. Southwest long after the 1848 signing of the Treaty of Guadalupe Hidalgo. In myths, legends, and especially the *corrido* (popular Mexican narrative songs that detail stories of oppression and peasant resistance), northern Mexicans and Mexican Americans in the Southwest valorized the men who participated in these activities, regardless of the dubiousness of their precise acts. They became folk heroes because they fought for their rights by any means against the imperialist North.[69] But Anglos had something of a different perspective: Mexicans and Mexican Americans who engaged in these rebellious and despicable acts, Anglos viewed as underhanded, exceptionally cruel, and duplicitous. Thus Anglos worked to demonize them. They also rendered the Mexican man as unmanly precisely for the treachery of his deeds.

One way that Anglos demasculinized the Mexican was by depicting him as a cross-dresser. In the years after Nash's demise, the borderland presented various tales of cross-dressing Mexican bandits. A notable example comes from Southern California and involves Sylvestro Morales, who established a reign of terror, so the newspapers say, that stretched across Orange County and lasted from February to September 1889. In addition to horse stealing, highway robbery, and the wanton killing of several people, he kidnapped a (willing biracial) "girl" preposterously named Nymphia Brown while holding her parents at bay with a gun. Morales gained a reputation for duplicity, unfairness, and bloodlust especially for stripping a man on the road of his money, gold watch, and horse and then shooting him; murdering "in cold blood" a sheepherder who otherwise kindly supplied Morales a hideout; and shooting full of holes, for apparently no reason at all, an old partner in crime. Authorities had a devil of a time apprehending Morales. Other Mexican Americans reportedly refused to provide any information about him and thereby became conflated with Morales's reputed perfidy, deceitfulness, and dishonor. But what made Morales particularly difficult to apprehend was that he often succeeded in escaping detection by wearing a black polonaise skirt, a red shawl, and a brown hat with a veil, and he further shielded his identity underneath the shadow of a "cheap parasol."[70] Such narratives questioning Mexican manliness that trace to the Mexican-American War (and obviously to events that occurred during the years subsequent to it) no doubt worked themselves, at least thematically, into later renditions of Nash, such as told by Katherine Gibson.

Mexican men and men from other nonwhite racial groups, whether in the Southwest or elsewhere, and whether they actually wore female attire, were in all cases feminized to varying degrees in the late nineteenth and early twentieth centuries through projects carried out by whites. The example of the Mexican-American War shows how this was at least partly done to Mexican men. Historians have well demonstrated how western whites feminized men of color in many other instances. Notably, whites repeatedly denied to nonwhite men basic legal and political rights, access to women and marriage, and freedom of movement (for example, confining Native Americans to reservations). These rights and privileges defined manhood in the late nineteenth-century West.

Denying these to men of color therefore demasculinized or feminized them. Of course, this had a racial element to it, too: these things defined not just manhood, but specifically white manhood.[71]

The classic example of the feminized male in the American West is the Chinese immigrant, whom whites hated.[72] During the latter half of the nineteenth century the vast majority of Chinese immigrants could be found in California. Whether there or elsewhere, Chinese males far outnumbered their female compatriots. In 1852 in California the ratio stood at 1,685 to 1. This declined precipitously over the next two decades, but in 1870 it still stood at a remarkably disproportionate 14 to 1.[73] The 1882 Chinese Exclusion Act altogether impeded the migration of Chinese women to America, and just two years before its adoption, California had prohibited the intermarriage of "Mongolians" and "whites." All this arrested the ability of Chinese men to create families.[74] Chinese men thus persisted longer than other groups of males in the region in homosocial or what is usually referred to as bachelor communities. It is true that through the nineteenth century men overall outnumbered women in the West and bachelor communities were common among all settler groups. But as the historian Robert G. Lee has explained, already by the 1870s in California (and this would apply to other parts of the West as the end of the nineteenth century approached), women had become considerably more common and society there had transitioned to more settled family life. In this atmosphere, the persistent Chinese bachelor society raised the specter of sexual deviance; it was, in Lee's words, "subversive and disruptive to the emergent heterosexual orthodoxy."[75] Simultaneously, by the turn of the twentieth century Americans had gained an international reputation for, as the German sexologist Magnus Hirschfeld put it, blaming "one or the other ethnic group for homosexuality."[76]

Excluding Chinese men from many avenues that would allow them to achieve a family and associating them with nonmanly sexuality were only two ways in which these immigrants faced feminization. Over the course of the same years, the Chinese were denied the ability to own land and to become citizens, thus in another way excluding them from what politically constituted manhood. Moreover, from the perspective of whites, Chinese men's outward appearance—their long braided queue, their relative smooth skin, their generally smaller stature, and their loose and flowing clothing— marked them as effeminate.[77] Additionally, whites routinely viewed Chinese men as womanly both in terms of their dexterity and their ability to perform certain tasks when working as miners, for example.[78] In time, when economic downturn and white working-class campaigns excluded Chinese men from traditionally male jobs, this group had little alternative but to move into types of employment more typically associated with women, for example in restaurants and laundries and as domestic servants. This all further worked to feminize the Chinese man.[79]

If Chinese men provide the classic example of the feminization of the non-white male in the American West, feminization happened in varying degrees to all racial minority males in the latter years of the nineteenth century and early years of the twentieth. Not surprisingly, then, news reports of non-Anglo men who were discovered in female attire described them as especially feminized in a racial context. The various considerations of Nash outlined earlier in this chapter constitute notable examples. So too was the report of Chin Ling, arrested in Oakland, California, in 1908, dressed as "a slave girl" to fool "some gullible Chinese who might pay a good price to obtain possession of the masquerader." News sources reported that Ling "presented a living picture of a handsome Chinese maiden of the better class." "Owing to the fact," the newspaper maintained, "that Chin Ling's features are more than ordinarily delicate for a Chinese, he had but little difficulty in making up as a woman."[80]

There are other examples, too, and not only of the Chinese. One is of Edward Martino, the "Spaniard" arrested in Denver in 1883 for wearing female attire. The Colorado press could not help but depict Martino along the lines of the period stereotype of the Mexican senorita: he came down the street "in a rich costume, and carrying a fan in the most approved fashion. He certainly made a very handsome looking woman and had made himself up in a most ravishing style."[81] Bill Smith, whom a Missouri newspaper noted "is an African," donned a "home-made linsey-woolsey frock." The use of the term "linsey-woolsey," which describes a blended cotton-woolen fabric, also connotes an odd or confused admixture. Clever newswriters likely intended it simultaneously to refer to Smith's race and, considering that here it literally referred to female clothing, to disparage his amalgam of female and male attributes.[82]

"Squaw Charley" or "Lady Jim," as the Nevada press alternately dubbed a cross-dressing Paiute Indian man, occasionally made the papers between 1874 and 1898. To explain the apparently inexplicable, residents of Virginia City, where Charley/Jim lived on the streets for years, created a story, spun out over some quarter of a century, that he had disgraced himself in the Pyramid Lake War of 1869. His tribe therefore forced him to wear women's clothing as punishment. In early years he reportedly dressed like a "squaw," but later accounts changed this, claiming that he wore the fashion of "white femininity" (a shawl, a hoopskirt, and crinolines), which supposedly meant a double ignominy for him.[83] Possibly referring to General Phil Sheridan's infamous racialized quip from the era that the only good Indian he ever saw was a dead Indian, one of the headlines at the time of Charley/Jim's death trumpeted, A DEAD COWARD.[84]

Even when not in women's clothing, Indian men could be feminized in reference to cross-dressing more generally. This happened in Missoula, Montana, when one night in March 1898 police chased a "mysterious man in female attire" who apparently vanished into thin air. The rest of the "boys" in the department joked about their colleague's inability to apprehend the suspect and laughed uproariously that the figure "was no woman" at all, "but an Indian, whose blanket was taken by the limbs of the law for a dress."[85]

In addition to an ethno-feminizing element, the racializing of cross-dressing males often had a more pointedly sexual component to it as well. Nash, supposedly a Mexican fugitive who escaped over the border by becoming a woman, also became the sexual submissive to a white man. The press called the "Spaniard" Edward Martino a "Male Miss Nancy," and claimed that his flirtations on the streets of Denver "nearly drove two or three young men of the dude order into hysterics."[86] Whether they actually intended to follow the charade through to its natural conclusion is perhaps less important than the fact that both Chin Ling in Oakland in 1908 and San Francisco's "Little Chinese" back in 1893 dressed to disguise themselves as women available for purposes of prostitution among their countrymen, or at least that is the way the press would have it.[87] The press's focus in 1891 on a Portland, Oregon, Chinese female impersonator's one-and-one-half-inch feet also had a sexual element to it. Not only did such a description serve to exoticize and feminize this performer, but it also not so innocently associated him with Chinese female sexual submissiveness, something that appealed to Chinese men, but also crossed racial boundaries to pique the fantasies of white men, too.[88]

Such descriptions further conflated male gender and sexual transgressiveness with race.[89] The Anglo or white penchant for racializing (what they viewed as) sexual and gender transgressiveness actually has a history that stretches far back before the late nineteenth century. Already in their initial encounters with Native Americans, Europeans harshly reacted to those Indians they called "berdache" or "hermaphrodites," that is, those male-bodied

Indians whose lives mixed female and male gender behaviors and clothing and who also often had sexual relations with men in their tribes.[90] While it is true that from the sixteenth century on, European explorers, travelers, and even missionaries might respond in a variety of ways, including somewhat neutrally and without apparent malice toward such Native Americans, their responses were more often tinged with venom and condemnation.[91] Moreover, they filled their descriptions of Native American gender and sexual behaviors with such shock and dismay that without actually saying it they made it quite clear that male effeminacy was not something one would find in European culture. Such responses would even provide justification for European conquest and extermination of Native Americans in the earliest years of Spanish encounters; likewise they justified assimilation programs that the U.S. government sponsored at the turn of the twentieth century.[92]

Over the years Europeans and Euro-Americans expanded their negative views on race, gender, and sexuality evoked by the male-bodied berdache to Native Americans generally.[93] In the 1750s, Frenchman Jean Bernard Bossu, for example, wrote of the "corrupt men, who have long hair and wear short skirts like women" among the Choctaw and denounced that "the people of this nation are generally of a brutal and coarse nature. . . . They are morally quite perverted, and most of them are addicted to sodomy."[94] In the 1830s Alexander Maximilian, Prince of Wied, encountered berdaches during his western travels along the Missouri, claiming that the Crow "exceed all the other tribes in unnatural practices."[95] A few years later, fur trapper Edwin Denig remarked on the "Berdêches" he encountered among the Crow as well as a woman among them who became a war chief and took wives. "Strange country this," Denig wrote expansively of the entire upper Missouri, "where males assume the dress and perform the duties of females, while women turn men and mate with their own sex!"[96]

For all its coverage of cross-dressing in the American West during the years surrounding the turn of the twentieth century, the popular press remained largely mute on the phenomenon among Native Americans.[97] But racialized and explicitly sexualized reports of male-to-female Native American cross-gendered practices and traditions nevertheless circulated widely. William Hammond, a onetime U.S. Army surgeon general and a president of the American Neurological Association, published such an account in the popular *American Journal of Neurology and Psychiatry*. Subsequently cited on numerous occasions, Hammond's piece concerned his 1850s encounter with two Pueblo men he called *mujerado* (a term that has been translated from its corrupted Spanish roots as "womaned," and obviously showing how Europeans influenced notions about such people).[98] One of these Hammond dismissed as having a "voice . . . of high pitch, thin and cracked, especially when he became excited, which he did very readily; and he indulged in more gesticulations than any Indian I had ever seen." Hammond also explained that the *mujerado* performed as the passive partner in sodomitical ceremonies, something he understood to be a regular part of Pueblo customs.[99]

In another instance, western historian Hubert Howe Bancroft published in 1874 a volume (in his long list of works) that he dedicated to "The Native Races" of North America. In it he asserted that "sodomy is common" among Alaska's Kodiak Indians, and then explained that (to him) "the most repugnant of all their practices is that of male concubinage." A handsome and promising boy, Bancroft related, is selected during his early years to dress and be reared as a girl in all ways "in order to render his effeminacy complete. Arriving at the age of ten or fifteen years, he is married to some wealthy man, who regards such a companion as a great acquisition."[100]

A final example is provided in 1889 by the physician A. B. Holder, who, in a widely cited medical article, wrote about his research on the Crow *bo-te*, who "wears the 'squaw' dress and leggins, parts the hair in the middle and braids it like a woman's, possesses or affects the voice and manner of a woman, and constantly associates with that sex as being of it." The *bo-te* also produces, Holder detailed, "sexual orgasm by taking the male organ of the active party in the lips . . . the bote probably experiencing the orgasm at the same time. . . . Of all the many varieties of sexual perversion, this, it seems to me, is the most debased that could be conceived of."[101]

It is true that as the nineteenth century ebbed, newspapers and other sources increasingly suspected gender inversion and transgressive sexuality among all males found in women's clothing regardless of the subject's race. And it is also true that newspapers largely remained silent on the gender and sexual diversity of Indians. Nevertheless, the press's intense focus on both racial and sexual/gender markers in the case of non-Anglo males who dressed as women and the wide circulation of non-news sources reporting in vivid detail about Native American men who dressed as women, performed female roles, and had sexual relations with men, all served to further feminize, sexualize, and exoticize nonwhite males in the West. The association of transgressive sexuality and gender behaviors with race had, of course, the effect of excluding male-to-female cross-dressers from the "real" West itself.

Contributing to this was the related and concomitant development in popular culture of the association of the American West with virile white masculinity.[102] Since the opening years of the nineteenth century, frontier tales of adventure involving Daniel Boone, Natty Bumpo, and Kit Carson, to name but a few, of course already marked the West as a place that tested and reinforced white manhood. By the latter years of the century, industrialization, the appearance of the impersonal modern corporate order, the spectacular growth of the city and of apparent disorder within it, the entrance of women into the public sphere, the frightening labor unrest, the freeing of slaves, and the arrival of large numbers of racially and ethnically different migrants all combined to alter the foundations on which hegemonic white middle-class manliness had recently been based—social control, patriarchy, self-restraint, and economic independence. Decreasingly able to mark manliness along these more traditional lines, during the last third of the nineteenth century white middle-class men instead turned to gender-exclusive outdoor activities, contact sports, bodybuilding, militarism, and adventure (whether experienced firsthand or vicariously) to establish and vivify their masculinity. The American West served as a prime locus for these and related activities.

Although many at this time widely promoted the West as a place of restorative masculinity, including fairly prominent individuals such as Owen Wister and Frederic Remington as well as the myriad authors of mass-produced dime novels, the most emblematic and perhaps influential to do so was the future president Theodore Roosevelt.[103] Reeling from accusations of effeminacy and even veiled allusions to homosexuality, smarting from snide remarks about his effete fashion sense, and mindful of his squeaky voice and asthmatic and underdeveloped body, in the 1880s Roosevelt purchased two ranches in the Dakota badlands and spent considerable time there making over his physique, his tenor, his health, his clothing, and his image. In fact, in the West the president-to-be engaged in open revolt against the older and now outmoded forms of middle-class masculinity exemplified by his father and with which he had been reared.[104] He then published extensively about his western experiences, lavishing details on how the frontier transformed him into a manly hero akin to the cowboy. Roosevelt's growing interest in the West also led him in the 1890s to complete a four-volume history, *The Winning of the West.* These white-, male-, and man-centric writings made him, some scholars have argued, the nation's most important historian of the region before the end of the century.[105]

Roosevelt's writings did more than promote the connections between white masculinity and the West, however; they also identified the twin aims of imperialism and nationalism as linked to manly frontier ventures. These also necessarily had a racial cast to them. In *The Winning of the West* series, in the words of historian Gail Bederman, Roosevelt depicted "the American West as a crucible in which the white American race was forged through masculine racial conflict."[106] All told, Roosevelt's "speeches and writings, and those of many of his contemporaries," explains sociologist Joane Nagel, "reflected a racialized, imperial masculinity, where adventurous, but civilized white men tame or defeat inferior savage men of colour, be they American Indians, Africans, Spaniards, or Filipinos."[107]

Roosevelt and others of his ilk popularized the association of virile white masculinity with the West and its superiority over peoples of color in that region at the very moment that Americans more generally began to accede to and lament the closing of the frontier. As the introduction of this book explained, they responded to the ensuing cultural crisis in a variety of ways. Among these is Frederick Jackson Turner's "The Significance of the Frontier in American History," perhaps the most notable, profound, and influential artifact of the frontier's (supposed) closing.[108] In this tribute, Turner did more than merely claim that the frontier "explained American development"; the cast of characters he identified as central to this development was composed of a succession of European or white men who headed west— explorers, hunters, traders, cattlemen, surveyors, and especially agrarians, each in his turn confronting the western wilderness.[109] Turner expelled from the frontier and its westward trek Hispanics, Asians, and African Americans. He all but ignored Native Americans, save to present them as an obstacle for western advancement that had to be overcome, and their villages serving only as sites on which later arose the great cities of the United States. Moreover, heteronormative assumptions underlay Turner's view of American history. His three principal settler-types were family men, responsible for ever-expanding and -increasing populations in the communities they founded. The first type was interested in the subsistence of their families; the second worked toward building up community and laying the foundations for its first institutions; and the third, which included some stay-behinds, developed fully civilized life with its complement of fields and gardens, brick buildings, and more elaborate institutions such as colleges and churches.[110]

While Turner developed his musings in libraries, lecture halls, and academic offices, they were in no way dissociated from an influence on and by popular culture. For one, Turner, like Roosevelt, both reflected and contributed to the period's whitening and masculinizing of America's frontier past. Furthermore, the U.S. government published "The Significance of the Frontier in American History" in its Senate documents, and after reading Turner's frontier thesis, Roosevelt in early 1894 sent the historian a congratulatory note, pointing out that he had "put into definite shape a good deal of thought which has been floating around rather loosely" for some time. He tellingly added that the appearance of Turner's exposition came at just "the right time for me, for I intend to make use of it in writing the third volume of my 'Winning of the West.'"[111]

By the end of the nineteenth century, broad popular opinion in the United States identified virile white masculinity with the American West. It had also literally transformed the frontier into the cradle of white American nationhood. Moreover, it had feminized non-Anglo men in the West by excluding them from social and political manhood there and identifying them with sexual deviance and certain elements of womanliness. It had also racialized male sexual inversion and cross-dressing. Simultaneously and purposely these related projects worked to push people like the Seventh Cavalry's Mrs. Nash from the region to its periphery, to its margins, indeed to its borderlands. On the one hand, in the late nineteenth century male-to-female cross-dressing was effectively removed from the defining narratives of the American West, the frontier, and thus the nation. On the other hand, male-to-female cross-dressing was obviously central, in a furtive sort of way, to the creation of these narratives.[112]

In the wake of Mrs. Nash's death, when all attention shifted to her husband, John Noonan, reactions to the cavalryman grew harsh. Likewise, the press would soon report sharply of his suicide. "There was a sigh of relief," one paper asserted, because "Noonan by his own hand had relieved the regiment of the odium which the man's presence cast upon them."[113] Corporal Noonan, the distant New York Herald disparaged, "blew out what little brains he had."[114] The sources and stories about Noonan generated over the weeks immediately following his wife's death and even over the next few years clearly show the insults and mockery this inconsolable cavalryman faced at the time.

None of these sources, however, questioned Noonan's sexuality, mental condition, or motives for his love life in terms of his race—he was white, after all. Some never even questioned his sexuality, insisting to the end that his marriage to Nash was purely one of convenience, based solely on his desire to line his pockets and feed his face (with Mexican cuisine).[115] And yet with regard to Nash and all these issues of character, motive, and sexuality, countless of these sources focused intensely on the very issue of race—she "was a Mexican," after all. In fact, some sources eventually came to treat Noonan with some measure of forgiveness and rehabilitation. For example, in time John Burkman remorsefully claimed that he and his fellow servicemen became terribly ashamed for treating Noonan so poorly, all the while thinking back on what a wonderful, lively, and popular fellow he had been. "It takes all kinds o' men to make an army," Burkman philosophically stated. "Nonan's troubles meant jist as much to him as though he'd been a Major. Hundreds of graves scattered over Dakota and Montana of men that's never been missed, never been writ up, but they was good soldiers jist the same, and without 'em thar wouldn't've been no country, maybe."[116] However inclusive this statement might seem, no such eulogies, at least free from the taint of racism, were ever offered up for Nash.

When period witnesses and later chroniclers explained that Nash's various husbands, whether Noonan or Nash or whoever, entered into marriage with the laundress for her money or her culinary skills, they of course normalized these men. This is not entirely unlike the passing mentions here and there in western American history of the transvestite habits of manly men in places and moments in the region's past—for example, the gold-rush frontier or some forlorn cattle trail—where the necessity of gender imbalance drove them fleetingly to dress as the opposite sex or at least stand in her place for purposes of good old wholesome fun. The cross-dressing and cross-gender habits of such men are understandable and, more to the point, acceptable thanks to "social context." That such men happened to be white (or are assumed so) has no doubt made their actions even more comprehensible.

All this helps point the way to which other "male" transgressive sartorial and sexual behaviors have been exoticized and racialized in western history and thus pushed to the margins there. Period sources clearly demonstrate this in the mentality of those who created them. But the exoticization, racialization, and marginalization in western history of men's trangressive sartorial behaviors, feminine gender activities, and homosexual habits remain uninterrupted to the present day, as seen in popular cultural renderings and even in the halls of academia. The great preponderance of scholarly and popular attention to male-to-female cross-dressers in what might loosely be called "western and frontier" history has principally centered on nonwhites and almost exclusively on Native Americans. One of the great exceptions to the latter, but not the former group, is Mrs. Nash. Over the years she has been the subject—whether as focal point or just in passing—of several scholarly and popular articles and books.[117] In part the interest in Nash is attributable to her association with the Seventh Cavalry, a regiment that has attained mythic proportions; Nash appears in a few of the most important firsthand accounts of that regiment, most notably Elizabeth Bacon Custer's *Boots and Saddles*, published already in 1885.[118] But more, Nash has demonstrated to historians who might otherwise prefer to forget the whole thing the inescapable reality that homosexuality can be found in the most masculine of western American bailiwicks: its military history and, in this case, the mythical Seventh Cavalry![119] In these cases, Nash has no doubt been employed because her national origins and her racial identity have made her less threatening to consider.

Most scholarly efforts devoted to (homo)sexuality and transgenderism in the historic trans-Mississippi West have rather concentrated on the so-called berdache, an important and fascinating subject to be sure.[120] Anthropologists have written extensively on them, at the same time generally ignoring the complexities of European/Euro-American gender-sexual life in western and frontier history, unless it is in terms of their reactions to Indians. What is more, academically inclined *western* historians have pretty much disregarded the berdache, thus abdicating the possibility of contextualizing and framing this element of Native American sexuality and gender within the region's history. Regardless of which scholars have done this and which scholars have done that, what has and has not been done has served to continue in the modern era something that has gone on since the earliest days of western and frontier American history: the racialization, exoticization, and marginalization of transgressive sartorial and sexual practices.[121] Likely this has been unintended. But that it is unintended demonstrates the power of the myth of the virile white masculine and heterosexual frontier to influence how we yet view and interpret America's western past.

Men who dressed as women have presented something of a thornier problem in western, frontier, and national history than have their female-to-male counterparts. As Chapter 3 explains, the ease with which the progress narrative could be invoked in the case of women who dressed as men made it a simple matter to re-imagine and remember them in western myth as both heterosexual and feminine, despite the very real evidence to the contrary. In the sense that it provides for rationally normative reasons to cross-dress, the progress narrative has also occasionally come in handy for making sense of the few hardy western male souls who wished to enjoy a dance from time to time and (supposedly because of being isolated from women) dressed as women. But the progress narrative largely breaks down when it has to account for other readings of these men's motives as well as of the myriad other male-to-female cross-dressers who lived in and passed through the Old West.

The male-to-female cross-dresser, his gender, and his sexuality all ran counter to cherished regional and nation-building myths, whereas the female-to-male cross-dresser could be accounted for in them. In light of this, the effort to forget the male-to-female cross-dresser in the history of the American West and in the foundational frontier narrative of the American nation has been at once more necessary, perhaps more hidden, and in some ways more complicated than for the female-to-male cross-dresser. In the story of Mrs. Nash and in the stories of other racialized, exoticized, feminized, and marginalized people like her we can see one fundamental way this exclusion has been accomplished. At best, Mrs. Nash has been seen as some misplaced figure in the grand narrative of western history, while at worst she has been depicted as a displaced and demasculinized Mexican border ruffian made subordinate to the penetrations of imperial white male heterosexuality. In fact, Nash was hardly an erratic on the western American landscape—rejected records, discarded documents, and marginalized memories speak otherwise.

The esteemed social/sexual theoretician Michel Foucault once very forcefully and cleverly argued that in the history of Western civilization, and contrary to popular belief, sex and sexuality have hardly been repressed, as commonly believed. In fact, Foucault claimed, the history of sex and sexuality has shown just the opposite propensity: through time, in the simple act of trying to remove sex and sexuality from sight, for example, there have been repeated discursive explosions about them, making sex and sexuality ubiquitous and creating sexual minorities. Clearly, documents that chronicle western American history reveal such discursive explosions there from the earliest days onward. And yet in historical writing and popular memory, these historic discursive explosions have been all but forgotten, regardless as to what Foucault might have once thought. The American West and its frontier antecedents simply have remained the most resistant of heteronormative ramparts.

CHAPTER 5

"Death of a Modern Diana"

Sexologists, Cross-Dressers, and the Heteronormalization
of the American Frontier

In 1855, a backcountry hunter named Joseph Israel Lobdell, who was twenty-six at the time and had piercing gray eyes and a full head of curly black hair, departed from his home in the Delaware River country of upstate New York and headed west to Minnesota Territory.[1] He was in search of wilder terrain, as the forests of his childhood and youth, in particular around Long Eddy, New York, had recently become somewhat crowded. In his baggage, Lobdell carried with him a lengthy heritage of frontier living. His ancestors had pioneered upstate New York in the late 1700s, and over the years they had made their living there from logging and farming. The area's still rough conditions during Joseph's childhood in the 1820s and 1830s provided him ample opportunity to become "conversant with hard work and with hard characters," not to mention the backwoods crafts of rafting, fishing, and handling firearms.[2] At about the age of eleven, the youthful Lobdell gained local notoriety when he hunted down a panther, doggedly tracking it for some ten miles. Over the years he honed his hunting skills as his father's ill health led the family to rely increasingly on what the young Lobdell could bring in with his rifle. By the time the hunter lit out for the Old Northwest, he had bagged, in addition to the panther, more than 160 deer, nearly half again as many bears, and any number of smaller game of the forest.

These experiences and skills served the backwoods New Yorker well in the Minnesota wilds. There he hunted, trapped, and chopped wood, first on the shores of Lake Minnetonka and then farther west near the village of Manannah in Meeker County. Soon known among the settlers for his "good

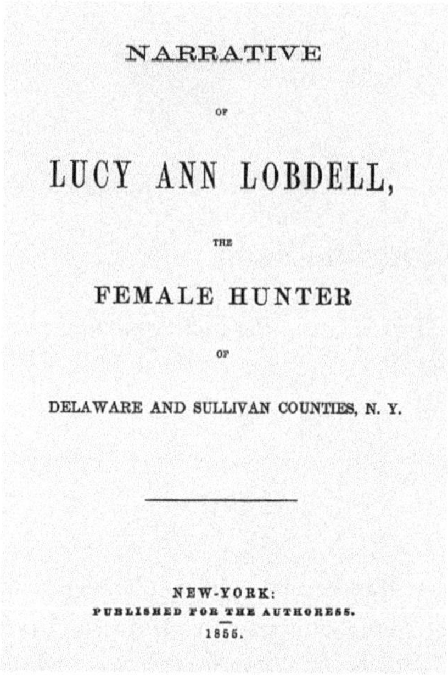

NARRATIVE

OF

LUCY ANN LOBDELL,

THE

FEMALE HUNTER

OF

DELAWARE AND SULLIVAN COUNTIES, N. Y.

———

NEW-YORK:
PUBLISHED FOR THE AUTHORESS.
1855.

FIGURE 12. *Narrative of Lucy Ann Lobdell*, 1855. In 1855, upstate New York's Joseph Lobdell published the story of his early life under his birth name of Lucy Ann Lobdell. He then permanently changed into male attire and headed to Minnesota Territory. Some mishap there in the summer of 1858 revealed him to have the body of a woman. Outraged local officials shipped him back East, where he resided until his death. *Narrative of Lucy Ann Lobdell* serves as a remarkable mid-nineteenth-century feminist tract as well as a defense of female-to-male cross-dressing.

company" and as a "hale fellow well met," Lobdell had a frontier reputation that also derived from being "handy at anything" and a "splendid hunter." His ability in the latter pursuit, however, did not go unrivaled in the Minnesota backcountry. Even so, the way it did only added more color to the woodsman's local celebrity: when the hunter's gun occasionally failed to provide, Lobdell's well-trained pet cat brought in squirrels that supplied sustenance for the two.[3]

In the wilder reaches of the Old Northwest, Lobdell spent considerable time with other woodsmen. In 1856 he and comrade Edwin Gribbel from St. Paul tramped "together through the woods in pursuit of game" and slept "together under the same blanket," wooing "the gentle goddess of slumber under the umbrageous forest trees around Minnetonka." With another companion, Lobdell held possession of the Kandiyohi town site during the winter of 1856–57 for Minneapolis investors. At other times, Lobdell's work in the northern wilds required him to bunk with any number of other laboring men.[4]

Lobdell truly was a frontiers*man's* frontiers*man*. At least, that is what Manannahites thought until some unrecorded indiscretion in the summer of 1858 revealed that Lobdell was no man at all, but a woman and, moreover, a mother! Shocked friends instantly turned bitter detractors. The scandal, replete with a trial for impersonating a man, entirely discredited Lobdell. Subjected to taunts and insults, he became an outcast. Uncertain exactly what to do, unnerved Meeker County officials finally scraped together enough train fare to return their charge to New York.[5]

When run out of northern Minnesota's backcountry in the summer of 1858, Joseph Lobdell walked directly into history. Truth be told, this was neither the first nor, more propitiously, the last time. Back in the winter of 1853, for example, while hunting in the snowy wilds of the Delaware Valley, Lobdell, already sporting male attire, crossed paths with an itinerant peddler known only as Talmage, whose discerning eyes figured out, to his satisfaction anyway, his acquaintance's true identity. So taken aback by the experience, the salesman wrote it up for a Connecticut newspaper, or so the story goes. The publication of the remarkable tale drew so many curiosity seekers to the Delaware Valley that Lobdell found it almost impossible to hunt there by the winter of 1854, the reason why he departed for the Old Northwest in the first place.[6]

Before doing so, however, Lobdell, as a woman, self-published an autobiography in which he considered his life up to the point that he finally took on a male identity. Viewed one way, *Narrative of Lucy Ann Lobdell, The Female Hunter of Delaware and Sullivan Counties, N.Y.,* is something of an early feminist tract. In it Lobdell complained specifically of an abusive marriage to George W. Slater and more generally about good-for-nothing and drunken husbands. In explaining that women, in caring for home, children, and their husbands, did considerably more than the latter to maintain the family, Lobdell decried that when on her own, even while raising a family, a woman could never earn the same wages as a man, the economic pressure often forcing her to surrender their children "to the charity of the world." "Help, one and all to aid woman," Lobdell demanded. "If she is willing to toil, give her wages equal with that of man. And as in sorrow she bears her own curse, (nay, indeed, she helps to bear a man's burden also,) secure to her her rights, or permit her to wear the pants, and breathe the pure air of heaven, and you stay and be convinced at home with the children how pleasant a task it is to act the part that woman must act."[7]

Lobdell's brushes with history multiplied after his 1858 forced retirement from Minnesota Territory's pioneer settlements. Continuing life as a man back in his old haunts, Lobdell took up a teaching position in Bethany, Pennsylvania, fatefully close to his childhood home of Long Eddy, offering courses in singing and dancing. His proficiency with the fiddle also made his attendance mandatory at local soirees. Reportedly popular with all the local young women, many of whom enrolled in his classes, by the end of his first term of teaching Lobdell had earned the love of, and an engagement to, one such pupil, the daughter of one of Bethany's leading lumber families. The night before the planned wedding, however, a rival for the girl's affections who had come into information from nearby Long Eddy about Lobdell's female alter ego planned to capture his opponent, tar and feather him, and then run him out of town on the rails. But before this nefarious scheme could be hatched, Lobdell's betrothed discovered the plans. Notwithstanding her reported mortification upon learning of her engagement to a woman, she nevertheless warned her fiancé, for whom she yet retained feelings. Lobdell safely fled in the night.

Not too much later, financial straits and failing health drove Lobdell to resume a woman's identity to secure shelter in the Delaware County almshouse in Delhi, New York, near her childhood stomping grounds. At about the same time and not so far away, a young Marie Louise Perry, graduate from a fine Boston school and daughter of a well-to-do Massachusetts family, eloped with a young and socially inferior railroad employee named James Wilson, really a scoundrel her parents had tried to prevent her from seeing. Within weeks of their marriage, James jilted Marie for the daughter of their landlady. Doggedly Marie tracked her unfaithful husband and his shameless partner as far as upstate New York until lack of funds forced her to abandon the chase. With too little money and too much pride to return to her parents, Marie threw herself on the benevolence of Delaware County and entered the local poorhouse.

Another version of Perry's life history claims instead that her mother went insane when Perry was but a newborn. In fact, this version explains that friends had to wrench the baby from the mother when the latter lost her mind and was discovered one morning clasping her child to her bosom while hiding behind a pile of wood at her Massachusetts farm. Perry matured into young womanhood, all the while displaying "a great liking for boyish games and attire." Persuaded to marry "a man to whom she became so repugnant that he deserted her and she sought refuge in a Pennsylvania almshouse."[8]

In either and both cases, at the almshouse she met Lobdell. The two reportedly took an instant liking to each other, "notwithstanding the difference in their habits, character, and intellect."[9] In the spring of 1869, the two took leave of their charitable domicile, were married by an unsuspecting local clergyman, and began roaming through the Delaware Valley countryside. They occupied caves, lean-tos, and bark huts, and tamed a bear that they led about on a leash, and Lobdell hunted and trapped and earned odd change as an itinerant preacher to supplement the berries, roots, and meager handouts on which they otherwise subsisted. At one point arrested as public nuisances in the hill country of Monroe County, Pennsylvania, the couple spent several weeks behind bars in Stroudsburg before shocked guards discovered Lobdell's female sex and then indignantly transported the peculiar pair back to New York.

A few years later, in 1876, and once again back on the Pennsylvania side of the Delaware, Lobdell landed in the Honesdale jail. Some sources claim it was for lunacy; another explains that Marie's uncle, for whom Lobdell did odd jobs, discovered his employee's biology and caused his arrest. Whatever the exact cause, Lobdell did another stint behind bars until either sympathetic neighbors or Marie secured his release. The story that holds to Marie's role claims that she used a split stick as a pen and pokeberry juice for ink to craft a heartfelt appeal that played on the sympathies of the local court. Of "neat penmanship and correct composition," the document had its intended effect; officials soon released Lobdell into Marie's care. A Damascus Township, Pennsylvania, farmer then took pity on the two and provided them a dwelling on some forgotten corner of his property.[10]

According to less reliable sources, around 1878 Joseph Lobdell wandered away from his and Marie's small Damascus, Pennsylvania, farm, disappearing into the forest. When human bones were discovered a year later in the nearby woods, some believed them to have belonged to Lobdell. In light of such evidence, a few well-respected newspapers rushed to report his demise. The *New York Times*, for example, did so in an 1879 extended obituary titled "Death of a Modern Diana."[11] But to paraphrase western humorist Mark Twain, reports of Lobdell's death, much like those of his life, had been greatly exaggerated. In fact, in October 1880, a "maniacal attack" forced Lobdell's commitment to New York's Willard Asylum for the Insane, on the shores of Lake Seneca.[12] His attending physician reported that over the next few years, Lobdell suffered "repeated paroxysmal attacks of erotomania and exhilaration, without periodicity, followed by corresponding periods of mental and physical depression." Dementia ultimately limited his ability to communicate. One report has him passing away at Willard in 1885. Another suggests his death occurred nearer to 1890, about the time of the so-called closing of the frontier. Yet another places his death in 1912.[13]

If newspapers can be believed, a highly suspect enterprise in light of what they reported on Lobdell's death and life, for a short time after Joseph's commitment to Willard, his wife, Marie, still using the name Mrs. Joseph I. Lobdell, her hair having turned a snowy white, continued to live on their secluded Damascus farm. On 18 May 1882, when she visited nearby Honesdale selling berries to raise some income, the local news editor took note. In the next issue of his paper he wrote of Marie and recalled her relationship with Joseph, deriding it as "strange." Marie wrote a spirited response. "I don't know," she shot back, "why the companionship of two women should be termed 'strange.'" Marie reportedly then returned to her childhood hometown of Whitman, Massachusetts, where she supported herself through employment she secured at Dunbar, Hobart & Company, a manufacturer of shoes and boots. All the while she "remained true to her first and only love" until passing away on 21 November 1890.[14]

Helen, Lobdell's daughter from his marriage to George Slater, had a life almost as unbelievable as her mother. Some accounts state that when Joseph headed out to Minnesota, he left Helen in the care of her grandparents. Others claim that she, like her mother, ended up in the Delaware County almshouse and was eventually adopted out from there to a local wealthy farmer. Several reports remarked on her own fantastic love life. One claimed that she unknowingly became involved with a young man and that neither she nor he knew during their courtship that they were in reality each other's half-sibling. The half-brother's mother, of course, did know, and tried to prevent the romance. Unable to do so by means of sheer will, she eventually faced the unsavory task of confessing her long-ago affair with George Slater, something that finally brought her son's romance to an end. Others claim that Helen became mixed up with a dissolute young man whose friends kidnapped, abused, and then dumped her ravished body in the Delaware River. She survived, however, washing up on the shore of a nearby island. Helen then wandered about in the woods in a state of mania. Eventually rescued, she recovered in mind and body only to become a respectable and happily married woman who had several of her own children.[15]

As for Lobdell's pet cat, known only as "Puss" and who hunted so well in the Old Northwest's backcountry, he was adopted by Noah White of Kandiyohi, Minnesota. A favorite in the settlement for many years, he eventually succumbed to old age. No doubt, as is typical with pets, Puss was likely neither aware nor particularly concerned about all the hoopla that so consumed for years, and in a few cases destroyed, the lives of those who lived in the domiciles and in the communities where he had long found a home.[16]

Three years after Lobdell entered Willard, Dr. Peter M. Wise, assistant physician at the hospital, reported on him and his long-term relationship with Marie Perry for the influential medical journal *Alienist and Neurologist*. Wise's article, "Case of Sexual Perversion," is one of the earliest American-based studies to be published on the subject. In it he referred to Lobdell's and Perry's love as "Lesbian," explaining that the two even had sexual intercourse made possible by the former's "enlarged clitoris," Lobdell disclosing to the physician that "I have peculiar organs that make me more a man than a woman."[17] From this first reporting in 1883 up to at least 1916, the extraordinary case of Lobdell and Perry would be pointed to at various times in the evolving American medical literature on homosexuality and transsexuality, sexual identities not fully differentiated from each other in the waning years of the nineteenth century and that were collectively referred to as sexual inversion, just one of any number of (so-called) sexual perversions identified at the time. Clothing, as a manifestation and indication of gender, was central to both the definition of sexual inversion and the identification of a sexual invert. Thus, cross-dressing and the cross-dresser took center stage in the sexologists' representations and medicalization of homosexuality during the last years of the nineteenth century.

In the years following Wise's publication, James G. Kiernan, one of the two most influential American sexologists of the time, referred to the case of Lobdell and Perry several times in his writings.[18] Thanks to Wise and Kiernan, this cross-dressing backwoodsman and sometime northwestern frontiersman played a fundamental role in the American medical profession's contributions to the creation of sexual inversion. Early on, for example, Lobdell's case provided the medical profession with some of the proof it needed to support the contention that an "enlarged" clitoris was stigmatic of sexual inversion in the female. Also, Lobdell's masculine inclinations and demeanor, including a predilection for dressing in male attire, but female body supported the prevalent view about the nature and characteristics of sexual inverts.[19]

Moreover, both sides of one of the principal early debates over the causes of sexual perversion drew evidence from Lobdell's case to support their arguments. On the one hand, Peter Wise explained in his 1883 report that Lobdell's homosexuality could be *acquired* by an individual within her lifetime. Those like Wise who held this view believed that one might lead an otherwise "normal" life until some misfortune, such as a turn toward alcoholism, a prolonged exposure to overstimulation, or some bad habit picked up here or there, rendered the nervous system weakened, making it susceptible to infection from perversions, of which sexual inversion was but one. In Lobdell's case, Wise speculated that sexual inversion was a byproduct of growing insanity. James Kiernan, on the other hand, utilized Lobdell over the years to support his view of the *congenital* nature of homosexuality—that is, it was something one had from birth. He further argued that as far as forensics was concerned, the fact that a sexual perversion was congenital relieved individuals in such a condition from legal responsibility for their actions.[20]

In time, the significance of Lobdell's case grew as the field of sexology in America evolved. But back in 1883, Peter Wise dismissed it as uncommon within the American context. "The subject possesses little forensic interest," Wise confidently announced, "especially in this country, and the case herewith reported is offered as a clinical curiosity in psychiatric medicine."[21] Just a few years later the situation and atmosphere in America (or at least the perception of these) had changed dramatically. Sexual inversion and other so-called perversions had apparently become more common. American sexologists took note and in the 1890s responded by producing a remarkable amount of interpretive literature about the phenomenon. Because sexual perversions seemed only now to be appearing and propagating in their nation, American sexologists naturally considered them, at least in part, as historical in nature and they focused some of their energy on determining the relationship between sexual perversion and America's past, present, and future.

American sexologists historicized sexual inversion precisely when there occurred notable developments in the field of American history and the ways in which professional historians understood that history. Significantly, in

1890 the superintendent of the U.S. census declared that he could no longer find a frontier line that stretched from north to south across the American West. For many years at the popular level, Americans had generally understood that their nation's constantly westward-moving frontier was the primary element that provided them their distinctive history and identity in the world; it had also given them a vast land of adventure and excitement, something that fed popular culture from late eighteenth-century biographies of Daniel Boone down to the late nineteenth-century Wild West shows produced by the likes of Buffalo Bill Cody. But now in the 1890s with the frontier vanished and no figurative place to escape to, the United States had seemingly entered a new age—one of modernity, replete with all its uncertainties, limits, and frightening manifestations, such as urbanization, industrialization, mechanization, electricity and steam power, rapid population growth, and so on. Historians in particular took note, and Frederick Jackson Turner produced his lyrical thesis about American history and development, in which he made the dramatic shift from a Eurocentric to an Americentric explanation for the history of the United States and the character of its institutions and people. Whereas previously, professional scholars had largely seen the country as an outgrowth of European developments, Turner argued that the United States uniquely evolved out of the North American environment, more specifically its frontier conditions. He also recognized that with the frontier's disappearance, the nation had entered a new epoch.[22] Just what the future would bring, however, was anyone's guess.

These historical developments, notions, and anxieties that affected Americans generally and Turner specifically likewise preoccupied American sexologists. In the waning of the nineteenth century, the latter employed ideas about the frontier and its passing to help explain the historical timing and the broader significance of the appearance of sexual inversion. By about 1900 or so, a segment of the American medical profession had concluded that the frontier epoch of U.S. history was largely void of sexual perversion—thus Peter Wise's conclusion back in 1883 that Lobdell's case was merely a curiosity in the American context—save in the interesting and unique case of Native Americans. They also proposed that the frontier had remedied sexual inversion in history when it might have otherwise appeared. They further contended that the frontier had immunized the country, at least for a short while, from the carnal decadence then largely believed to be sweeping through

Europe that was a sure sign of that civilization's overall degeneracy in the fin de siècle. Soon the American medical profession gave in to the evidence supporting the spread of sexual inversion within the United States, attributing the phenomenon in part to the passing of the frontier and to the nation's entry into the modern era.

In light of this, it might seem paradoxical that a cross-dressing frontiersman and sometime resident of the Old Northwest would provide one of the very first reported cases of sexual inversion in America—and an influential case at that. The facts of Joseph Lobdell's life as a backwoodsman and his association with the wilds of upstate New York and the frontier of territorial Minnesota would, however, eventually be lost on American sexologists as they explained sexual inversion from a chronological and regional perspective. Deeply held cultural views of the frontier influenced the science of sexology in America at the end of the nineteenth century, working to remove Lobdell and others like him from America's mythic frontier history and thus, in an essential way, from the most celebrated and powerful of our national narratives. Sexologists also dealt with the troubling reality of Native Americans' diverse sexual system. Just as Frederick Jackson Turner excluded Indians (except to see them as a barrier to be overcome) from the meaning and effects of the frontier on European-American history, sexologists exempted "perverse" Native American sexual practices from the salubrious effects they believed the frontier bore for white Americans.

For a variety of social, cultural, and economic reasons, both popular and scientific concepts of sexuality underwent significant alteration in the nineteenth century.[23] At the medical level, as historian Harry Oosterhuis has summarized, developments in criminology and forensics by mid-century stimulated the psychiatric profession and its interest in discovering underlying emotional and instinctual reasons for people's behaviors. Among the behaviors of greatest interest were the sexual; they increasingly became matters of jurisprudence when growing public concern accompanied the apparent spread of prostitution, public indecency, and other transgressive sexual activities as the nineteenth century advanced. The developing psychiatric discipline would view these sexual behaviors less and less as indicative of moral choices or as symptomatic of one's intelligence, as they had tended to be viewed in the past, but increasingly as characteristics of individuals, whether innate or acquired.[24]

The exact origins of sexual impulses remained something of a mystery. Charles Darwin's theory of evolution, which included notions of natural selection and the propagation of the species, provided a timely and "natural" rationale for opposite-sex attraction and relations, something that had been viewed for some time in Western civilization as normal and moral, albeit under the appropriate circumstances, namely within the confines of marriage.[25] Scientists concluded that "abnormal" impulses were acquired mental or neurological disorders. They could also influence evolution. Or, rather, they could result in reverse evolution. Since they were abnormal and inheritable, they could pass quickly to subsequent generations, resulting in the decay of a species in a relatively short period of time.[26]

This reverse evolutionary biological theory, popularly known as degeneration, fits hand-in-glove with elements of nineteenth-century social thought generally. Though social progress remained the reigning belief in Europe through the century, an exceptionally strong undercurrent of pessimism existed there. It only grew in force as an increasing number of European intellectuals came to feel by the twilight of the 1800s that their civilization had reached its apex and had actually entered a period of decline, recapitulating a cycle that ultimately resulted in downfall, as in the case of great civilizations of the past. Contributing to the fear that Western civilization had entered a period of decline were various events and developments, including rapid urbanization and industrialization and their accompanying ills, escalating national antagonisms during the age of imperialism, periodic world depressions, and increasing luxury, wealth, and indolence among certain classes and social unrest among others. The belief in this so-called degeneration partly constituted the fin-de-siècle malaise (or end-of-the-century melancholy) so prevalent at the time. It also explained for the developing psychiatric and neurological professions, particularly in Europe, why sexual perversion and in particular sexual inversion appeared and spread at that time.[27]

Among the many who accepted degeneration theory to account for sexual inversion was the German sexologist Richard von Krafft-Ebing. One of the leading European sexologists of the day, Krafft-Ebing had a singular influence on his American counterparts; they had already begun citing Krafft-Ebing as early as 1881 and within a couple years he had generally emerged in American medical literature as the most important authority on the subject of sexual perversions.[28] The first of twelve ever-expanding editions of his magnum opus,

Psychopathia Sexualis, appeared in 1886, though only in German and accompanied by a smattering of Latin to obscure from lay readers the publication's more spicy details. *Psychopathia Sexualis* became something of a bible for sexologists, especially for Americans when in 1893 the seventh edition became the first translated into English.[29] By that edition, Krafft-Ebing had fully adopted degeneration theory as the principal explanation for sexual inversion, arguing that it was a manifestation of an ancestor's acquired and transmittable abnormality.[30] While Krafft-Ebing accepted the era's basic tenet that society continuously progressed, he also admitted that it experienced fluctuations. Thus, he could link degenerative sexualities to downward cycles within civilization:

> Periods of moral decadence in the life of a people are always contemporaneous with times of effeminacy, sensuality, and luxury. These conditions can only be conceived as occurring with increased demands upon the nervous system, which must meet these requirements. As a result of increase of nervousness, there is increase of sensuality, and, since this leads to excesses among the masses, it undermines the foundation of society,—the morality and purity of family life. When this is destroyed by excesses, unfaithfulness, and luxury, then the destruction of the state is inevitably compassed in material, moral, and political ruin. Warning examples of this character are presented in Rome, Greece, and France under Louis XIV and XV. In such time of political and moral destruction monstrous perversions of the sexual life were frequent, which, however, may in part be referred to psycho-pathological or, at least, neuro-pathological conditions existing in the people.[31]

This translation of Krafft-Ebing did not introduce American sexologists to degeneration theory; they had generally accepted it as an explanation for mental and neurological disorders, and eventually sexual inversion, since the early 1880s.[32] Nevertheless, its appearance in the United States in 1893 is significant for a few reasons. First, its translation, completed by Charles Gilbert Chaddock, a St. Louis professor of nervous and mental disorders, partially constitutes the remarkable American literary outpouring on sexual inversion and various other sexual maladies in the decade of the 1890s. Second, the volume would influence that literature, notably the way in which American sexologists interpreted the relationship between the rise and spread of sexual perversions and the past, present, and future of the United States. And third, it appeared precisely at the moment that Frederick Jackson Turner promulgated his thesis about the closing of the frontier.

At first glance it might seem something of a paradox that the appearance in America of Krafft-Ebing's fully developed and influential articulation of degeneration theory should coincide with Turner's powerful and concise expression of ideas about the frontier and its relationship to American history. After all, degeneration theory derived from the very European social, intellectual, and historical currents Turner revolted against. Also, while it is true that to some degree the fin-de-siècle malaise that affected Europe and made degeneration theory so influential there did penetrate America, that pessimism in the United States was, in the words of historian John Higham, "neither general nor profound. Sourness and irony Americans could sometimes stomach; they had little taste for despair." Rather, Americans maintained "a triumphant belief in evolutionary progress."[33]

Evolutionary progress indeed underlay Turner's frontier thesis. In fact, one might call his view of American development "regenerative" (he even used the term in his work). He saw it as one of advancement from a state of savagery and wilderness to that of civilization. At the local level, the line moved directly from one to the other. At the national level, the process repeated itself over and over as settlement constantly moved westward, encountering more wilderness awaiting transformation. Turner defined the frontier itself as the point where civilization met savagery. As such, it was the point "of most rapid and effective Americanization" and in its repetition—a "perennial rebirth," to use Turner's phrasing—it moved America away from Europe and established all positive political and social attributes assumed to be American in nature.[34]

At times this view of the frontier's effects that powerfully affirmed American development transcended the nation's borders and influenced how Europeans who worked in degeneration theory understood the United States. Notable among them was the Austrian social critic Max Nordau. His sensational book *Degeneration*, which first appeared in German in 1892 (an English translation came out in 1895), argued passionately that Europe had passed its pinnacle of development and had entered into a period of decline. He did not feel the same about America. "Why should Americans degenerate?" he rhetorically responded in an interview with a Chicago newspaper. "They have a new country, new opportunities, a boundless future, a restless and resistless activity; their eyes are fixed upward, their impulses are toward better and higher things, their ambition is healthier. How can Americans be degenerates?" "With boundless room for expansion," Nordau continued elsewhere in his interview, "with new ideals, with the restless activity and push bred amid such conditions, there cannot be degeneration."[35]

In drawing on ideas and beliefs that anticipated by a year essential elements of Turner's progressive view of American development, Nordau pointed out the substantive problem of applying degeneration theory to the United States. Thus, it would seem contradictory that Krafft-Ebing's degeneration theory should appear in America and have the influence it did precisely at the moment when Turner issued his influential regenerative thesis of American history. In fact, it was not. The two were culturally linked and complemented and reinforced each other. Turner's thesis historically interpreted an American epoch that had come to an end in 1890. In its sometimes romantic sentiments about the past, the frontier thesis directly responded to the increasing complexities of the transitional era during which Turner produced it. Krafft-Ebing's views made real sense in this transitional time; his was a cautionary tale told during an anxious era about an uncertain future for individuals, societies, and nations. In adopting degeneration theory, American sexologists adapted it to their own nationalistic vista, to their nation's specific historical circumstances in relation to its European cousins, and to the current situation in the United States in terms of sexuality.

For example, from the early 1890s Krafft-Ebing's references to the connection between moral decadence and the fate of civilizations struck American sexologists.[36] His consideration of Rome proved particularly poignant because of that civilization's dramatic rise and its equally calamitous fall replete with its arresting stories of sexual license, orgies, and perversions. American sexologists, in the tradition of Krafft-Ebing, also commented time and again on the decadence and fates of Greece and early modern France. In the former case, they noted sodomy and pederasty and remarked on how these perversions supposedly spread across the Mediterranean to Italy and to France. Early modern France, decapitated during the French Revolution, furnished an excellent example of how effeminacy in a population supposedly leads to downfall; sexologists singled out for comment the effeminate dress and immoral sexual behaviors of courtiers in the opulent times of Louis XIV and XV and against which the French later revolted. Medical and social commentators also made mention of ancient Egypt, Babylon, and Nineveh, but they found equally persuasive examples from contemporary times, particularly in the older and larger European cities. Some American sexologists viewed Paris as the "throne" of "satiety and vice." London they noted for its notorious sex scandals of the 1880s.[37] The conclusions American sexologists drew from the histories and examples of these debauched civilizations, nations, and urban centers resembled those of Krafft-Ebing: "Sexual perversion," to quote the American physician William Lee Howard, "both in its congenital and acquired form seems to be correlated with the cycles of civilization, for its recrudescence from sporadism to recognition, then to national adoption, is seen in ancient times and the influence of wealth gradually brought about luxury, luxury vice, and vice degeneracy."[38]

The rise and fall of ancient civilizations that went hand in hand with increased sensuality provided cautionary tales for American sexologists in the 1890s. "Effemination has occasioned the downfall of many nations," warned Kentucky physician James Weir in 1893. "Let us guard against it with all our power. Let us train up our boys to be manly men, and our girls to be womanly women." In a similar warning just a few years later, Dr. Emanuel Stuver of Wyoming and Colorado wrote, "Moral excellence and virtue are of the greatest importance to a nation. If we would avert the fate of Rome, we must avoid the vices which led to her downfall."[39]

These admonitions intimate one central tenet of American sexology in the 1890s: degeneracy had not yet enveloped the United States, at least not to the extent it had contemporary Europe or ancient Rome. Reasons varied; among the most crucial, sexologists traced degeneracy's absence to the nation's frontier heritage and, more generally, to American exceptionalism. In 1892, G. Frank Lydston (along with Kiernan the most influential American sexologist of the era) claimed that vice, which he felt typically first infected the weakened higher classes in a debauched nation, had not yet appeared in the United States because of its republican form of government as opposed to "those in which an effete monarchical and aristocratic system of control exists."[40] James Weir very closely reflected the sentiments of Max Nordau and, in a more general way, Frederick Jackson Turner. In speaking in 1893 of effemination in men and masculinization in women, Weir asserted that they "are more prevalent in the Old World than in the United States. The civilization and settlement of the United States are, comparatively speaking, new. The people are, as yet, a young, strong, and vigorous nation. Years of luxury and debauchery have not yet brought the penalty of enervation and neurasthenia to the masses."[41]

And yet, American sexologists could not ignore the evidence in the 1890s that sexual inversion had begun to appear in the United States. Already in

1894, Dr. A. J. Bloch of New Orleans claimed that perversion "is progressively increasing; its taint is entering into the homes of our most elegant and refined; this contagion exists in our schools, seminaries and asylums; its handiwork is shown by our many obscure and unrecognized nervous disorders."[42] Because American sexologists generally accepted the positive, progressive, exceptional view of their nation's history, when sexual inversion did appear, they only hesitantly equated American conditions with the decadence of fallen civilizations of the past. Instead, American medical experts tended to find the cause of perversity in their nation in other places. One of these was the debilitated nervous system; they argued it provided the underlying etiological explanation for sexual inversion. By 1894, in fact, "all observers," according to Charles Gilbert Chaddock, "agree in the conclusion that a neuropathic nervous system, congenital or acquired, is a prerequisite for the development of sexual instinct for the same sex (homosexuality)."[43] And if nervous exhaustion existed in the United States, it was not due to the cycles of civilization, but rather to new conditions that weakened the nervous system, precisely the "hurry and fret of American life," to use the words of G. Frank Lydston.[44]

Nervous exhaustion, what was also called neurasthenia, left one open to an atavistic attack that caused one's psychical sex to become reversed from one's anatomical sex (i.e., caused sexual inversion), a view that James Kiernan, for example, promoted widely. His theory began with the assumption that the far distant ancestors of humans, for example at the cellular level, were bisexual—that is, hermaphroditic—as they singly reproduced themselves. He argued that residual psychical elements of this earlier stage of human evolution were handed down to subsequent generations and when disease or congenital defect interfered with normal development, one could revert psychically to the other sex.[45] James Weir put it more succinctly: effemination in males and masculinization in women (something then called viraginity) "are due directly to the influence of that strange law . . . reversion to ancestral types. It is an effort of nature to return man to the old hermaphroditic form from which he was evolved. It is an effort on the part of nature to incorporate the individualities of the male and female, both physical and psychical, in one body." He added that the "phenomenon of atavism is more apt to occur in feeble types than in strong, healthy and well-developed types."[46]

Already by the 1870s American medical experts had identified neurasthenia and began studying it due to its apparent growth and spread. New England physician George M. Beard became the authority when he published, in rapid succession, *A Practical Treatise on Nervous Exhaustion* (*Neurasthenia*) in 1880, *American Nervousness* in 1881, and (posthumously) *Sexual Neurasthenia* in 1884. He called neurasthenia the American disease, asserting that it had "first taken root under an American sky," and he explained that Americans were the most nervous people in the world. Moreover, Beard posited that "no age, no country, and no form of civilization, not Greece, nor Rome, nor Spain, nor the Netherlands, in the days of their glory, possessed such maladies" as does America. Only recently would he concede that neurasthenia had started to appear in Europe, reversing the prevalent view of degeneration's geography.[47]

Even Turner commented on American nervousness, noting in his frontier thesis that the otherwise well-known phlegmatic nature of the colonists led commentators to wonder "how such a people could have developed that strained nervous energy now characteristic of them." Turner posited that the transition from the one characteristic to the other began at the close of the War of 1812 when "the development of the West" took off.[48] Beard agreed. In language strikingly similar to Turner's, he accounted for neurasthenia as the result of the "opportunities and necessities of a rising civilization in a new and immense continent." He also laid a heavy emphasis on the dryness and violent temperature extremes of the North American climate as an underlying cause of American nervousness.

In Beard's mind, however, debilitating neurasthenia resulted from the effects of "modern civilization" and not from frontier conditions or the climate. He distinguished modern civilization by five characteristics: steam power, the periodical press, the telegraph, the sciences, and the mental activity of women.[49] These quickened the pace of life, introduced people immediately and constantly to the sorrows of others around the world, caused increased amounts of cerebral labor, and led people into activities not naturally suited to their gender. Collectively and individually they induced exhaustion of the nervous system. Over the next several years, any number of other American physicians, sexologists, and social critics fretted over the effects of encroaching modernity and its connection to neurasthenia and, in its most degenerative phase, sexual inversion.[50]

American sexologists' allowance for the spread of degeneracy and sexual perversions in the United States already in the 1890s and George Beard's reference in the previous decade to neurasthenia as a distinctly American disease would seem contrary to the contention that medical experts attributed salutary sexual effects to the frontier and claimed American superiority in this regard compared to Europe and ancient civilizations. In fact, the works of Beard and others demonstrate that medical experts viewed degeneracy and sexual inversion as neither associated with the frontier past nor even with the contemporary American West, but rather squarely with modernity and older regions of the nation. When Beard spoke of those suffering from neurasthenia, he made certain to point out that he referred "only to a fraction of American society" and particularly those living within the "Northern and Eastern portions of the United States," where the conditions he associated with modernity were most advanced. The majority of Americans, on the other hand, he yet saw as "muscle-workers rather than brain-workers; have little education, and are not striving for honor, or expecting eminence or wealth," thus they escaped nervous exhaustion.[51]

One of the earliest to write on American neurasthenia, neurologist Silas Weir Mitchell, likewise associated the disease with geography and history. He argued that Americans' colonial ancestors had filled their lives with daily activities that brought them close to the earth. In doing so, they had built up a store of vigor, which they bequeathed to subsequent generations. In Mitchell's estimation, that a multitude of Americans still lived similarly to their colonial ancestors helped to maintain the population's overall energy and force. But the prodigality of those living in the city and chiefly on the Atlantic Coast, he warned, had depleted these stores, exhausting their nervous energy, and now presented in themselves "the peculiarities of an old nation."[52]

George Beard also detected a profound sexual difference between those of the Northeast and the city on the one hand, and the "farming population" and "those who live out-doors" on the other. In doing so, he drew directly on evidence supplied by the "great number" in New York City who suffered "sexual perversion." He outlined for his readers the shocking condition of one specifically. That was a male patient who came to him for "a number of symptoms of nervous trouble" and whose "constant desire was to attain sexual gratification . . . by performing the masturbating act on some other person." In comparison to "the delicate, finely-organized lads of our cities and of higher civilization," Beard maintained that "the strong, the phlegmatic, the healthy, the well-balanced temperaments—those who live out-doors and work with the muscle more than with the mind—are not tormented by sexual desire to the same degree or in the same way as the hysterical, the sensitive, the nervous—those who live in-doors and use mind much and muscle very little."[53]

Others agreed, blaming the city especially for whatever sexual inversion existed in America. Already in the early 1880s a correspondent of the *Alienist and Neurologist* called attention to the large number of people arrested for dressing as the opposite sex in "large cities." Before the decade was out, G. Frank Lydston felt comfortable enough in these views to make such off-handed comments as "There is in every community of any size a colony of male sexual perverts," and there "exists in every great city so large a number of sexual perverts." Just a couple years later, Irving C. Rosse explained that the "degrading" sexual conditions he found in Washington, D.C., applied "more or less to other American large cities." Not long afterward in 1899, G. J. Monroe would claim that sodomy had become "quite common in our large cities." A few years later Charles H. Hughes would assert that the "perverted creatures" he studied in St. Louis "appear to be features of million peopled cities." About the same time, James Weir described large cities as "the hotbeds and breeding-places of the various neuroses. There general paresis treads closely upon the heels of sexual neurasthenia, while the victims of hysteria and kindred ills are almost countless in their number."[54]

The association of sexual inversion with urbanization was part of a larger, late nineteenth-century anti-urban sentiment that saw the city generally as the breeding ground for degeneration. As early as 1872, one commentator in *Popular Science Monthly* blamed whatever physical degeneracy existed in America on the urban air, breathed many times over by the sickly and healthy alike. He also faulted the city's thick-walled, narrow-windowed, high residences and warehouses for blocking out the healthy rays of the sun. Steam-powered appliances he held responsible for wealthy city dwellers' lack of exercise. But more, he negatively compared these to the "sun-penetrated tents" of an earlier era and, in ways revealing a penchant for frontier-like setting, asked his readers to "contrast the myopic and weak-eyed men of the day with the eagle-eyed men of the plain and forest." A quarter century later, Henry Childs Merwin asserted that those boys who leave the countryside for the city to take up positions in law, politics, medicine, and ministry retained their "strength only by perpetually renewing . . . contact with Mother Earth." If they failed to do so, they became "over-civilized," "effete," and "perverted," ultimately leading to the same catastrophe that befell Rome.[55]

But something more specific than urban atmospheric conditions led to the belief that American cities fostered conditions that contributed to perversion. The historian Jennifer Terry determined that American sexologists also believed sexual perversity was endemic to American urban areas because of the social disorder that (they believed) prevailed there. As members of America's educated middle classes who worried about the loss of social control as their nation became increasingly more diverse and complex, physicians discovered social disorder in any number of guises, but especially in the dissolution of the traditional boundaries that separated the races and the classes. Physicians maintained that the working classes, nonwhite racial groups, and ethnic immigrants were by nature sexually perverse and degenerate, having never fully reached the stage of civilization. These people appeared attracted in ever-increasing numbers to America's urban centers as the twentieth century approached. There they readily mixed and mingled with one another as well as with recent arrivals from the American countryside. It was through these means, in the minds of American medical experts, that sexual perversion spread.[56] Sexological and social commentaries on the city, therefore, did not attribute sexual perversion there just to the fret and hurry of life in the urban setting, nor only to atmospheric and environmental conditions one encountered in the metropolis. They also felt it very much had to do with the city's so-called dissolute racial and class composition.

In connecting neurasthenia to the city and the perceived social disorder there, to the Northeast, and to the Atlantic Coast, American medical experts distanced degeneracy and its sexual manifestations from the out-of-doors, rural America, the frontier, and the West, as well as from white, middle-class America. Obviously this view drew from and contributed to the notion that the American frontier was a white and morally chaste place. In this light, it is hardly surprising that some period physicians even recommended the outdoors, both its social and environmental context, as a cure-all for nervous exhaustion. If the outdoors and the frontier had produced health, energy, and vigor for those who regularly lived there, then hikes in the woods, daily plunges into rivers and lakes, hunting for food, exploration, mountaineering, boat rowing, and sleeping in tents should provide the antidote to those riddled with the disease.[57] In 1877, Silas Weir Mitchell colorfully dubbed this the camp cure.[58] If "civilization has hurt," in Mitchell's estimation, "barbarism shall heal" and "one could reverse the conditions of his life" by taking the camp cure and, in the process, coming into "contact with the guides, woodmen and trappers, and the simple-minded, manly folk who live on the outposts of civilization—'the lords of the axe and the rifle'"[59] (as long as they stayed away from Lake Minnetonka, one would presume). This was the very advice that individuals such as Theodore Roosevelt and his friends Owen Wister (author of the first western American novel) and Frederic Remington (the great artist of western American life and landscapes) followed and then championed.

Early in his work, Mitchell even specified outdoor activity and exercise for nervous women, but he is better known for his later prescription of the rest cure, which entailed bed rest, overfeeding, and passive exercise, such as massage and the use of electricity to stimulate muscles.[60] Middle-class women commonly suffered neurasthenia in the late nineteenth century and, consequently, sexologists believed that sexual inversion was increasing among them. They attributed these developments to certain qualities of the era, namely women's growing independence from men as a result of the vastly changing economic world. Women who lessened their reliance on men, sexologists argued, turned to their own for relationships. The era's New Woman, with her efforts to achieve equal rights and suffrage, moreover, squandered her nervous energy, leaving her open to atavistic attack. As for women's reformist efforts, such as suffrage, some medical experts felt they were an attempt to reinstate a matriarchal system that, as a form of social organization relegated to the dustbin of history, contributed in the modern age to society's overall retrogression. Should the "female possessed of masculine ideas of independence . . . be unfortunate enough to become a mother," William Lee Howard further warned, "she is . . . a menace to civilization, a producer of nonentities, the mother of mental and physical monstrosities who exist as a class of true degenerates until disgusted Nature, no longer tolerant of the woman who would be a man . . . allows them to shrink unto death."[61]

Though these beliefs prevailed, the West and its people, on the other hand, remained unsullied. In 1899, journalist Rollin Lynde Hartt wrote for the *Atlantic Monthly* an arresting series on degeneracy in small-town New England. In his articles he compared his pseudonymous northeastern example of "Sweet Auburn" with the West's very real Billings, Montana. In the latter he claimed he discovered hope, a future, a golden age awaiting, while in the former he found none of these. If anything, the golden age in Sweet Auburn lay in the distant past. In language that reflected Max Nordau, American sexologists, and Frederick Jackson Turner, Hartt summed up the differences between Montana and New England: "Montana has youth, courage, elasticity, and ambitious, expansive energy. Its progress is the normal result of resident forces. Sweet Auburn, on the other hand, has already spent its vitality. It is bowed and bent. Its blood runs tepid. Its sight is dim. It is garrulous and egotistic. It promises nothing from resident forces."[62]

Not surprisingly, medical experts argued that although physical degeneracy existed in the West by the end of the 1890s, it was considerably less pronounced than what they observed plaguing the East. A year prior to publishing his better known *Degeneracy: Its Causes, Signs, and Results* (1899), Eugene S. Talbot produced a comparative study of degenerative stigmata among the criminal youth in the state reformatories of Elmira, New York (what he referred to as the East), and Pontiac, Illinois (which he described as the West). He determined that those in the latter showed fewer physical signs of degeneracy than those in the former, attributing the differences to what might be called external and internal influences. In the former case, he claimed that less active degenerate European immigrants tended to remain in the East where they first arrived, while the more fit headed to the interior of the country. Moreover, the "rush and roar of city life" in the East attracted to it homegrown degenerates of the countryside, while the stronger and healthier, like their more robust foreign immigrant counterparts, headed West. The result, according to Talbot, was that the migrant "of better physique goes westward," thus accounting for less advanced degeneracy in that region.[63]

As noted above, sexologists generally shared Talbot's beliefs about new immigrants at the end of the nineteenth century. "The Old World has gotten rid of [its degenerate] people as rapidly as possible," James Weir contended in 1894, "by unloading them on our shores. Year after year, practically without restriction, thousands of these antisocial men and women have swarmed into our country, until we, comparatively speaking a nation just born, contain as many of these undesirable citizens as any of the older nations." In the early twentieth century, G. Frank Lydston complained that "the degenerate flotsam and jetsam of Europe have entered our country in a continuous stream. Paupers, inebriates, insane, beggars, and known criminals have been deposited upon our shores, until this country has become practically a dumping-ground for the sweepings of Europe."[64]

In earlier years frontier conditions might have ameliorated the perverse tailings of humanity that Europe dumped on North America. But by the turn of the twentieth century, with the frontier having passed, some sexologists grew worried that this amelioration would no longer be likely, just when immigrants in larger numbers than ever crowded onto American shores and into American cities.[65] In theorizing about how frontier-like conditions prevented sexual perversions up to the 1890s, sexologists took something of a different approach toward another group of people, Native Americans. On the one hand, at least one neurologist, George Beard, used Native Americans to exemplify "those who live out-doors and have well-balanced constitutions of the old-fashioned sort" who are not annoyed by sexual desires "to the same degree as the delicate, finely-organized lads of our cities and of higher civilization." He further explained that a medical doctor he knew who had "much experience" among the Native Americans told him "that Indian boys do not masturbate, and do not, as a rule . . . commit excesses in sexual indulgence prior to marriage."[66]

And yet almost in the same breath, Beard acknowledged the Pueblo *mujerado*, whom the medical doctor William Hammond reported on in 1882. Drawing from Greek mythology about the Scythians and on what he was able to learn from the Pueblo when among them in the 1850s, Hammond explained that "certain New Mexican inhabitants" who "changed from male to female . . . assumed the garb of a woman, lived with women and followed their occupations." These he understood the Pueblo to call *mujerados*, individuals whom in his research he determined that the Pueblo actually created. "For the making of a *mujerado*," Hammond explained, "one of the most virile men is selected, and the act of masturbation is performed upon him many times every day." He is then forced "to ride continuously on horseback." The purpose is to exhaust the recruit's sexual energy, making it impossible for him to have an emission, and eventually an erection. Once this point is achieved, his "penis and testicles begin to shrink, and in time reach their lowest plane of degradation." The eventual effect is that the *mujerado* loses his interest in sports, his courage evaporates, he becomes timid, and essentially transforms into a woman, though not entirely in the physical sense. The Pueblo created the *mujerado*, Hammond contended, specifically to fulfill purposes of their "saturnalia orgies." Those ceremonies were part of the rite of spring and revolved about sodomy being repeatedly performed on the *mujerado* by several men.[67]

Beard reconciled his views of the lack of sexual perversions among Native Americans (due to their "savage" nature) with his acknowledgment of the cross-dressing and sexually perverse *mujerado*; he explained that the latter was created "intentionally for religious purposes." This accounting did not typically accord with what other sexologists (as well as a number of others who encountered them over the years) thought about Indians, their cross-dressing, and their same-sex sexual activities. Simply, sexologists saw Indians as racially inferior, at a lower stage of development, and thus prone to vice regardless of the setting. A. B. Holder, who at one time had medical charge of the Crow and became familiar there with the bo-te (what others might have termed "berdache"), chalked up this person's "perversion" to "his own perverted lust." The Crow countenanced such an individual, Holder concluded, due "to the debased standard of the people among whom he lives."[68] The British sexologist C. G. Seligmann, writing about "primitive races" generally and using Native Americans to support his views, explained that cross-dressing and the cross-dressers' (presumed) sodomitical habits were not at all unusual "among people in the barbarous stage."[69] And the American Charles H. Hughes likewise claimed that vice explained Native American perversion. When he stated that "sanity in a savage may be lunacy in a civilized being," Hughes agreed with Beard, who claimed that the Pueblo mujerado, "who knows he is a man, not a woman, though dressed as a woman and partakes of feminine occupations," was not truly insane according to Western standards. Other sexologists agreed.[70]

In the face of the berdache, hermaphrodites, mujerados, and other so-called sexual perversions they observed among Native Americans, sexologists (George Beard excepted) had to conclude, as did Irving C. Rosse, that "lubricity and civilization" did not necessarily "march hand in hand, since travelers have noticed that many facts to the contrary exist among primitive people, especially our North American Indians."[71] This position obviously contradicted what American sexologists argued about the relationship between modern civilization and the appearance of sexual inversion among (presumably) white Americans at the end of the nineteenth century. Also contradicting the perceived impact of civilization on sexual inversion among (again, presumably) white Americans, sexologists sometimes made the hopeful assertion, as William Hammond did in 1882, that the Indian cross-dressers who engaged in same-sex sexual activities, "will doubtless disappear ere long before advancing civilization."[72] In these sentiments, Hammond reflected those earlier made by famed western artist George Catlin, who in the 1830s observed the "dance to the berdashe," performed among the Sioux, Sac, and Fox. The celebration apparently venerated the "man dressed in woman's clothes," as his peculiar habits suggested to his tribesmen that he was looked upon as "sacred." Thoroughly disgusted with the custom, Catlin wished "that it might be extinguished before it be more fully recorded."[73]

American sexologists generally agreed that same-sex sexual perversions among Indians were due less to disease and insanity than to vice and perverted practice endemic to primitive peoples. This view likewise reflected those having long been made by travelers and observers in the interior of North America. In making these calculations, sexologists accounted for Indian perversity differently from how they did so for (white) Americans, whose apparently increasing rates of sexual inversion in the waning of the nineteenth century must have been related to the onset of modernity. This was not a matter of the sleight of hand or the dismissal of inconvenient facts that got in the way of beautiful theory. Sexologists' view of the frontier and what it did was every bit as racialized as those of Frederick Jackson Turner. He spoke specifically of the frontier's transforming Europeans into Americans. Indians were not part of that process, save that they presented the savagery that westering Euro-Americans struggled against. To sexologists, the frontier process attenuated potential sexual perversion among earlier European immigrants and among later American populations, at least those who continued to live in frontier-like conditions, a process that secured heterosexuality for Euro-Americans. Indian perversity, on the other hand, could be accounted for differently, and Indian reform would conversely come about through advancing civilization.[74]

Remarkable change came to America during the twilight of the nineteenth century—increasing immigration of peoples seemingly different from those who had come before; singular economic alterations resulting in the concentration of capital, the rise of combinations and trusts, severe depression, agricultural crisis, and changed relations between women and men; industrialization, urbanization, and the perceived rapid depletion of natural resources; troubling social unrest and class conflict as well as wars for empire; and altered gender behaviors, proliferating vice, and increasing sexual deviance. All these factors affected Americans who pondered their nation's past, its present, and its future.

Viewing these troubling developments as unprecedented, Frederick Jackson Turner logically separated them from all of American history that had come before. "And now," Turner proclaimed of the 1890 closing of the frontier, "four centuries from the discovery of America, at the end of a hundred years of life under the Constitution, the frontier has gone, and with its going has closed the first period of American history." In arriving at this conclusion, Turner conveniently defined the first epoch of American history as the counterpoint to the growing complexities of his age, locking away the frontier in a place and time where it would forever remain unchanged.

Scholars have criticized Turner for this conclusion, as well as for any number of other problems they have found with his thesis. And yet Turner's view of the frontier has endured for the very reason that through the years it has provided to those who need it a simplified past, one bereft of troubling stories, one filled with similar people engaged in a similar mission, one with pristine environmental conditions, and one that thankfully concludes before modern problems could befall it. We cannot give Turner all the credit; we have long known that during the era when Turner lived and wrote, popular writers and Wild West show directors, painters and sculptors, dude-ranch proprietors, filmmakers, chambers of commerce, and even would-be presidents contributed to ossifying the frontier in place and time and with a particular cast of heroic characters.

American sexologists were also very much affected by the unprecedented and troubling developments that beset their nation. Like Turner, they worked to separate them from all of American sexual history that had come before. Something of an exception, at least later in his career, was James Kiernan. In an article he wrote for *The Urologic and Cutaneous Review* in 1916, for example, he strongly countered an American informant who, in recently providing his own views on the subject to the famed British sexologist Henry Havelock Ellis, made the claim that sexual inversion was increasing among the people of the United States.[75] In responding to this assertion, Kiernan did not contend that the frontier had immunized America from sexual inversion. Rather, he plainly pointed out that sexual inversion had always been a part of America's history, even noting the tradition of crossdressing women in the American West as evidence to support this view. Precisely, Kiernan argued that early on "pederasty" had been brought to America "by English emigrants not to speak of other emigration (containing similar defectives)."[76] He drew particular attention to early eighteenth-century London mollies—men who had sexual relations with other men, who dressed as women, and who behaved and acted in effeminate ways— specifically mentioning "'Molly houses,' where male harlots resorted in great numbers."[77] He further noted that England's early eighteenth-century "punishment for sodomy was then death," but explained that both "male and female harlots as well as other criminals were however sold as bond servants to the [North American colonies] as a means of public revenue."[78] Such European sexual depravity foisted onto early America became legally apparent, Kiernan contended, by the fact that even the Old Northwest territories found it necessary early on to legislate against sodomy.

From this, Kiernan drew an important conclusion. Contrary to what this chapter has argued as the general view of sexologists at the time, Kiernan in fact explained that in America's "frontier agricultural communities homosexuality was much in evidence." In making this point, Kiernan wished to show that homosexuality's long history in America was evidence that it had not suddenly appeared on the scene at the end of the nineteenth century and, furthermore, had not necessarily increased in the early years of the twentieth century (as Havelock Ellis's informant had claimed).[79]

But very much in keeping with what this chapter has argued, in fact helping to prove its point, Kiernan went on to note something else in 1916. He argued that the fact of homosexuality's existence in frontier America demonstrated that "an American 'golden age' ere 'foreign demoralization'" was in fact a "myth." Kiernan singled out the work of George M. Beard as particularly instrumental in fabricating this lie about America's frontier past.[80]

What Kiernan did not own up to in 1916 were the considerable contributions he had made earlier that helped create the very myth he now argued against. Take for example two complementary articles he published in 1895 and 1896 in the most influential psychiatric journal of the day, the *Alienist and Neurologist*. In the 1896 piece, Kiernan accepted Max Nordau's claim that Americans could not degenerate. He reinforced such a conclusion by citing Darwin's assessment that the United States' singular progress came as the result of natural selection—that is, because "restless and courageous men from all parts of Europe" had migrated to American shores.[81] He also explained in both 1896 and 1895 that from the time of "earliest colonization the defective classes [had also] poured into the United States."[82] Kiernan further claimed in 1895 that "Great Britain, whence most American settlers came . . . had been a refuge for degenerates for centuries."[83] (As an aside, while some of these settlers and their descendants did forcibly make the transatlantic migration as little more than slaves, Kiernan maintained that something less tangible brought others to North America: "The stir of the west," in Kiernan's mind, also "attracted hysterics, paranoiacs and other defectives" and it did so "as light house lanterns do birds.")[84]

But most important in all this was Kiernan's argument about what had happened to these defectives once they arrived in America. To make his point, he cited the census. The 1880 census, which he criticized for underestimating the true number of those suffering mental disorders in the United States, showed 1 insane person for every 543 sane persons in the country. The 1890 census, on the other hand, Kiernan lauded for its accuracy due to the supervision of the "ablest American statistician of these classes"; it revealed a ratio of only 1 to 583, "a slight apparent but really enormous decrease." With regard to other forms of defect, Kiernan claimed that the 1890 census likewise demonstrated the same positive trends. And thus, he concluded, "While forced decrease in importation of defectives has affected the result slightly, still the home manufacture and propagation of defectives has clearly decreased. In other words, the race has here so improved that the United States have assimilated and approximated to normal the enormous mass of defective humanity poured into them for nearly three centuries."[85]

Regardless of what he may have argued in 1916, early in his publications Kiernan contributed to the sexological myth that early American conditions had a positive effect on defectives of all stripes. In this view, he echoed Turner's contention that American conditions transformed Europeans, imbuing them with all manner of positive character traits. Also like Turner, Kiernan pointed to the 1890 census for evidence to support his argument. It is obvious, then, that in the 1890s many sexologists had sensed much of what Turner and other Americans did about their exceptional and frontier heritage.

It is time that we acknowledge the role that American sexologists played in creating the frontier myth. It is also time that we admit to the myth's sexual presumptiveness. The great changes occurring in the late nineteenth century concerned sexologists in the United States every bit as much as they did Turner. As products of America, sexologists shared in Turner's progressive view of their nation's history, one of constant advancement and distinctly different from Europe. At the same time, these physicians practiced an incipient field of study that had even less of a tradition in America than in Europe, and struggled with the available science to make sense of the various and proliferating mental and emotional disorders that, because they only now appeared, seemed to be related to history. Degeneration theory emanating from European psychiatric and neurologic discourse provided a model for understanding that historical relationship. While degeneration theory's association of sexual perversion with the fall of civilizations did not exactly suit American sexologists' progressive view of their nation's history, its focus on the timing and occurrence of nervous exhaustion, something that underlay sexual inversion, made perfect sense against the backdrop of the remarkable changes of the late nineteenth century. Historically, American sexologists would attribute sexual inversion to modernity, urbanization, and to both higher civilization and to the lower, primitive classes. Geographically, when it appeared in the United States, they identified it with the large city, the older Atlantic seaboard, and the Northeast. As such, they viewed the frontier past, frontier-like conditions, and the American West as the historical and geographic counterpoints to the periods and places when and where sexual inversion appeared. And thus, not unlike the residents of Minnesota Territory who banished the cross-dressing Joseph Israel Lobdell from the Old Northwest in the 1850s, American sexologists eliminated people with non-heteronormative sexualities, the cross-dresser representing the central figure among these, from the frontier myth they had helped to create.

Sierra Flats and Haunted Valleys

Cross-Dressers and the Contested Terrain of America's Frontier Past

In 1854, later celebrated American writer Bret Harte, who was all of eighteen, journeyed west to California, right near the tail end of the gold rush's heyday. He was propelled to fame in 1868 when his short story "The Luck of Roaring Camp," about life and social relations in gold-rush California, appeared in the recently founded West Coast literary journal *Overland Monthly*, a journal that Harte himself soon edited.[1]

In 1873, Harte published yet another short story, "The Poet of Sierra Flat."[2] Like so many of Harte's pieces, this one takes place in the heart of gold-rush country, near Calaveras and within the county of Tuolumne. It concerns "an awkward young man," as Harte describes his protagonist, Milton Chubbuck, who gains local fame when his doggerel is published, for a price, in the community newspaper, the *Sierra Flat Record*.[3]

Soon Milton, with his newfound fame and confidence, forms an admiring relationship with a local actress named California Pet, a "saucy, pretty brunette" whose notoriety came from her deft footlight impersonations of a white street boy and a male African-American dancer.[4] When Milton and Pet finally meet in chaperoned privacy, the poet reportedly comes alive: known for his reticence among other males, in the presence of California Pet he becomes "exceedingly voluble" in his praise of his heroine—he even impetuously beseeches the actress to "take him with her" so he can join her acting company.[5] In the face of such admiration from a person about whose identity California Pet grows suspicious, the actress wonders aloud "if it were as a boy or a girl that she was the subject of [such] flattering admiration."[6]

In concert with locals who have made something of a mascot of Milton and want to play a practical joke on him, the actress persuades her admirer to appear on her stage, where he would recite an original poem. After doing so, the audience planned to pelt Milton with "unsavory articles" and then carry him through town in a processional that would dump him at the outskirts, where he would be instructed never to return.[7] But just as his recitation commences, stage fright overwhelms the poet and he collapses. California Pet, now racked with guilt, rushes to him and loosens his shirt and collar and at that moment "burst into an hysterical laugh," though what she finds so amusing, Harte did not reveal to readers, at least right then.[8] With the help of her assistant, Manuela, Pet rescues Milton from the agitated crowd and elopes with him, disappearing from Sierra Flat, to the consternation of locals who have lost their saucy, pretty brunette, her cross-dressing performances, and their mascot Milton as well as the fun they had planned to perpetrate on him. The men of Sierra Flat grumble for some time, but the real outrage of the actress-poet elopement comes sometime later. Only at the very end of the story does a Sierra Flat local, using western dialect, shockingly learn and announce to the others that Milton "war a woman."[9]

"The Poet of Sierra Flat" is a story of same-sex love and multiple crossings of gender boundaries. But as it unfolds, Harte leads readers to believe that opposite-sex attraction and gender conformity are the case. We learn of Milton's infatuation with California Pet when we understand Milton to be a male, for example. But throughout the piece, Harte toys with prevalent opposite-sex attraction and concomitant gender compliance. Early in the story the *male* editor of the *Sierra Flat Record*, which publishes Milton's doggerel, is so taken by the poet's "sweet and musical" voice that he "looked at him curiously, and wondered if he had a sister."[10] California Pet's fame comes from her impersonations of boys and men. In her response to the male Milton's fervent admiration of these performances, Pet wonders if he worshipped her as a boy or as a girl. Although we never know exactly what becomes of California Pet and Milton Chubbuck and the exact nature of their relationship once they disappear from Sierra Flat (which is another way Harte plays with sexual certainty), we do know this in retrospect: California Pet literally disrobed Milton's secret identity when unbuttoning his collar and shirt to provide him more air after he fainted. Shockingly, it is at that very moment that Pet decides to assist the poet, forsake her successful career, and elope with her *female* admirer. We do not learn of Milton's female sex, of course, until the last line of the story, long since we had likely forgotten Harte's subtle mentioning of Pet's raucous laughter upon loosening Milton's shirt behind the drawn curtains of Sierra Flat's stage.

Just two years before Harte wrote "The Poet of Sierra Flat," another soon-to-be famed American writer, Ambrose Bierce, published his first story, "The Haunted Valley," also in the *Overland Monthly* and when Harte served as its editor.[11] Bierce ended up in San Francisco after the Civil War; at the time he headed West with the U.S. Army, inspecting military installations along the way. He remained in California for a few years before departing for London, where he stayed until 1875 and then returned to the Pacific Coast.[12]

Told in the first person by an unnamed narrator, "The Haunted Valley" is a considerably darker tale than "The Poet of Sierra Flat." A searing indictment of the rabid anti-Chinese sentiment that Bierce witnessed firsthand in California, the story involves racism, morbid jealousy, and even murder. But like Harte's piece of two years later, it is set in California and concerns sexual uncertainty and cross-dressing, or at least it never fully clarifies suspected cross-dressing and homosexuality.

The narrator tells the story of relative old-timer and alcoholic Jo. Dunfer, who lived in a "hermaphrodite habitation, half residence and half groggery" somewhere between "Hutton's" and "Mexican Hill."[13] Dunfer's "most obvious characteristic was a deep-seated antipathy to the Chinese," making such racist remarks as, "They're a flight of devouring locusts, and they're going for everything green in this God blest land." He also casts aspersions on "liberal ideas about immigration" and asserts that those who hold them are unable to tell the difference between a Chileño and a Kanaka.[14]

Some years back, before his anti-Chinese sentiments came to overwhelm his life, Dunfer began to construct a cabin. He hired two men to do much of the work, Ah Wee and Gopher. The former he later claims did not take orders and directions very well. Dunfer describes him, in fact, as "the perversest scoundrel outside San Francisco."[15]

The narrator of "The Haunted Valley" soon departs from his encounter with Dunfer and heads out of town. On his travels he chances upon the Californian's old cabin. He discovers nearby a fairly well-kept grave, marked with a headstone whose inscription astonishingly reads:

AH WEE—CHINAMAN
Age unknown. Worked for Jo. Dunfer
This monument is erected by him to keep the Chink's
memory green. Likewise as a warning to Celestials
not to take on airs. Devil take 'em!
She Was a Good Egg.

"The meagre inscription but sufficient identification of the deceased," the narrator relates in shocked tones, "the impudent candor of confession; the brutal anathema; the ludicrous change of sex and sentiment—all marked this record as the work of one who must have been at least as much demented as bereaved."[16]

The narrator does not return to the valley for four years, Dunfer having meanwhile passed away. During this second visit he runs across Gopher, who fills him in on the details of the story that he had only surmised from the headstone inscription he had stumbled across during his previous sojourn in the valley. Gopher relates that Dunfer, whom he called "W'isky," had indeed murdered Ah. Everyone knew he did and he even admitted it at the time. But the local justice of the peace, considering the racial element, found him not guilty. "But the fact is," Gopher continues about Dunfer, he "'was jealous o' *me* . . . thought a lot o' that Chink; nobody but me knew 'e doted on 'im. Couldn't bear 'im out of 'is sight. . . . And w'en 'e came down to this clearin' one day an' found him an' me neglectin' our work . . . W'isky laid hold of my axe and let us have it, good an' hard!" The jealous rampage, of course, resulted in Ah's death, but Gopher survived. After the gruesome ordeal, Dunfer hit the bottle but hard, drinking for years till his death, when he was laid to rest next to Ah, of all people, Gopher explaining that in reality Ah was "the woman who loved [Dunfer] better than she did me!"[17]

The story approaches its conclusion with Gopher describing Ah as a woman—Dunfer reportedly won her in a poker game in San Francisco years before and forever remained "ashamed to acknowledge 'er and treat 'er white!"[18] And yet Ah's sex is never entirely clear; feminine and masculine pronouns interchange readily right up to the story's conclusion, Gopher explaining near the very end, for example, that he had not wanted to visit "'er" grave as he did not want to meet "'im" in that way.[19] Thus, Ah Wee may have been a Chinese woman dressed as a man, or a (typically) feminized Chinese man; Bierce's use of the term "hermaphrodite" to describe Dunfer's abode early in the story suggests his desire to leave Ah's identity a mix of the two. That both

Dunfer and Gopher had passionate feelings for 'er/'im makes the story all that more remarkable because of the very probability of homosexuality—though it might have been female homosexuality, too, as Bierce always curiously rendered Dunfer's first name as "Jo."

Bierce and Harte wrote their stories of sex, sexuality, and gender uncertainty right at the cusp of the modern era, just when sexualities became identities and the medical profession began developing etiologies and pathologies for same-sex sexuality and the gender nonconformity believed to accompany it. This is also the time when popular as well as medical anxieties grew over the rise of the masculine New Woman, the perceived growing effeminacy of males associated with over-civilization, the supposed increase of sexual inversion, and of course the popular press's widespread coverage of an equally widespread cross-dressing.

Both Bierce and Harte presciently tapped into these developments and uncertainties. In Harte's case, for example, he wrote that the community of Sierra Flat believed that California Pet's decision to elope with Milton was the result of "inherent moral depravity."[20] Only at the end of Harte's story do we learn of same-sex attraction, but the moral depravity conclusion is arrived at earlier for other, though historically related, reasons: First, the angry men of Sierra Flat cannot believe Pet would run off with someone so unmanly as Milton—he would not stand in his own defense, but instead fainted and fled. Second, Harte juxtaposes California Pet's turpitude against the story of a white Philadelphia heiress who dumped her husband, a Southern congressman, for a black man. The local man who relates this news does so to put into perspective California Pet's actions (while it was still believed she ran off with a less-than-manly fellow rather than a woman). But in telling this story its narrator becomes so upset—indeed horrified—by the sexual impropriety of a white woman and a black man that he is unable to complete his yarn, being reduced to a blubbering idiot: "unintelligible and inaudible," in Harte's descriptive phrasing.[21]

Questions of improper sexual behavior, same-sex attraction, and "inherent moral depravity" are especially notable in Harte's piece considering when the story takes place and when he produced it. Published in 1873, the story was both written during and is set in what might reasonably be called the post-frontier, at least with regard to its California locale—the socially tumultuous period of the gold rush had long passed and California had really settled into a new era. Harte even describes the atmosphere of Sierra Flat when Milton Chubbuck first comes forward as many months "since the last vigilance committee" and since "nothing had transpired to dispel the listless *ennui* begotten of stagnant business and growing civilization."[22]

As Americans grew discomfited by the gender and sexual changes they witnessed, as they became troubled by the passing of the frontier and what they thought that meant, and as they witnessed a remarkable amount of cross-dressers in the West, they began to re-imagine, reinterpret, and redefine both the cross-dresser and the frontier and the West of which s/he was a part. The most significant chronicles of female-to-male cross-dressers they created at this time described these individuals according to two dominant ideas about the West and the frontier. One was the West as a (particularly colorful) masculine space. The other was the frontier as a place that followed an advancing trajectory from a state of wilderness and savagery to an acceptably settled landscape fully integrated into the nation. Both these views inscribed onto the bodies and into the biographies of female-to-male cross-dressers a regional history broken into stages that successfully concluded when order was established, namely when the subject's heterosexuality, femininity, and true womanhood are restored. In this way, turn-of-the-twentieth-century Americans both in the West and elsewhere gave considerable effort to using the myths of the region to normalize their female-to-male cross-dressers: they created elaborate biographies for them, scarcely related to fact, that transformed their transgendered behaviors (and eased suspicions about their sexuality) by explaining these behaviors as merely due to a westering process that, thank goodness, was as ephemeral as the frontier.

Because of the history and nature of women's oppression and the exigencies of the frontier, it was relatively simple for people to re-imagine the female-to-male cross-dresser within a western and frontier context—this has, however, continued into the contemporary era as western historians of female-to-male cross-dressers persist in hiding behind the skirts of the progress narrative to do so. The male-to-female cross-dresser presented something of a different problem back at the turn of the twentieth century. Difficult to account for within any sort of progress narrative, Anglo Americans instead had to find a way to remove these troubling people from western and frontier history altogether. Or, that is, at least remove them from the white, virile, masculine, and heteronormative version of that history. They accomplished this, at least in part, through racializing the cross-dresser and feminizing the non-Anglo male (regardless of whether he actually cross-dressed).

In either and both cases, this made the troubling subjects peripheral to the central story of the region, the frontier, and the nation. For that reason the male-to-female cross-dresser has continued to elude historians of the West and frontier to the present day.

In "The Poet of Sierra Flat," Bret Harte captured the late nineteenth-century projects that racialized and feminized the cross-dresser, describing Milton as unmanly and then associating him/her with the sexual improprieties of a black man. Ambrose Bierce went further. He witnessed firsthand how the racializing of cross-dressing and the feminizing of non-Anglo males actually played out in post-gold-rush California, and he made these central to "The Haunted Valley." There Bierce vividly captured vehement racism against the Chinese, but also against Chileans and Pacific Islanders. With this as his social backdrop, Bierce utilized the term "hermaphrodite," a concept that so well captured for the period the uncertainty Bierce leaves his readers with as to the sexual and gender identity of Ah Wee. Bierce's story also shows the ways in which the racialized cross-dresser and the feminized non-Anglo male were pushed to the periphery of the American West, not just in recalling Ah Wee's murder, but also by explaining that his murderer faced no justice at all precisely because he was white and his victim Chinese. The "Chink," the "hermaphrodite," was dispensable. An even deeper reading might suggest that these western characters had to be pushed to the margins because they had become the subject of white male homosexual desire, another concept the West and the evolving frontier and national narrative could not countenance.[23]

While Bierce and Harte tapped into popular concerns about sexuality, gender, and cross-dressing, they drew upon and anticipated developing sexological explanations of these as well. Harte referred to "inherent moral depravity." Bierce spoke of Ah Wee's "change of sex" and the decay of civilizations, and he used terms and phrases such as "hermaphrodite," "reverted to his original type," "queer little man," "demented," "perverted," and "perverse." Sexology at the time likewise used such words and concepts; it also would soon hold that sexual deviance could not be associated with America's frontier past, a past that had rather bequeathed to the nation all sorts of positive characteristics, for example those that Frederick Jackson Turner identified in his highly influential 1893 paper, "The Significance of the Frontier in American History." Furthermore, to sexologists, frontier conditions had to some degree immunized the country from perversions, but that perversions were starting to appear by the 1890s was due to the declining influence of the frontier as the nation entered the modern era. Collectively, sexologists constructed a frontier America devoid of sexual inversion due to, among other things, its population distribution, its "wild" conditions, and the effects of its climate and outdoor living.

In the end, the concerted efforts at both the medical/scientific and popular levels to rid America's frontier past from troubling questions about gender and sexuality as represented by the cross-dresser best expose the fact of these people's ubiquitous presence and central importance to the history of the American West and the American nation. America's frontier past was clearly a place and process where gender and sexuality were unstable, contentious, and transgressive. It was a place where a wide variety of people who did not conform to gender and sexual expectations lived, loved, and died. Many today may yet find it humorously incongruent to juxtapose the classic Old West with gender transgressiveness and same-sex sexuality. In fact, same-sex sexuality and gender fluidity represented in and by the cross-dresser actually lay at the very heart of the classic Old West. Likewise, buried deep within ideas and understandings about sexuality and gender in today's modern America lay the very fact of the nation's mythic frontier past.

NOTES

INTRODUCTION

Portions of this introduction first appeared in "Go West Young Man, Go East Young Woman: Searching for the *Trans* in Western Gender History," *Western Historical Quarterly* 36 (Winter 2005): 477–97. Copyright by the Western History Association. Reprinted by permission.

1. Much uncertainty and debate surrounds Horace Greeley's association with "Go West, young man," a phrase for which he has been popularly credited. Fred R. Shapiro, ed., *The Yale Book of Quotations* (New Haven, CT: Yale University Press, 2006), 322–23, found that the earliest source to attribute this to Greeley was likely one in 1870, though the phrase plausibly can be attributed to him as early as 1853.

2. Horace Greeley, *An Overland Journey, from New York to San Francisco, in the Summer of 1859* (New York: C. M. Saxton, Barker & Company, 1860), 85.

3. Ang Lee, director, *Brokeback Mountain*, Focus Features, 2005; Annie Proulx, "Brokeback Mountain," *New Yorker*, 13 October 1997, 74–80, 82–85.

4. See Daniel Kurtzman, "Brokeback Mountain Jokes: Late-Night Jokes about *Brokeback Mountain*," About.com: Political Humor, http://politicalhumor.about .com/od/brokebackmountain/a/brokebackjokes.htm (accessed 27 May 2010); Guy Trebay, "Cowboys, Just Like the Movies," *New York Times*, 18 December 2005, www .nytimes.com/2005/12/18/fashion/syndaystyles/18BROKEBACK.html (accessed 27 May 2010); Dan Savage, "Don't Let Your Babies Grow Up to Be Ex-Gay Cowboys," *New York Times*, 10 February 2006, www.nytimes.com/2006/02/10/opinion/10savage .html (accessed 27 May 2010).

5. Alfred C. Kinsey, Wardell B. Pomeroy, and Clyde E. Martin, *Sexual Behavior in the Human Male* (Philadelphia: W. B. Saunders, 1948), 457, 459 (quoted), 631.

6. Frederick J. Turner, "The Significance of the Frontier in American History," *Annual Report of the American Historical Association for the Year 1893*, Congress,

Senate, Miscellaneous Document No. 104, 53rd Cong., 2d sess., 1894 (Washington: Government Printing Office, 1894), 199.

7. Thomas Laqueur, *Making Sex: Body and Gender from the Greeks to Freud* (Cambridge, MA: Harvard University Press, 1990).

8. The standard history of sexuality in America is John D'Emilio and Estelle B. Freedman, *Intimate Matters: A History of Sexuality in America*, 2d ed. (Chicago: University of Chicago Press, 1997).

9. A good general study of the emergence of the concepts of homosexual and heterosexual, and thus the sexual system they are part of, is Jonathan Ned Katz, *The Invention of Heterosexuality* (New York: Plume, 1995).

10. Deeply imbued with this tradition, modern-day historians and popular writers of the American West's female-to-male cross-dressers have been unable to look for transgressive sexuality and gender identities among them. Examples of this work that are otherwise very useful are Evelyn A. Schlatter, "Drag's a Life: Women, Gender, and Cross-Dressing in the Nineteenth-Century West," in *Writing the Range: Race, Class, and Culture in the Women's West*, ed. Elizabeth Jameson and Susan Armitage (Norman: University of Oklahoma Press, 1997), 334–48; Sally Zanjani, *A Mine of Her Own: Women Prospectors in the American West, 1850–1950* (Lincoln, NE: Bison Books, 1997), especially chapter 3; DeAnne Blanton, "Cathy Williams: Black Woman Soldier, 1866–1868," *MINERVA: Quarterly Report on Women and the Military* X (Fall/Winter 1992): 1–12; Mary Chaney Hoffman, "Whips of the Old West," *American Mercury* 84 (April 1957): 107–10; Mildretta Adams, *Historic Silver City: The Story of the Owyhees* (Homedale, ID: Printed by the Owyhee Chronicle, 1960), 56–59; Joyce Roach, "Horse Trader," in The Western Writers of America, *The Women Who Made the West* (Garden City, NY: Doubleday, 1980), 178–85; Gordon Morris Bakken and Brenda Farrington, eds., *Encyclopedia of Women in the West* (Thousand Oaks, CA: Sage, 2003), 91–92; Phillip Thomas Tucker, *Cathy Williams: From Slave to Buffalo Soldier* (Mechanicsburg, PA: Stackpole Books, 2002); Vardis Fisher and Opal Laurel Homes, *Gold Rushes and Mining Camps of the Early American West* (Caldwell, ID: Caxton Printers, 1968), 109.

On the other hand, there are a few more critical studies of western female-to-male cross-dressers, albeit written by scholars neither western nor necessarily historians. They include Louis Sullivan's *From Female to Male: The Life of Jack Bee Garland* (Boston: Alyson, 1990); Sharon O'Brien, *Willa Cather: The Emerging Voice* (New York: Oxford University Press, 1987); Clare Sears, "'A Dress Not Belonging to His or Her Sex': Cross-Dressing Law in San Francisco, 1860–1900" (PhD diss., University of California, Santa Cruz, 2005).

Scholars of locations other than the West have created a remarkably rich and critical literature on cross-dressers. Among the most significant works are Vern L. Bullough, "Transvestites in the Middle Ages," *American Journal of Sociology* 79 (May 1974): 1381–94; Judith C. Brown, *Immodest Acts: The Life of a Lesbian Nun in Renaissance Italy* (New York: Oxford University Press, 1986); Rudolf M. Dekker and Lotte C. van de Pol, *The Tradition of Female Transvestism in Early Modern Europe* (London: St. Martin's, 1989); Kathleen Brown, "'Changed . . . Into the Fashion of Man': The Politics of Sexual Difference in a Seventeenth-Century Anglo-American Settlement," *Journal of the History of Sexuality* 6 (October 1995): 171–93; Patricia Crawford and Sara Mendelson, "Sexual Identities in Early Modern England: The Marriage of Two Women in 1680," *Gender & History* 7 (November 1995): 362–77; James Vernon, "'For Some Queer Reason': The Trials and Tribulations of Colonel Barker's Masquerade in Interwar Britain," *Signs* 26 (Autumn 2000): 37–62; Mary McGinn Blanchette, "Dressing Across the Great Gender Divide (1850–1901): Dr. Mary Edward Walker and Murray H. Hall" (M.A. thesis, Sonoma State University, 2001).

11. Turner, "The Significance of the Frontier in American History," 199–227. Of course, more than just the 1890 census inspired Turner; see Ray Allen Billington, *The Genesis of the Frontier Thesis: A Study in Historical Creativity* (San Marino, CA: Huntington Library, 1971).

12. I further explore the heterosexual assumptions of frontier myth in "Thinking Like Mount Rushmore: Sexuality and Gender in the Republican Landscape," in *Seeing Nature Through Gender*, ed. Virginia J. Scharff (Lawrence: University Press of Kansas, 2003), 40–59.

13. Ki Namaste, "'Tragic Misreadings': Queer Theory's Erasure of Transgender Subjectivity," in *Queer Studies: A Lesbian, Gay, Bisexual, and Transgender Anthology*, ed. Brett Beemyn and Mickey Eliason (New York: New York University Press, 1996), 183.

14. Thomas M. Lauderdale and Tom Cook, "The Incredible Life and Loves of the Legendary Lucille Hart," *Alternative Connection* (Portland, OR), September 1993, 1; J. Allen Gilbert, "Homo-Sexuality and Its Treatment," *Journal of Nervous and Mental Disease* 52, no. 4 (October 1920): 299; *The National Cyclopaedia of American Biography* (New York: James T. White & Co., 1969), 51: 604; Manuscript Population Census Returns, Kingman County, Kansas, 1880, Enumeration District 305, page 9, lines 16–21.

15. Gilbert, "Homo-Sexuality and Its Treatment," 300–309.

16. Ibid., 304–6.

17. *The Takenah* (Albany, OR: Albany College, 1911): 18.

18. Ibid., 18, 20; Lauderdale and Cook, "The Incredible Life and Loves of the Legendary Lucille Hart," 1.

19. *The Takenah*, 20.

20. Gilbert, "Homo-Sexuality and Its Treatment," 308–10.

21. Ibid., 310–11; Gerard Koskovich, "Private Lives, Public Struggles," *Stanford* 21, no. 2 (June 1993): 33.

22. Gilbert, "Homo-Sexuality and Its Treatment," 312–13, 317.

23. Ibid., 311, 313–17.

24. Ibid., 310–18; Lauderdale and Cook, "The Incredible Life and Loves of the Legendary Lucille Hart," 1, 4–5.

25. Gilbert, "Homo-Sexuality and Its Treatment," 297, 298 (quoted), 302.

26. Such reasoning was in keeping with the era's notion of sexual inversion (Gilbert used the term "homosexual" in his analysis of Hart): the belief was that a female invert was someone who had a man's brain and mind, but a woman's body.

27. Gilbert, "Homo-Sexuality and Its Treatment," 319–21, 321 (quoted).

28. *Albany (Oregon) Daily Democrat*, 26 March 1918, 1.

29. "AMAZING SEX DISCOVERY," *Medical Sentinel* 26, no. 6 (June 1918): 253.

30. Gilbert, "Homo-Sexuality and Its Treatment," 321.

31. "AMAZING SEX DISCOVERY," 253.

32. *Portland (Oregon) News*, 3 August 1917, 1.

33. *Albany (Oregon) Daily Democrat*, 26 March 1918, 1; Gilbert, "Homo-Sexuality and Its Treatment," 321; Lauderdale and Cook, "The Incredible Life and Loves of the Legendary Lucille Hart," 5; *The National Cyclopaedia of American Biography*, 51: 604.

34. Alan Hart, *The Undaunted* (New York: Norton, 1936), 262.

35. *The National Cyclopaedia of American Biography* 51: 604–5; "Dr. Hart Dies, X-Ray Director, State TB Unit," *Hartford (Connecticut) Times*, 2 July 1962, 36.

36. Tom Cook and Thomas M. Lauderdale, "Lucille Hart Marries a Woman," *Alternative Connection* (Portland, OR), October 1993, 1, 4.

37. Gilbert, "Homo-Sexuality and Its Treatment," 321.

38. When historians began to investigate lesbian and gay history in the 1970s and 1980s, they did not always properly historicize those they resurrected from documents. Thus, they claimed even as late as 1998 that Alan Hart was a woman and a lesbian (who just happened to dress as a man). Such works include Jonathan Ned Katz, *Gay American History: Lesbians & Gay Men in the U.S.A.*, rev. ed. (New York: Meridian, 1997), 258–79; Jonathan Ned Katz, *Gay/Lesbian Almanac: A New Documentary* (New York: Harper & Row, 1983), 516–22; Margaret Gibson, "The Masculine Degenerate: American Doctors' Portrayal of the Lesbian Intellect, 1880–1949," *Journal of Women's History* 9 (Winter 1998): 81, 91–92; and Koskovich, "Private Lives, Public Struggles," 33.

In time methodological and theoretical developments permitted historians and other scholars to see that some of these so-called gays and lesbians may have been transsexual. Those who have seen Hart in this light are Joanne Meyerowitz, "Sex and the Popular Press: Historical Notes on Transsexuality in the United States, 1930–1955," *GLQ* 4 (1998): 161–62; Susan Stryker, "Local Transsexual History," *TNT: The Transsexual News Telegraph* 5 (Summer/Autumn 1995): 14–15; and Cook and Lauderdale, "Lucille Hart Marries a Woman," 4–5.

Transsexuals have recovered Hart from gay and lesbian history, including in some very high-profile efforts. Beginning in the 1980s, gays and lesbians in Portland, Oregon, hosted an annual fund-raiser dinner to support the work and campaigns of politicians sympathetic to their cause. They called the affair the "Lucille Hart Dinner." It honored someone they believed to be a lesbian and they held up "her" life as an example of the prejudices, difficulties, and secretiveness that lesbians and gays historically have had to endure in America. By 1995, transsexual activism had crystallized and members of the movement boldly picketed the Lucille Hart Dinner, arguing that Hart was no lesbian, should not be called Lucille (but rather Alan), and was rather a transsexual who took to men's clothing not to hide her identity but to fully express it. The controversy eventually led the dinner's organizers to remove the name "Lucille Hart" from their fund raiser. See Tom Bates, "Decades Ago, an Oregon Doctor Tried to Redefine Gender," *Oregonian*, 14 July 1996, B1, B5.

Why dinner organizers did not re-imagine it as the Alan Hart Dinner and promote Hart as a hero for all peoples oppressed because of their gender and sexual identities is somewhat of a fraught proposition. Probably this was due to hard feelings; it might have also been due to prejudice: transsexuals and transgender people have often felt left out of mainstream lesbian and gay activism, their presence being discomfiting to some lesbians and gays.

39. Henry S. Rubin, "Phenomenology as Method in Trans Studies," *GLQ* 4 (1998): 276; Suzanne Kessler and Wendy McKenna, "Who Put the 'Trans' in Transgender? Gender Theory and Everyday Life," *International Journal of Transgenderism* 4 (July–September 2000): www.symposium.com/ilt/gilbert/kessler.htm (accessed July 2005); Vern L. Bullough, "Transgenderism and the Concept of Gender," *International Journal of Transgenderism* 4 (July–September 2000), www.symposium .com/ijt/gilbert/bullough.htm (accessed July 2005); Judith Halberstam, "Transgender Butch: Butch/FTM Border Wars and the Masculine Continuum," *GLQ* 4 (1998): 303; Gordene Olga MacKenzie, *Transgender Nation* (Bowling Green, OH: Bowling Green State University Popular Press, 1994).

40. *Albany (Oregon) Daily Democrat*, 26 March 1918, 1.

41. "AMAZING SEX DISCOVERY," 253.

42. *Albany (Oregon) Daily Democrat*, 26 March 1918, 1.

43. Ibid.

44. Judith Butler, *Gender Trouble: Feminism and the Subversion of Identity* (New York: Routledge, 1990, 1999), 179. See also Butler, *Bodies That Matter: On the Discursive Limits of "Sex"* (New York: Routledge, 1993).

45. Butler, *Gender Trouble*, 179.

46. An indication of severity of the disruption to the two-sex/two-gender system that cross-dressers pose, and an attempt to bring it back into conformity, can be seen in the increase of laws that prohibited people from wearing the clothing of the opposite sex. During the course of the second half of the nineteenth century, some thirty major American municipalities adopted ordinances or codes prohibiting people from wearing clothing accustomed to the opposite sex. Perhaps it is a measure of how many cross-dressers appeared in America's various regions at that time that a majority (eighteen) of these municipalities were located in the trans-Mississippi West, twelve in the trans-Missouri West alone. See William N. Eskridge Jr., *Gay Law: Challenging the Apartheid of the Closet* (Cambridge, MA: Harvard University Press, 1999), Appendix A2, 338–41. It should be added, however, that municipalities across the country without such specifically worded ordinances and codes nevertheless routinely arrested and prosecuted cross-dressing offenders under other generic laws—for example, those dealing with vagrancy and public indecency.

47. For a consideration of the role played by the late nineteenth-century mass-circulation press in shaping views on transgressive sexuality and gender identity, see

Lisa Duggan, *Sapphic Slashers: Sex, Violence, and American Modernity* (Durham, NC: Duke University Press, 2000), 1–6.

48. *Albany (Oregon) Daily Democrat*, 26 March 1918, 1.

49. Marjorie Garber, *Vested Interests: Cross Dressing & Cultural Anxiety* (New York: Routledge, 1992), 68–70. Garber has also pointed out that the progress narrative, in explaining away cross-dressing as nothing but a rational choice considering social circumstances, reinforces the idea that there are two sexes (the male/female binary).

50. Examples of scholarly studies on the West that hold fast to the progress narrative are Evelyn A. Schlatter, "Drag's a Life," 334–48; DeAnne Blanton, "Cathy Williams: Black Woman Soldier, 1866–1868," *MINERVA: Quarterly Report on Women and the Military* 10 (Fall/Winter 1992): 1–12; The San Francisco Lesbian and Gay History Project, "'She Even Chewed Tobacco': A Pictorial Narrative of Passing Women in America," in *Hidden from History: Reclaiming the Gay and Lesbian Past*, ed. Martin Duberman, Matha Vicinus, and George Chauncey Jr. (New York: Plume, 1989), 189–92; Phillip Thomas Tucker, *Cathy Williams: From Slave to Buffalo Soldier* (Mechanicsburg, PA: Stackpole, 2002); Tania Modleski, "A Woman's Gotta Do . . . What a Man's Gotta Do? Cross-Dressing in the Western," *Signs* 22 (Spring 1997): 525.

51. An excellent consideration of these and other aspects of "West" is Walter Nugent, "Where Is the American West? Report on a Survey," *Montana: The Magazine of Western History* 42, no. 3 (Summer 1992): 2–23.

52. Kerwin Lee Klein, "Reclaiming the 'F' Word, or Being and Becoming Western," *Pacific Historical Review* 65, no. 2 (May 1996): 179–215, provides an excellent overview of the history of the term "frontier" in the American context and debates about it.

CHAPTER I

1. Portland, *Morning Oregonian*, 4 June 1912, 12; *Portland Evening Telegram*, 4 June 1912, 8; Portland, *Oregon Journal*, 4 June 1912, 6. Information on weather conditions is from the *Morning Oregonian*, 4 June 1912, 1.

2. *Morning Oregonian*, 4 June 1912, 4 (quoted); *Oregon Journal*, 4 June 1912, 6; *Ada (Oklahoma) Evening News*, 11 October 1911, 4; *Portland News*, 10 April 1912, 3; Manuscript Population Census Returns, Spokane County, Washington, 1910, Enumeration District 183, Sheet 8B, line 57. While by 1912 Nell Pickerell went by the name Harry Allen, a few years earlier he regularly used the name Harry Livingstone. Although how he chose Allen has not yet come to light, the 1900 census for Seattle shows Pickerell living as a roomer in the McMatt household, where there also lived a Harry Livingstone. See Manuscript Population Census Returns, King County, Washington, 1900, Enumeration District 100, Sheet 13A, lines 40 and 41.

3. *Portland News*, 8 June 1912, 1; Portland Police Department's Women's Auxiliary Reports, 19 June 1912, Lola G. Baldwin Papers, Portland Police Museum, Portland, Oregon. Authorities released Allen prior to the completion of his sentence;

Portland Police Department's Women's Auxiliary Reports, 19 August 1912, Lola G. Baldwin Papers.

4. *Portland News*, 11 June 1912, 1 (quoted); *Morning Oregonian*, 4 June 1912, 12 (quoted); *Oregon Journal*, 4 June 1912, 6; *Portland Evening Telegram*, 4 June 1912, 8; *Portland News*, 8 June 1912, 1, 10 June 1912, 1, 12 June 1912, 1, and 6 June 1912, 1.

5. According to the death certificate, "Nell Pickerell" was born on 11 September 1882. Nell Pickerell, Certificate of Death, Record No. 3002, Washington State Board of Health, Center for Health Statistics, Olympia.

6. *Saint Paul (Minnesota) Globe*, 13 May 1900, 26. Other early local and distant newspapers that covered Allen include the *Minneapolis Journal*, 30 December 1901, 3; *San Francisco Call*, 26 December 1901, 7, 5 November 1903, 9, and 21 February 1906, 10; Boise, *Idaho Statesman*, 27 December 1901, 2; Olympia, Washington, *Morning Olympian*, 1 June 1902, 3; *Seattle Mail and Herald*, 9 September 1905, 2, and 19 December 1903, 2; *Oakland (California) Tribune*, 4 June 1912, 12; *San Jose (California) Mercury News*, 4 June 1912, 8; *Norfolk (Nebraska) Weekly News-Journal*, 22 September 1911, 8; and *Ada Evening News*, 11 October 1911, 4.

7. "Girl in Man's Clothing Goes A-Wooing Women," *Washington (D.C.) Times*, 23 February 1908, Magazine Section, 7.

8. Dolly Quappe is not named in this piece. For more on the suicides, see *Minneapolis Journal*, 30 December 1902, 3; *San Francisco Call*, 5 November 1903, 9; Salt Lake City, Utah, *Salt Lake Telegram*, 6 November 1903, 2; *Anaconda (Montana) Standard*, 6 November 1903, 1; and somewhat later *San Francisco Daily News*, 21 June 1915, 6. The various stories contain contradictory information, including the dates and nature of the suicides, in particular the second one, which was reported both as Hazel Walters' shooting herself in the chest or the head in Seattle's Denny Park or jumping from a cliff at Seattle's Madrona Park. Whatever the actual details, Portland policewoman Lola G. Baldwin provided independent verification of the suicides in 1912 in Portland Police Department's Women's Auxiliary Reports, 19 June 1912, Lola G. Baldwin Papers. A source that questions the suicides altogether is Miriam Van Waters, "The Adolescent Girl Among Primitive Peoples," *Journal of Religious Psychology* 7, no. 1 (January 1914): 107.

9. In order quoted: *Portland News*, 11 June 1912, 1, and 10 June 1912, 1; *Norfolk Weekly News-Journal*, 22 September 1911, 8; *Seattle Mail and Herald*, 9 September 1905, 2; *Ada Evening News*, 11 October 1911, 4; *San Francisco Daily News*, 21 June 1915, 6; *Portland News*, 8 June 1912, 1.

10. News reports on her marriage and its effect include *San Francisco Daily News*, 21 June 1915, 6; and "Girl in Man's Clothing Goes A-Wooing Women."

11. *San Francisco Daily News*, 21 June 1915, 6.

12. *Oregon Journal*, 4 June 1912, 6.

13. Examples are: *Oakland Tribune*, 4 June 1912, 12; *Morning Oregonian*, 4 June 1912, 12; *Oregon Journal*, 4 June 1912, 6; *Portland Evening Telegram*, 4 June 1912, 8; *Portland News*, 11 June 1912, 1.

14. The foregoing is a paraphrasing of Estelle B. Freedman's summary of "The Adolescent Girl Among Primitive Peoples," in *Maternal Justice: Miriam Van Waters*

and the Female Reform Tradition (Chicago: University of Chicago Press, 1996), 54. In her thesis, which she published, Van Waters refers to Pickerell as "Case I" and "H.A." No doubt "H.A." is Harry Allen, Pickerell's preferred moniker; various information included in the case study also matches biographical information from Pickerell's life collected independently. See Van Waters, "The Adolescent Among Primitive Peoples," 107–10.

15. Van Waters, "The Adolescent Among Primitive Peoples," 108.

16. On Van Waters, see Estelle B. Freedman, *Maternal Justice.*

17. King County Birth Register, Vol. 1, 206, Record No. 5265, Washington State Digital Archives, www.digitalarchives.wa.gov (accessed 24 November 2009).

18. Van Waters, "The Adolescent Among Primitive Peoples," 108.

19. Ibid.

20. Ibid., 109 (quoted), 110 (quoted).

21. Portland Police Department's Women's Auxiliary Reports, 19 June 1912 and 19 August 1912, Lola G. Baldwin Papers.

22. San Francisco Lesbian and Gay History Project, "'She Even Chewed Tobacco': A Pictorial Narrative of Passing Women in America," in *Hidden from History: Reclaiming the Gay & Lesbian Past,* ed. Martin Duberman, Martha Vicinus, and George Chauncey Jr. (New York: Meridian, 1990), 183–94; John D'Emilio and Estelle B. Freedman, *Intimate Matters: A History of Sexuality in America* (New York: Harper & Row, 1988), 228; Jonathan Ned Katz, *Gay American History: Lesbians and Gay Men in the U.S.A.,* rev. ed. (New York: Meridian, 1992), 209–12; Esther Newton, "The Mythic Mannish Lesbian: Radclyffe Hall and the New Woman," *Signs* 4, no. 4 (Summer 1984): 557–75; Elizabeth Lapovsky Kennedy and Madeline D. Davis, *Boots of Leather, Slippers of Gold: The History of a Lesbian Community* (New York: Routledge, 1993); Lillian Faderman, *Odd Girls and Twilight Lovers: A History of Lesbian Life in Twentieth-Century America* (New York: Penguin, 1992), 39–45.

23. Joan Nestle, "Lesbians and Prostitutes: An Historical Sisterhood," in *A Restricted Country* (Ithaca, NY: Firebrand Books, 1987), 157–77; Faderman, *Odd Girls and Twilight Lovers,* 37.

24. *Morning Oregonian,* 4 June 1912, 12.

25. "Girl in Man's Clothing Goes A-Wooing Women."

26. *Seattle Mail and Herald,* 9 September 1905, 2.

27. *Portland News,* 11 June 1912, 1.

28. Ibid., 13 June 1912, 1.

29. Nell Pickerell, Certificate of Death, Record No. 3002, Washington State Board of Health, Center for Health Statistics, Olympia; *Seattle Post-Intelligencer,* 28 December 1922, section 2, 16.

30. *Anaconda Standard,* 12 December 1908, 1 (quoted); *Idaho Statesman,* 21 December 1908, 4. See also *Idaho Statesman,* 19 December 1908, 2; *Oakland Tribune,* 20 December 1908, 21; *Grand Forks (North Dakota) Herald,* 16 December 1908, 1.

31. *Oakland Tribune,* 20 December 1908, 21; *Ocala (Florida) Evening Star,* 22 December 1908, 9.

32. 21 December 1908, 4.

33. For example, on Mary Walker, see *Idaho Statesman*, 30 September 1891, 2. Also see "In Male Attire. Famous Women Who Have Doffed Petticoats Because They Preferred Trousers," *Idaho Statesman*, 30 January 1890, 1; and "Disguised as Men. Women Who Have Lived for Years in Male Attire," *Idaho Statesman*, 1 April 1897, 4. A quick search through this newspaper reveals no fewer than forty stories related to cross-dressing appearing between 1890 and the time of Sammy Williams's case.

34. *Idaho Statesman*, 24 October 1908, 4. These more interesting quotations come from the *San Francisco Call*, 5 October 1908, 2.

35. 24 October 1908, 4; 11 March 1908, 3.

36. 2 May 1857, 1.

37. 26 July 1878, 1.

38. Albert D. Richardson, *Beyond the Mississippi: Life and Adventure on the Prairies, Mountains, and Pacific Coast* (Hartford, CT: American Publishing Co., 1869), 200.

39. St. Louis, *Daily Missouri Republican*, 23 April 1851, 2.

40. *Idaho Falls Times*, 22 June 1893, 5. Likewise, and years later, when Grace Hyde came under arrest in San Jose, California, for wearing men's clothes, she told the papers that her health compelled her to camp in the open air. In doing so, she "felt safer from molestation in male attire." *San Francisco Call*, 3 July 1910, 29.

41. *Perry (Iowa) Daily Chief*, 6 October 1896, 2. Some years later, in July 1913, Pearl Roberts dressed as a boy. While passing through Ellensburg, Washington, while returning to her Seattle home, she came to the attention of the local press. Having set out in March to tour the world, she seems to have made it only as far as the East Coast. Although then on her way home, the possibility of traveling more widely remained open: "I have had such a good time on the trip," she said, "I am sure I will want to take another one in the near future." *Spokane Spokesman Review*, 11 July 1913, 13.

42. Examples are the *Kansas City (Kansas) Post*, 30 December 1910, 2; *San Francisco Chronicle*, 1 November 1913, 2; *Spokane Spokesman Review*, 11 July 1913, 3; *Ellensburg (Washington) Evening Record*, 8 July 1913, 2; *Kansas City Post*, 7 May 1915, 3.

43. Quintard Taylor, *In Search of the Racial Frontier: African Americans in the American West, 1528–1990* (New York: W. W. Norton, 1998), Chapter 6.

44. The news item from which the quotation comes was published in the *St. Louis Daily Times* on 2 January 1876 and reprinted in Phillip Thomas Tucker, *Cathy Williams: From Slave to Female Buffalo Soldier* (Mechanicsburg, PA: Stackpole Books, 2002), 223. On Cathy or Cathay Williams, see also DeAnne Blanton, "Cathay Williams: Black Woman Soldier 1866–1868," *Minerva: Quarterly Report on Women and the Military* 10, nos. 3 and 4 (Fall/Winter 1992): 1–12.

Other examples of women who wore men's clothing to find better paying employment are Canadian Mary Johnson, who became Frank Woodhull; South Dakota's Delia Lahmon, who became Michael Harmon; Nebraska's Shirley Martin, who changed into Charley Taylor; and Portland's Carmen Fells. See *Idaho Statesman*, 24 October 1908, 4; *San Francisco Call*, 5 October 1908, 2; *Laramie Boomerang*,

2 June 1908, 1; *Portland Oregonian*, 29 August 1911, 9; Portland Police Department's Women's Auxiliary Reports, 24 June 1911, Lola G. Baldwin Papers.

Many women changed clothing to more easily follow their husbands about the region as they searched for employment. When Arla Marshall's husband, an Omaha machinist, lost his job in late 1913, he decided to hitch a freight train to the Pacific in search of new employment. Rather than staying put, Arla put on men's clothing and loyally accompanied him, despite a perilous trip that included freezing her feet when traveling through the cold of the western mountains. See *San Francisco Chronicle*, 1 November 1913, 2.

Similarly, the next year when Lincoln, Nebraska, authorities arrested May Daring for wearing men's attire, she explained to them that she wore such clothing to more comfortably follow her husband, a structural steel and iron worker, who was traveling the state in search of work. She did not know cross-dressing transgressed the law and admitted that her husband opposed her choice of clothing; he reportedly cried when she cut short her hair. See *Lincoln Daily Sun*, 27 August 1914, 6.

In 1927, Dorothy Halling, who also went by the name Bob Watson, came to light in Mandan, North Dakota. For years she and her husband traveled the West as transient laborers while she wore men's clothing. As a man, she had found employment as a hotel clerk, a cement worker, a rodeo rider, and a copper miner. See *Moab (Utah) Times-Independent*, 13 January 1927, 3.

45. *San Francisco Evening Bulletin*, 22 September 1862, 1. Another example, coming from the *San Francisco Evening Bulletin*, 18 August 1871, 4, concerns one of the three prostitutes who worked Bradshaw City, an Arizona mining town with only two hundred inhabitants. Like her Cariboo counterparts, this woman "swaggered and swore about in male attire equal to the occasion." Similarly, San Francisco's *Daily Evening Bulletin*, 20 November 1857, 3, reported the arrest of the "rather fair-looking but infamous" Sophia Sherwood for promenading in the streets dressed as a man and in the company of William Brown.

46. *Bismarck (Dakota) Daily Tribune*, 27 September 1887, 1 (quoted); *Cheyenne (Wyoming) Daily Leader*, 28 January 1891, 1.

47. *San Francisco Daily Morning Call*, 16 September 1876, 3.

48. Ibid.

49. San Francisco, *Daily Alta California*, 1 August 1874, 1, 23 August 1874, 1, and 20 July 1875, 1; *San Francisco Chronicle*, 12 May 1876, 2, and 12 July 1876, 3; *Daily Alta California*, 16 September 1876, 1; *San Francisco Chronicle*, 16 September 1876, 2; *San Francisco Evening Bulletin*, 16 September 1876, 4; *San Francisco Daily Morning Call*, 16 September 1876, 3; *San Francisco Chronicle*, 17 September 1876, 8; *San Francisco Daily Morning Call*, 17 September 1876, 5; *Daily Alta California*, 17 September 1876, 1; *San Francisco Chronicle*, 20 September 1897, 1; *St. Louis Globe-Democrat*, 23 September 1876, 2, and 14 December 1876, 2; Nestle, *A Restricted Country*, 167.

During her short time in San Francisco, Bonnet's celebrity grew to such proportions that local newspapers sometimes linked her infamy to cross-dressing more generally. For example, in September 1876, about a week after Bonnet's assassination, the local court fined the two Brown sisters, Lizzie and Nelly, $20 apiece for "emulating Jeanne Bonnett [sic] by wearing male attire." See *San Francisco Daily Evening Bulletin*, 20 September 1876, 3.

50. New York City, *Pomeroy's Democrat*, 2 November 1870, 3. A year after Susie, Marie Sweiz found no steady work as a respectable woman in San Francisco and so "determined to don the apparel of the sterner sex and fight life's battle as a man." As such, she left for California's interior working as a farmhand and miner. After some twenty years, Sweiz returned to San Francisco to spend her money and "see life as men see it." Unfortunately, while relaxing in a saloon on her homecoming, something about "her manner was unlike that of a man, and led to her arrest." *San Francisco Daily Evening Bulletin*, 19 April 1871, 1.

51. *San Francisco Daily News*, 21 May 1915, 6. The same went for Ilene Shaw in 1913. Arriving in San Francisco from Portland, she changed her "petticoats for trousers and took a job as a bell hop." "There seemed to be no way," she added, for "a girl to get a living wage and keep her womanhood." See *Portland News*, 3 July 1913, 6.

52. *San Francisco Call*, 24 May 1903, 18.

53. *Oakland Tribune*, 12 February 1915, 9.

54. *Reno (Nevada) Evening Gazette*, 11 February 1881, 2. Along similar lines, in 1900 in Sausalito, California, where gambling resorts did not permit women, Alberta La Moyne, who had something of a gaming addiction, grew weary of losing money to men she asked to place bets for her who then would abscond with her winnings. So, she dressed as one herself and thereby gained access to pool halls, where she had more control over her losses; she gave free rein to her gambling habit and quickly went into debt. See *Anaconda Standard*, 22 July 1900, 12.

55. *St. Louis Globe-Democrat*, 11 October 1876, 5.

56. Denver, *Rocky Mountain News*, 5 April 1892, 2; *Albuquerque Morning Democrat*, 6 April 1892, 3.

Not all such holdups occurred in rural settings, nor in Arizona: in Los Angeles in 1914, a bandit held up a streetcar, liberating watches and money from the conductor and motorman. The two shaken victims reported their belief that the "bold highway man was really a woman": although dressed as a man, she wore a "flimsy lace handkerchief as a mask," which gave away her identity. See *Oakland Tribune*, 12 December 1914, 7.

57. *Idaho Statesman*, 16 September 1912, 1.

58. *Cheyenne Daily Sun*, 15 July 1878, 2 (quoted); *Central City (Colorado) Weekly Register-Call*, 26 July 1878, 1.

59. *Galveston (Texas) Daily News*, 27 November 1892, 2; Correctville, Iowa, *Sioux Valley News*, 1 December 1892, 1; *Castle Rock (Colorado) Journal*, 7 December 1892, 2; *Idaho Statesman*, 27 November 1892, 1.

Not all horse-stealing crimes took place in the Southwest. Roseburg, Oregon's eighteen-year-old Myrtle Tipton, who reportedly preferred men's to women's attire, was arrested in Colfax, Washington, in 1905; the ingrate stole three horses, a wagon, and a harness from a Coeur d'Alene Indian man in Idaho who had recently employed her as a male farmhand. See *Portland Oregonian*, 31 October 1905, 4.

Some female-to-male cross-dressers proved inveterate criminals. Nina Patchens, described in papers as quite an accomplished masquerader as well as a "short-haired morphine and snuff fiend," stole, burglarized, picked pockets, and may have even poisoned a man all in the Denver area in the 1890s. See *Rocky Mountain News*, 13 January 1896, 6.

60. *Davenport (Iowa) Gazette*, 24 April 1883, 4.

61. For example, Della Earl came before Portland police in 1904, saying that she met a certain Frank Allen at a dance in Lansing, Michigan. Allen then compelled her to elope with him, dress in men's clothing, and travel first to Chicago, then by wagon to Iowa, and finally by boxcar out West. In Portland, Frank held Della captive. Living in a hut along the Willamette River, all the while disguised as a man, she subsisted by fishing. At night Frank tied her to his body, regularly beat her, infected her with "repulsive diseases," and threatened her life should she try to escape. See *San Francisco Call*, 23 September 1904, 6; *Portland Oregonian*, 23 September 1904, 8.

Similarly, after having been rescued from a freight train in Belleville, Kansas, Beatrice Fanning told the local police that she had become the captive of an abusive Cameron Keener. The two met in her hometown of Toledo, Ohio. Promising marriage, Keener forced Fanning to accompany him to Steamboat Springs, Colorado, where he claimed his mother lived. Fanning soon found her intended's intentions somewhat different from what he had originally professed. He burned her clothes and made her wear a set of his own. He beat her, choked her, and threatened to kill her. Near Topeka, Kansas, she finally got word to fellow tramps about her troubles and they successfully intervened in her favor. *Lincoln Evening News*, 7 July 1910, 6.

62. Loraine Moore of Butte, Montana, told officials in 1912 that one day her husband, William, returned from his job in the mines and mistreated her. So, she dressed as a boy, fled to Lewistown, Montana, and took a job there as an elevator operator. Everything went well, including dalliances with local girls to make her cover complete, until one day her disguise failed her. She was soon back in Butte, with authorities compelling her to try to patch things up with William. See *Anaconda Standard*, 5 May 1912, 1.

In North Dakota in 1911, in order to dump her husband and run off with a hired hand, Belmora Monserud cropped her hair and put on men's clothes. The disguise worked, but in time she grew weary of having to maintain it, not to mention laboring in the fields as a man with her paramour to support themselves. A visit to her sister in nearby Canada finally persuaded her to return to her husband. See *Grand Forks Herald*, 25 August 1911, 1.

63. *St. Louis (Missouri) Globe-Democrat*, 1 October 1878, 7. Similar was the case of a young couple from Columbus, Ohio, whom police arrested in Sacramento in 1875. The woman, who was dressed as a man at the time, claimed that her parents had tried to prevent her marriage and so she disguised herself and ran off with her lover. The couple planned to marry once they reached California. Suspicious of the story, Sacramento authorities compelled the two to get a license immediately. And then,

not wasting any time, the police held the wedding right at the station. *San Francisco Daily Evening Bulletin*, 8 April 1875, 1.

64. Cheyenne, *Wyoming Tribune*, 16 November 1906, 1.

65. *Portland Oregonian*, 23 December 1889, 2.

66. *Morning Oregonian*, 8 March 1889, 3.

67. Ibid.

68. *Portland Oregonian*, 23 December 1889, 2.

69. For example, in reporting on Sammy Williams's death in December 1908, the *Anaconda Standard*, 12 December 1908, 1, called him a "queer character." Inveterate cross-dresser Betty Ann Arnold was "a queer tramp woman," *Idaho Statesman*, 12 October 1892, 4; a lower Mississippi River female-to-male cross-dresser was "the queerest fish that ever was seen out of water," *Daily Alta California*, 22 February 1856, 1.

70. Lisa Duggan, *Sapphic Slashers: Sex, Violence, and American Modernity* (Durham, NC: Duke University Press), 2. See also Duggan, "The Trials of Alice Mitchell: Sensationalism, Sexology, and the Lesbian Subject in Turn-of-the-Century America," *Signs: Journal of Women in Culture & Society* 18, no. 4 (Summer 1993): 791–814.

These turn-of-the-century sexologists, moreover, as historian Lillian Faderman has shown, typically conflated cross-dressing with sexual inversion, failing to realize that women donned male clothing for all sorts of reasons. The medical community's findings influenced the broader populace. As such, by the end of the nineteenth century both would link cross-dressing to sexual inversion. By the onset of the twentieth century, the desire to dress as a man was seen to be as much of a masculine desire as was the romantic or sexual desire for women. See Lillian Faderman, *Odd Girls and Twilight Lovers*, 39–45.

71. St. Louis, *Daily Missouri Republican*, 23 April 1851, 2; Sarah Josepha Hale, *Woman's Record, Or, Sketches of All Distinguished Women*, 2nd ed. (New York: Harper & Brothers, 1855), 809–11.

72. *Aspen (Colorado) Daily Times*, 11 May 1889, 4.

73. *St. Louis Globe-Democrat*, 1 October 1878, 7.

74. Reno, *Daily Nevada State Journal*, 29 December 1879, 2.

75. *Helena (Montana) Independent*, 30 August 1882, 4.

76. *Galveston News*, 17 October 1891, 2.

77. *St. Louis Globe-Democrat*, 1 October 1878, 7; *Daily Nevada State Journal*, 29 December 1879, 2; *Helena Independent*, 30 August 1882, 4.

78. It should also be noted that censorship traditions and laws no doubt also affected, over time, how newspapers reported the sexual angle of cross-dresser stories. See Jennifer Terry, *An American Obsession: Science, Medicine, and Homosexuality in Modern Society* (Chicago: University of Chicago Press, 1999), 76–77.

79. *Sioux Valley News*, 22 October 1896, 4.

80. *Rocky Mountain News*, 12 October 1891, 1 (quoted); *Atchison (Kansas) Champion*, 5 November 1891, 7. The same arrest led to Clark's long-term incarceration. At that point, Helen reformed and became a missionary for the Salvation Army in Portland. After a while she drifted back to Helena. Still grieving over the loss of her

beloved, at least as newspapers tell it, she committed suicide there in 1896. See *Rocky Mountain News*, 12 October 1891, 1; *Atchison Champion*, 5 November 1891, 7; *Morning Oregonian*, 21 August 1892, 11; *Atchison Daily Globe*, 10 November 1896, 3.

81. *Morning Oregonian*, 21 August 1892, 11.

82. *Oakland Tribune*, 18 December 1912, 9.

83. *Helena Independent*, 7 September 1927, 16.

84. Portland Police Department's Women's Auxiliary Reports, 24 August 1911, Lola G. Baldwin Papers.

85. *Iowa City Citizen*, 10 September 1909, 3.

86. *Morning Oregonian*, 21 August 1892, 11.

87. *Helena Independent*, 7 September 1927, 16.

88. *Lincoln Daily News*, 17 July 1914, 9. Another instance, back in the mid-1890s, concerns Harrisburg, Nebraska's William J. Wallace. As a young woman, Wallace moved to the area with her aunt and uncle. To gain employment with the U.S. postal authority, she took on a male guise. She then found she had to keep up the deception, so much so that her behaviors became entirely those of a rogue, to the point of dissipation. William, papers reported, "could drink, chew, smoke and gamble and in fact led a decidedly fast life." Such behaviors made it difficult for those in the community to believe he was anything but a man—including a fellow who filed a divorce suit against his wife, claiming she had become too close of a friend with Wallace. Only the expert testimony of a few witnesses close to the cross-dresser convinced the community and the disaffected husband that Wallace indeed was a woman. As an aside, this paved the way for the divorce suit to be dropped and a happy reunion of husband and wife to be achieved. See Lincoln, *Nebraska State Journal*, 21 October 1901, 1.

89. *San Francisco Chronicle*, 2 January 1880, 3. In Parkhurst's case, the press in fact maintained that he had never had a love interest in another woman, though such a claim suggests a certain level of anxiety over the issue already at this early date.

90. *Atchison Daily Globe*, 22 February 1893, 1.

91. *Portland News*, 27 March 1914, 1.

92. *Helena Independent*, 30 November 1926, 3.

93. *Lincoln Evening News*, 17 January 1912, 1.

94. *Oakland Tribune*, 12 September 1913, 1.

95. On the New Woman and viraginity, see, for example, Lillian Faderman, *Odd Girls and Twilight Lovers*, 45–48; and James Weir Jr., "Viraginity and Effemination," *Medical Record* (16 September 1893): 359–60. On New Women and sexual perversion generally, see Terry, *An American Obsession*, 97–100.

96. *New York Times*, 6 November 1885, 4.

97. *Oakland Tribune*, 20 November 1912, 1.

98. *Washington Times*, 23 February 1908, Magazine Section, 7; *Minneapolis Journal*, 30 December 1901, 3.

99. *Morning Oregonian*, 4 June 1912, 12.

100. *Oakland Tribune*, 1 November 1912, 1.

101. *San Francisco Chronicle*, 27 January 1895, 14; *San Francisco Morning Call*, 27 January 1895, 4, and 28 January 1895, 1; *San Francisco Examiner*, 28 January 1895, 12; and 29 January 1895, 3; *San Francisco Chronicle*, 29 January 1895, 9; *San Francisco Examiner*, 30 January 1895, 3; *San Francisco Morning Call*, 30 January 1895, 6; *San Francisco Examiner*, 7 February 1895, 16, and 10 February 1895, 26.

102. *San Francisco Chronicle*, 27 January 1895, 14.

103. *San Francisco Morning Call*, 28 January 1895, 1.

104. *San Francisco Examiner*, 7 February 1895, 16, and 10 February 1895, 26.

105. *San Francisco Morning Call*, 30 January 1895, 6.

106. *San Francisco Examiner*, 7 February 1895, 16.

107. *Oakland Tribune*, 3 September 1915, 1.

108. *San Jose Mercury News*, 2 September 1915, 1; Wilbur Fisk Stone, ed., *History of Colorado*, vol. 1 (Chicago: S. J. Clarke Publishing, 1918), 689, 690.

109. *San Jose (California) Evening News*, 3 September 1915, 3 (quoted); and *Oakland Tribune*, 3 September 1915, 1.

110. *Oakland Tribune*, 3 September 1915, 1; *San Jose Mercury News*, 2 September 1915, 1–2.
About the same time, when local authorities learned that cobbler Ray Leonard of Lebanon, Oregon, had a female body, they forced him to wear dresses, eventually even remanding him to the state asylum for treatment. Newspapers reported that upon release from the Oregon State Hospital Leonard was "cured." But after having attired himself and lived as a man for nearly a half century, Leonard was not ready to give up what he felt was his true identity. He continued to wear trousers, but beneath his assigned skirts. He also once protested to local physician Mary Rowland, as Rowland herself recounted in her memoirs, "Look at me, Dr. Rowland, do you think I have one feminine feature?" Rowland had to admit, with no reluctance, that Leonard in fact did look like a man. See *Portland Oregonian*, 15 November 1911, 1; Mary Canaga Rowland, *As Long as Life: The Memoirs of a Frontier Woman Doctor, Mary Canaga Rowland, 1873–1966*, edited with a foreword by F. A. Loomis (Seattle: Storm Peak, 1994), 107.

111. This also is the case with Artie Baker, who ended up in San Quentin prison in 1916 on a fourteen-year sentence for various crimes. Baker reportedly masqueraded as a man his whole life. His well-worn disguise not only made it easier for him to avoid detection after numerous instances of defrauding and robbing California banks, but also made it possible for him to be sent to prison as a man for some time before flustered officials discovered his female body. See *San Francisco Daily News*, 12 August 1916, 1.

112. *Stockton (California) Evening Mail*, 17 September 1897, 6.

113. See various articles in *Stockton Evening Mail*, 2 August 1897, 1, through 16 May 1898, 8; and Louis Sullivan, *From Female to Male: The Life of Jack Bee Garland* (Boston: Alyson, 1990).

114. *Stockton Evening Mail*, 9 December 1897, 5.

115. Beebe Beam, "My Life as a Soldier," *San Francisco Sunday Examiner Magazine*, 21 October 1900, n.p. See also James G. Hutcheson, "Was It Jack Bee

Garland on City of Para?" letter to the editor, *San Francisco Chronicle*, 24 September 1936, 10.

116. "Death Ends Charities, 'Samaritan' Garland Succumbs, 'Jack Bee' Was Woman," *San Francisco Chronicle*, 21 September 1936, 1; *Oakland Tribune*, 22 September 1936, 4.

117. *San Francisco Chronicle*, 2 January 1880, 3 (quoted); *Providence (Rhode Island) Daily Journal*, 22 January 1880, 4; *Nevada State Journal*, 4 January 1880, 2. For more on Charley Parkhurst, see Ed Sams, *The Real Mountain Charley* (Ben Lomond, CA: Yellow Tulip Press, 1995); Craig MacDonald, *Cockeyed Charley Parkhurst: The West's Most Unusual Stagewhip* (Palmer Lake, CO: Filter Press, 1973); and Mary Chaney Hoffman, "Whips of the Old West," *American Mercury* 84, no. 399 (April 1957): 107–10.

118. *Trinidad (Colorado) Advertiser*, 12 November 1907, 1, 6 (tells of the nuns' naming him "Grandpa"); *Tucson Daily Citizen*, 25 October 1905, 1; *Eagle (Colorado) Valley Enterprise*, 15 November 1907, 5; Castle Dale, Utah, *Emery County Progress*, 16 November 1907, 4.

119. *Eagle Valley Enterprise*, 15 November 1907, 5.

120. Rowland, *As Long as Life*, 107. See also Manuscript Population Census Returns, Linn County, Oregon, 1910, Enumeration District 195, Sheet 11B, line 64.

121. *Santa Cruz (California) Sentinel*, 10 January 1880, 3.

122. Because so many could not believe Pollard was a woman, a news story published Marancy's sworn affidavit to the fact. See *San Francisco Bulletin*, 24 May 1878, 4. A later report claimed that Marancy retracted her statement and then reunited with Pollard, to the chagrin of local men hoping that she would soon be back on the market, "as woman are scarce in that mining town." *Cincinnati Daily Gazette*, 14 June 1878, 4 (quoted); *Kalamazoo (Michigan) Gazette*, 11 August 1880, 2.

123. 3 January 1880, 3.

124. 10 January 1880, 1.

125. 15 June 1878, 2.

126. *Nevada State Journal*, 7 May 1879, 2. Silver City, Idaho's *Owyhee Avalanche* also "ridiculed the story as a hoax." But some years later the editor of Tuscarora's *Times-Review* provided a sincere defense of the account as true. See *Owhyee Avalanche*, 12 April 1879, 3; and *Salt Lake Tribune*, 12 November 1885, 6. The 1880 federal census also shows an S. M. Pollard, listed as a male, living in the Tuscarora area. See Manuscript Population Census Returns, Elko County, Nevada, 1800, Enumeration District 4, page 4, line 2.

127. "What is it" is used in *Owyhee Avalanche*, 12 April 1879, 3; *Nevada State Journal*, 7 May 1879, 2; *Nevada State Journal*, 14 August 1879, 2; *Kalamazoo Gazette*, 11 August 1880, 2 (quoted as the "Tuscarora What-Is-It"); *Reno Evening Gazette*, 10 January 1881, 3. "Man-woman" is used in *Owyhee Avalanche*, 3 May 1879, 3; and *Nevada State Journal*, 26 June 1884, 3.

128. *Meeker (Colorado) Herald*, 20 September 1913, clipping in Marriage and Obituary files, Meeker Public Library.

129. *Yuma (Colorado) Pioneer*, 6 October 1911, 3 (quoted); *Wray (Colorado) Rattler*, 5 October 1911, 1.

130. *Meeker Harold*, 20 September 1913, clipping in Marriage and Obituary files, Meeker Public Library.

131. Ibid., 25 November 1912.

132. Ibid., 27 September 1913.

133. Ibid., 20 September 1913. Other information in this paragraph is from *Summit County Journal and Breckenridge (Colorado) Bulletin*, 26 September 1913, 8; Golden, *Colorado Transcript*, 25 September 1913, 3. For an examination of a Texas physician's use of medical language to explain female homosexuality in his 1895 western dime novel, *Norma Trist; or, Pure Carbon: A Story of the Inversion of the Sexes*, see Kim Emery, "Steers, Queers, and Manifest Destiny: Representing the Lesbian Subject in Turn-of-the-Century Texas," *Journal of the History of Sexuality* 5 (July 1994): 26–57.

CHAPTER 2

1. The following story and quotations are from Case II that B. S. Talmey related on pages 365–66 of "Transvestism: A Contribution to the Study of the Psychology of Sex," *New York Medical Journal* 99 (February 21, 1914): 362–68.

2. *Littleton (Colorado) Independent*, 31 January 1913, 3. Though this story may seem farcical, the U.S. census lends it credence. The 1910 census for Victor, Colorado, lists the husband and wife Tim and Mary Manahan, who had been married for twenty-four years. During that time, Mary had given birth to seven children, five of whom were living when the census was taken. Of these, four were listed in the Manahan household. The oldest child living with Tim and Mary at the time was a son named Willie, who was sixteen. The second oldest was Irene, a daughter, who was listed as fourteen years old, the very age the Moynihan son-turned-daughter described in the 1913 news account would have been. Newspapers of the period often mangled names and so while the press reported in January 1913 that Irene was the mother, in fact Irene may very well have been the youth who caused so much consternation. Additionally, the 1900 census, which has the Manahans living in Salt Lake City, Utah, shows another son, Daniel, who was older than either William or Irene. So, Mary had at least two sons before Irene was born. In 1920, Tim and Mary were living in Cochise County, Arizona (recall from the news story that the Moynihan son/daughter was on his/her way to Arizona in 1913 to visit his/her father). Unfortunately, the censuses' Manahan family was without their "daughter" Irene in 1920 and there is no son her age (so we cannot check up on what sex she was going by then). See U.S. Department of Commerce, Bureau of the Census, Fourteenth Census, 1920, Manuscript Population Census Returns, Cochise County, Arizona, Enumeration District 31, Sheet No. 16B, line 100, and Sheet No. 17A, lines 1 through 4; U.S. Department of Commerce, Bureau of the Census, Thirteenth Census, 1910, Manuscript Population Census Returns, Teller County, Colorado, Enumeration District 188, Sheet No. 4B, lines 58 through 63; U.S. Department of Commerce, Bureau of

the Census, Twelfth Census, 1900, Manuscript Population Census Returns, Salt Lake County, Utah, Enumeration District 25, Sheet No. 9B, lines 82 through 87.

3. In fact, for many years beyond the 1910s, the medical profession, especially psychoanalysts, as well as the general public would continue to associate cross-dressing with same-sex sexuality. See Vern L. Bullough and Bonnie Bullough, *Cross Dressing, Sex, and Gender* (Philadelphia: University of Pennsylvania Press, 1993), 207–21, 253.

4. Denver, *Rocky Mountain News*, 2 July 1883, n.p.

5. George D. Dornin, *Thirty Years Ago: Gold Rush Memories of a Daguerreotype Artist*, ed. Peter E. Palmquist (Nevada City, CA: Carl Mautz Publishing, 1995), 21, 6.

6. Boise, *Idaho Statesman*, 24 February 1868, 2.

7. J. D. Borthwick left what has become a classic description of an all-male miners' dance, though this one in California's Angel's Camp in 1852 did not have any men dressed in women's clothing. "Dancing parties such as these were very common, especially in small camps," Borthwick explained. "Wherever a fiddler could be found to play, a dance was got up." Borthwick's dance was attended solely by "long-bearded men, in heavy boots and flannel shirts." But none dressed as women; rather, those who played the part of the "ladies" wore canvas patches over their "inexpressibles." "These patches" Borthwick described as "rather fashionable, and were usually large squares . . . showing up brightly on a dark [back]ground." J. D. Borthwick, *Three Years in California* (Edinburgh and London: William Blackwood and Sons, 1857), 320, 321.

8. Hikozo [Hamada], *Hyoryu Ki: Floating on the Pacific Ocean*, trans. from the 1863 edition by Tosh Motofuji (Los Angeles: Glen Dawson, 1955), 23–28 (28 quoted). Western observer J. D. Borthwick also witnessed such a San Francisco masquerade. "The company was just as might be seen in any gambling-room," Borthwick related, "save for "the presence of a half-dozen-masks in female attire." He felt the charade well worth attending if only to watch the men being stripped at the door of all manner of weapons, from bowie knives to pistols, that they tried to smuggle into the affair. See Borthwick, *Three Years in California*, 77 (quoted), 78.

9. Bullough and Bullough, *Cross Dressing, Sex, and Gender*, 232–33; Robert C. Toll, *Blacking Up: The Minstrel Show in Nineteenth-Century America* (New York: Oxford University Press, 1974), 139–45; Sharon Ullman, *Sex Seen: The Emergence of Modern Sexuality in America* (Berkeley: University of California Press, 1997), 40; Anthony Slide, *The Vaudevillians: A Dictionary of Vaudeville Performers* (Westport, CT: Arlington House, 1981), 50; F. Michael Moore, *Drag! Male and Female Impersonators on Stage, Screen and Television* (Jefferson, NC: McFarland & Company, 1994), 55–86.

10. San Francisco, *California Star & Californian*, 9 December 1848, 3; *San Francisco Daily Evening Bulletin*, 5 June 1858, 1; Edwin Le Roy Rice, *Monarchs of Minstrelsy, from "Daddy" Rice to Date* (New York: Kenny Publishing, 1911), 68. Some historians place the first San Francisco blackface minstrel shows in 1849, but the 1848 newspaper listed above advertises for one already in the year before. See Lynn M. Hudson, "Entertaining Citizenship: Masculinity and Minstrelsy in Post-Emancipation San Francisco," *Journal of African American History* 93, no. 2 (Spring 2008): 178, 180.

11. *Sacramento (California) Daily Union*, 10 August 1857, 3

12. Rice, *Monarchs of Minstrelsy*, 180.

13. Pueblo, *Colorado Daily Chieftain*, 14 June 1876, 2.

14. Richard Erdoes, *Saloons of the Old West* (New York: Alfred A. Knopf, 1979), 172.

15. Bismarck *(North Dakota) Daily Tribune*, 29 May 1886, 3.

16. *Portland Oregonian*, 23 October 1889, 6.

17. Portland, *Morning Oregonian*, 31 August 1891, 5.

18. *Daily Central City (Colorado) Register*, 4 June 1871, 4

19. *Reno Evening Gazette*, 9 September 1882, 3.

20. San Francisco, *Daily Alta California*, 6 May 1852, 2.

21. *San Francisco Daily Evening Bulletin*, 18 March 1870, 3.

22. Ibid., 21 September 1874, 4.

23. Ibid., 14 December 1874, 1.

24. *Daily Alta California*, 26 December 1875, 1.

25. *San Francisco Daily Evening Bulletin*, 7 August 1879, 3.

26. Ibid., 20 February 1882, 3; U.S. Department of Commerce, Bureau of the Census, Tenth Census, 1880, Manuscript Population Census Returns, San Francisco County, California, Enumeration District 16, page 15, lines 36 and 37.

27. *San Francisco Call*, 2 November 1907, 15.

28. *Galveston (Texas) Daily News*, 21 April 1881, 1.

29. *Atchison (Kansas) Daily Globe*, 12 December 1884, 4.

30. Ibid., 2 January 1891, 4.

31. *Rocky Mountain News*, 9 October 1891, 3.

32. *Morning Oregonian*, 13 September 1892, 5.

33. *Atchison Daily Globe*, 2 December 1895, 1.

34. *Bismarck Daily Tribune*, 18 August 1896, 2.

35. *San Antonio Daily Express*, 21 October 1903, 8.

36. *Anaconda (Montana) Standard*, 24 July 1901, 8.

37. Willard's troupe got into an altercation with another young man on the street and when Willard told their antagonist to "go to Helena," he received a severe beating. See *Anaconda Standard*, 25 July 1906, 12.

38. *Fort Worth Morning Register*, 13 December 1901, 7.

39. *Sacramento Daily Union*, 9 May 1859, 2.

40. *San Francisco Daily Evening Bulletin*, 17 January 1877, 3.

41. Ibid., 7 August 1879, 3.

42. *Omaha World Herald*, 20 February 1893, 2. Also on a fling in 1890, sons of three of Southern California's finer families, one dressed in heels and a "fashionable French dress with poodle, paint and black stockings," drove about Los Angeles in a carriage. Apparently passing under the nose of unsuspecting police, the threesome might have escaped detection had a quarrel not broken out among them. See *Los Angeles Times*, 25 October 1890, 3.

A year later in San Francisco, police there arrested John Harvey, described as a "'funny' young man who enjoys a joke." He dressed in women's clothing to fool his friends on the street, but he did not fool the police, and paid a steep $50 fine. See *San Francisco Daily Evening Bulletin*, 2 July 1891, 3.

It seems that joking cross-dressers kept the San Francisco police particularly busy in 1891, as later that year they nicked fourteen-year-old John Wilsey for parading on the streets in female attire. Apparently he did so as part of a birthday-party prank. See *San Francisco Daily Evening Bulletin*, 3 September 1891, 2.

43. *Fort Worth Morning Register*, 13 December 1901, 7.

44. *St. Louis Globe-Democrat*, 22 January 1877, 2.

45. *Rocky Mountain News*, 7 March 1886, 8. Other such cases include Charles Latterner, wanted for forgery in Durango, Colorado, in 1893, who made his escape to Santa Fe by wearing women's clothing. But recognized by those who knew him on the streets of the New Mexico town, he soon found himself behind bars awaiting extradition to the north. See *Santa Fe New Mexican*, 9 October 1893, 4.

In September 1898, police in San Jose, California, found themselves searching for a person disguised as a woman and who passed a counterfeit five-dollar piece at a local millinery shop. The person turned out not to be a woman at all, but a man with a big, bushy wig and women's clothing. Apparently he had worked several stores in the area and then returned to his lodgings, where he made a quick change of clothing. See *San Jose Evening News*, 16 September 1898, 5.

Back in 1886, and while on their way to one of San Francisco's masquerade balls one winter's evening, three young men, including A. J. Fisk, who costumed himself as a woman, stopped off at a saloon for a drink. Shortly after Fisk "flirted" there with a young Frenchman by the name of M. Pousche, the three partygoers continued on to the ball while Pousche found his wallet with its contents of $18.50 missing. The Frenchman immediately made his own way to the ball and there told the policeman at the door his suspicions. The officer suggested Pousche ask Fisk to dance. As a newspaper reported, he did and the "promenade" ended at the police station, where Fisk found himself charged with grand larceny and appearing on the streets in female attire. See *San Francisco Daily Bulletin*, 3 February 1886, 2.

46. *Lincoln (Nebraska) Evening Star*, 6 September 1923, 4. Other reports of men dressing in women's clothing to escape from jail or prison include those contained in the *Oakland (California) Tribune*, 19 October 1913, 17, and 31 March 1915, 20; and *Reno Evening Gazette*, 28 July 1916, 9.

47. *Bismarck Daily Tribune*, 15 October 1885, 3.

48. *Denver Evening Post*, 3 January 1898, 5.

49. *Anaconda Standard*, 18 July 1905, 7.

50. Ibid., 1 September 1906, 13.

51. *Omaha World Herald*, 9 July 1899, 28.

52. *San Francisco Call*, 16 April 1895, 7 (quoted), 17 April 1895, 11, and 3 July 1895, 8 (quoted).

53. *Anaconda Standard*, 1 January 1914, 4.

54. Ibid.

55. *San Francisco Call*, 3 July 1895, 8.

56. Talmey, "Transvestism," 366.

57. For example, San Francisco's *Daily Evening Bulletin*, on 14 December 1874, 1, reported that John Roberts "has a mania" for parading in the streets in female attire. Jennifer Terry, *An American Obsession: Science, Medicine, and Homosexuality in Modern America* (Chicago: University of Chicago Press, 1999), 77, explains how medical doctors of the era also equated sexual perversion with lunacy.

58. *Reno Evening Gazette*, 15 October 1906, 3.

59. *Anaconda Standard*, 28 February 1913, 3.

60. *Rocky Mountain News*, 1 November 1889, 3.

61. *Anaconda Standard*, 28 February 1913, 3.

62. *Denver Evening Post*, 3 January 1898, 5.

63. Ullman, *Sex Seen*, 45–71, 150 fn. 6 (quoted).

64. Ibid., 51, 56–57 (quoted), 58–59. On Bothwell Browne as well as Julian Eltinge and sexuality and gender performance, see also Slide, *The Vaudevillians*, 17–18, 46–47. On the general issue of female impersonators needing to emphasize their masculinity offstage, see also Bullough and Bullough, *Cross Dressing, Sex, and Gender*, 237.

65. *Atchison Globe*, 4 November 1880, 3.

66. Albert Barrère and Charles G. Leland, *A Dictionary of Slant, Jargon & Cant* (London: Bell & Sons, 1897), 77–78; *A Standard Dictionary of the English Language* (New York: Funk & Wagnalls, 1895), 1176. On Nancy Dawson, see Julie Peakman, Alexander Pettit, and Patrick Spedding, eds., *Whore Biographies, 1700–1825*, vol. 4 (London: Pickering & Chatto, 2006), 287–390.

67. *Atchison Daily Globe*, 17 December 1884, 4.

68. See *The Alyson Almanac: A Treasury of Information for the Gay and Lesbian Community* (Boston: Alyson, 1990), 129.

69. *Atchison Daily Globe*, 5 October 1885, 3.

70. Ibid., 3 October 1885, 4.

71. Ibid., 15 December 1890, 1.

72. *Omaha Daily Bee*, 29 November 1884, 8.

73. *Bismarck Daily Tribune*, 7 October 1899, 3.

74. *Atchison Daily Champion*, 26 February 1889, 7.

75. *Oakland Tribune*, 15 November 1907, 12.

76. *San Jose Evening News*, 25 January 1907, 5.

77. The same holds true for elsewhere in the western world at about the same time. For example, the 1870 Boulton-Park case in London, wherein two men publicly paraded in women's clothes, propositioned other men for sexual relations, and participated in female impersonation on the stage, raised public concerns about how these all blended together about a decade before western Americans expressed similar concern. The Boulton-Park case also appeared in the western regional press, sometimes in lurid detail, already initiating the public there to anxieties raised locally in the next decade. On Boulton-Park and on- and offstage female impersonation and homosexuality, see Laurence Senelick, "Boys and Girls Together: Subcultural Origins of Glamour Drag and Male Impersonation on the Nineteenth-Century Stage," in

Crossing the Stage: Controversies on Cross-Dressing, ed. Lesley Ferris (London: Routledge Press, 1993), 86–88. An example of the extensive coverage of the Boulton-Park case in the American West is *Sacramento Daily Union*, 4 July 1870, 3.

78. *Rocky Mountain News*, 2 July 1883, 1.

79. Ibid., 1 November 1889, 3.

80. *Omaha World Herald*, 21 May 1891, 6.

81. *Atchison Daily Globe*, 28 May 1891, 4.

82. Elizabeth Jameson, *All That Glitters: Class, Conflict, and Community in Cripple Creek* (Urbana: University of Illinois Press, 1998), 38–39; Elizabeth Jameson, "Of Cabbages and Queens: Gender in the Hardrock American West," *Book of Proceedings, 5th International Mining History Congress*, Milos Island, Greece, 12–15 September 2000, ed. J. E. Fell, D. Nocolaou, and G. D. Xydous (Milos, Greece: Milos Conference Center—George Eliopoulos, 2001), 480–82. I wish to acknowledge Professor Elizabeth Jameson's assistance with this case. McPherson's exact identity is unknown, though the 1900 census, which Professor Jameson has pointed out undercounted miners in the Cripple Creek area, does list a "Dugless McPherson" as a resident of Altman, the town where 1901 news items always placed him. He is living with his "pardner" (a not unusual designation for the relationship miners provided the census enumerator), William Millar, who was thirty-eight at the time and also an immigrant from Scotland. A news item in the Cripple Creek and Victor, Colorado, *Daily Press*, 26 July 1901, 5, explains that "Billy Mercer" and McPherson threw a dinner party at their home for friends. The closeness of the names in the newspaper in 1901 and the census in 1900 leads me to the tentative conclusion that "Dugless McPherson" is Countess McPherson and Billy Mercer and William Millar are one and the same. See U.S. Department of Commerce, Bureau of the Census, Twelfth Census, 1900, Manuscript Population Census Returns, Teller County, Colorado, Enumeration District 124, Sheet 7A, lines 13 and 14. On the use of the term "partners" among miners, see Jameson, "Of Cabbages and Queens," 482.

83. Jameson, *All That Glitters*, 38–39; *Daily Press*, 14 July 1901, 5, 26 July 1901, 5, and 27 July 1901, 5.

84. *Daily Press*, 20 July 1901, 5.

85. Jameson, "Of Cabbages and Queens," 481.

86. On this issue, see George Chauncey, *Gay New York: Gender, Urban Culture, and the Making of the Gay Male World, 1890–1940* (New York: Basic Books, 1994), 47–97.

87. Ralph Werther—Jennie June ("Earl Lind"), *The Female Impersonators* (New York: Medico-Legal Journal, 1922), 253, fn. 1.

88. Ibid., 254, fn. 1.

89. Historians have demonstrated for the American West and elsewhere in the United States in the late nineteenth and early twentieth century that working-class men were relatively accepting of male-to-female transgendered identities and behaviors, and readily willing to participate in same-sex sexual activities under certain circumstances. See Chauncey, *Gay New York*.

90. The stories of these affairs are recounted in Peter Boag, *Same-Sex Affairs: Constructing and Controlling Homosexuality in the Pacific Northwest* (Berkeley: University of California Press, 2003), and Ullman, *Sex Seen*, 61–70.

91. *Denver Evening Post*, 25 April 1895, 2.

92. From the earliest years of exploration well into the nineteenth century, Europeans and Euro-Americans employed this particular meaning when they used the term for the Native American men they encountered and who wore women's clothing and participated in women's tasks and duties. For example, Joseph François Lafitau, a French missionary in Canada between 1711 and 1718, explained that Indian men who "dressed as women" confused the first explorers; they could not figure out why men would become women, save that they must be "hermaphrodites," individuals in which "the two sexes were confounded" (quoted in Jonathan Ned Katz, *Gay American History: Lesbians & Gay Men in the U.S.A., A Documentary History*, rev. ed. [New York: Meridian, 1992], 289). Also in the eighteenth century, Juan Agustín de Morfi in the Southwest discovered in one Indian nation "many boys ... whom the Spaniards of Béjar call hermaphrodites; but it is not known whether they are actually hermaphrodites or not" (see Father Juan Agustín de Morfi, *Excerpts from the Memorias for the History of the Province of Texas*, with a prologue, appendix, and notes by Frederick C. Chabot [San Antonio, Texas: Naylor Printing Company, 1932], 55).

Examples from the nineteenth century include Alexander Maximilian, Prince of Wied, who applied the term "hermaphrodite" to certain Crow men. In the 1850s, Edwin Thompson Denig did the same. And then in the early twentieth century, anthropologists also used "hermaphrodite" when discussing the Crow third-gender males. It is unclear if these various individuals meant hermaphrodite to mean one who had both female and male genitalia. But likely this is exactly what they meant, as suggested by William Hammond, an army physician stationed among the Pueblo in the early 1850s who had the chance to examine a male-to-female person among the Laguna. He explained that when he inspected his patient's genitals, he fully "expected to see some form of hermaphrodism, or at least cryptorchism." The persistence of this expectation continued in the work of at least one anthropologist in 1911. He wrote, "It is said that the Indian name for these persons, *who are invariably supposed to be* hermaphrodites, is translated 'split testicles.'" See William A. Hammond, "The Disease of the Scythians (Morbus Feminarum) and Certain Analogous Conditions," *American Journal of Neurology and Psychiatry* 1, no. 3 (August 1882): 345. Also see Alexander Maximilian, Prince of Wied, *Travels in the Interior of North America: 1832–1834*, vol. 22 of *Early Western Travels, 1748–1846*, edited with notes, introduction, and index by Reuben Gold Thwaites (Cleveland, Ohio: A. H. Clark, 1904–1907), Part I, 354; Edwin Thompson Denig, *Five Indian Tribes of the Upper Missouri*, edited with an introduction by John C. Ewers (Norman: University of Oklahoma Press, 1961), 187; S. C. Simms, "Crow Indian Hermaphrodite," *American Anthropologist*, new series, 5, no. 3 (July–September 1903): 580; Alanson Skinner, *Notes of the Eastern Cree and Northern Saulteaux*, Anthropological Papers of the American Museum of Natural History, vol. 9, pt. 1 (New York: The Trustees, 1911), 151.

93. On hermaphroditism in nineteenth-century America, see Elizabeth Reis, *Bodies in Doubt: An American History of Intersex* (Baltimore, MD: Johns Hopkins University Press, 2009), esp. 23–81.

94. Werther—June ("Earl Lind"), *The Female Impersonators*, 254, fn. 1.

95. *Omaha World Herald*, 4 April 1890, 8.

96. Oklahoma City, *Daily Oklahoman*, 21 May 1913, 10.

97. *Longmont (Colorado) Ledger*, 24 November 1911, 2; Fairbanks, *Alaska Citizen*, 1 January 1912, 7.

98. *Portland Oregonian*, 21 May 1913, 1.

99. *Daily Oklahoman*, 21 May 1913, 10.

100. Ibid., 21 May 1913, 10.

101. *Lincoln Evening News*, 4 October 1901, 1; Lincoln, *Nebraska State Journal*, 5 October 1901, 4.

102. *Lincoln (Nebraska) Evening News*, 4 October 1901, 1, and 5 October 1901, 4.

103. Ibid., 4 October 1901, 1, and 4 October 1901, 1; Harrisburg, Nebraska, *Banner County News*, 11 October 1904, 4.

104. *Nebraska State Journal*, 5 October 1901, 4; *Ashland (Nebraska) Gazette*, 11 October 1901, 5; *Nebraska State Journal*, 8 October 1901, 5.

105. *Nebraska State Journal*, 6 October 1901, 1; Bassett, Nebraska, *Rock County Leader*, 11 October 1901, 1; *Lincoln Evening News*, 4 October 1901, 1; *Nebraska State Journal*, 4 October 1901, 1.

106. *Nebraska State Journal*, 5 October 1901, 4.

107. *Senate Journal of the Legislature, 1903* (Lincoln, NE: State Journal Company, 1903), 96.

108. Nebraska, Bert Martin, Inmate #3656, Department of Correctional Services State Penitentiary, Descriptive Record of Inmates, vol. 2, January 7, 1891–December 17, 1902, #1883-4010, microfilm RG86, Nebraska State Historical Society, Lincoln.

109. U.S. Department of Commerce, Bureau of the Census, Tenth Census, 1880, Manuscript Population Census Returns, Nodaway County, Missouri, Enumeration District 256, page 10, lines 46, 47, 48; *Nebraska State Journal*, 8 October 1901, 5.

110. *Nebraska State Journal*, 6 October 1901, 1.

111. *Lincoln Evening News*, 4 October 1901, 1.

112. Reis, *Bodies in Doubt*, 32–33.

113. Des Moines, *Daily Iowa State Register*, 16 February 1868, 2.

114. U.S. Department of Commerce, Bureau of the Census, Twelfth Census, 1900, Manuscript Population Census Returns, Saunders County, Nebraska, Enumeration District 122, Sheet 18B, lines 56 and 57.

115. Ibid., Thirteenth Census, 1910, Manuscript Population Census Returns, Woodbury County, Iowa, Enumeration District 168, Sheet 13A, lines 3–6.

116. Ibid., Fourteenth Census, 1920, Manuscript Population Census Returns, Otoe County, Nebraska, Enumeration District 131, Sheet 2A, lines 9–12.

117. Chicago, *Inter Ocean*, 9 November 1878, 4.

118. Werther—June ("Earl Lind"), *The Female Impersonators*, 253–54, fn. 1.

CHAPTER 3

Portions of this chapter first appeared in "Go West Young Man, Go East Young Woman: Searching for the *Trans* in Western Gender History," *Western Historical Quarterly* 36 (Winter 2005): 477–97. Copyright by the Western History Association. Reprinted by permission.

1. *Boise (Idaho) Evening Capital News*, 13 January 1904, 1, 5; Boise, *Idaho Daily Statesman*, 19 June 1904, 5, and 12 January 1904, 1; U.S. Department of Commerce, Bureau of the Census, Twelfth Census, 1900, Manuscript Population Census Returns, Malheur County, Oregon, Enumeration District 26, page 4A, lines 2–7.

2. *Boise Evening Capital News*, 13 January 1904, 5.

3. U.S. Department of Commerce, Bureau of the Census, Ninth Census, 1870, Manuscript Population Census Returns, Silver City, Owyhee County, Idaho Territory, page 17, line 27; U.S. Department of Commerce, Bureau of the Census, Tenth Census, 1880, Manuscript Population Census Returns, Owyhee County, Idaho Territory, Enumeration District 29, page 19, line 46, lists Monahan's birthplace as England; Silver City, Idaho Territory's *Owyhee Avalanche* on 8 May 1875 (p. 2), 18 December 1875 (p. 3), 28 April 1877 (p. 2), 11 August 1877 (p. 2), and 25 May 1878 (p. 2) lists "Monahan J" having not picked up letters at the Silver City post office; *Owyhee Avalanche*, 4 September 1880, 3, notes that Monahan voted in the Republican primary; *Idaho Daily Statesman*, 19 June 1904, 5, for example, carries a notice of the sale of the cattle from Monahan's estate.

4. *Buffalo (New York) Evening News*, Three O'clock Edition, 11 January 1904, 1.

5. Ibid., Five O'clock Edition, 12 January 1904, 1.

6. *Idaho Daily Statesman*, 13 January 1904, 5; *Boise Evening Capital News*, 13 January 1904, 5.

7. Some female-to-male cross-dressers did indeed borrow the names of real people they knew. Back in 1900, for instance, Seattle's Nell Pickerell roomed in a home where also resided a boy whose name, Harry Livingstone, Pickerell soon assumed. U.S. Department of Commerce, Bureau of the Census, Twelfth Census, 1900, Manuscript Population Census Returns, King County, Washington, Enumeration District 100, page 13A, lines 40–41.

8. U.S. Department of Commerce, Bureau of the Census, Eighth Census, 1860, Manuscript Population Census Returns, 8th Ward, City of Buffalo, Erie County, New York, page 102, lines 6–10. Sources placing Monahan's arrival in Silver City in 1867 include *Idaho Daily Statesman*, 13 January 1904, 5, and *Owyhee Avalanche*, 15 January 1904, 4.

9. *Idaho Daily Statesman*, 12 January 1904, 1, and 9 April 1904, 6 (quoted).

10. *Buffalo Evening News*, Three O'clock Edition, 11 January 1904, 1; *Idaho Daily Statesman*, 12 January 1904, 1, and 13 January 1904, 5; *Boise Evening Capital News*, 13 January 1904, 1, 5; *Olympia (Washington) Record*, 14 January 1904, 1; *Owyhee Avalanche*, 15 January 1904, 4.

11. *Olympia Record*, 14 January 1904, 1.

12. *Buffalo Evening News*, Three O'clock Edition, 11 January 1904, 1.

13. U.S. Department of Commerce, Bureau of the Census, Tenth Census, 1880, Manuscript Population Census Returns, Owyhee County, Idaho Territory, Enumeration District 29, page 19, line 46, and page 20, line 3.

14. *Buffalo Evening News*, Three O'clock Edition, 11 January 1904, 1.

15. *Owyhee Avalanche*, 20 March 1875, 3 (quoted), and 5 August 1875, 3.

16. Ibid., 3 October 1891, 3.

17. *Buffalo Evening News*, Three O'clock Edition, 11 January 1904, 1.

18. For example, "Desperate Women," *New York Post*, 21 December 1952, clipping in Joe Monahan File, Idaho State Historical Society, Boise; *Idaho Statesman*, 24 January 1954, clipping in Joe Monahan File, Idaho State Historical Society; Mildretta Adams, *Historic Silver City: The Story of the Owyhees* (Homedale, ID: Owyhee Chronicle, 1960), 56–59; Vardis Fisher and Opal Laurel Holmes, *Gold Rushes and Mining Camps of the Early American West* (Caldwell, ID: Caxton, 1968), 109; Roger Rickert, "Little Jo," *Frontier Times* 45 (July 1971): 39, 52–53; Betty Penson, "Death Ended Cowboys' Masquerade," *Idaho Statesman*, 17 December 1978, clipping in Joe Monahan File, Idaho State Historical Society; Betty Penson, "Little Joe, Idaho Cowboy with a Secret: Part II," *Idaho Statesman*, 4 February 1979, clipping in Joe Monahan File, Idaho State Historical Society.

19. *Little Joe Monaghan* (1981).

20. Free Line Features, 1993.

21. The *American Journal Examiner*'s "Cowboy Jo—Was a Woman!" appeared in, for example, Denver's *Rocky Mountain News*, 23 March 1904, clipping in Joe Monahan File, Idaho State Historical Society.

22. Ibid.

23. *Helena (Montana) Independent*, 15 March 1884, 5.

24. On the general contours of eighteenth- and nineteenth-century American literature, including the role of sensation and seduction in it, see Jane Tompkins, *Sensational Designs: The Cultural World of American Fiction, 1790–1860* (New York: Oxford University Press, 1985), and Nina Baym, *Woman's Fiction: A Guide to Novels By and About Women in America, 1820–1870* (Ithaca, NY: Cornell University Press, 1978). On western dime-novel cross-dressers and their character development as related to the domestic seduction novel, see Nicole Tonkovich, "Guardian Angels and Missing Mothers: Race and Domesticity in Winona and Deadwood Dick on Deck," *Western American Literature* 32, no. 3 (Fall 1997): 240–64. On the seduction novel in the eighteenth- and early nineteenth-century cross-dressing female-warrior ballad, see *The Female Marine and Related Works: Narratives of Cross-Dressing and Urban Vice in America's Early Republic*, edited with an introduction by Daniel A. Cohen (Amherst: University of Massachusetts Press, 1997), 18.

25. Over the years, Parkhurst's life has been the subject of many studies, for example, Mary Chaney Hoffman, "Whips of the Old West," *American Mercury* 84, no. 399 (April 1957): 107–10; Mabel Rowe Curtis, *The Coachman Was a Lady* (Watsonville, CA: Pajaro Valley Historical Association, 1961); Craig MacDonald, *Cockeyed Charley Parkhurst, The West's Most Unusual Stagewhip* (Palmer Lake, CO: Filter

Press, 1973); Patty Haden Stoker, *The Burden of Charley Parkhurst* (Watsonville, CA: Pajaro Valley Historical Association, 1975); Ed Sams, *The Real Mountain Charley* (Ben Lomond, CA: Yellow Tulip Press, 1995).

26. For example, *San Francisco Chronicle*, 2 January 1880, 3; *Santa Cruz (California) Sentinel*, 3 January 1880, 3; *Watsonville (California) Pajaronian*, 8 January 1880, 3; *Providence (Rhode Island) Daily Journal*, 22 January 1880, 4.

27. *Santa Cruz Sentinel*, 2 January 1880, 3.

28. *Watsonville Pajaronian*, 8 January 1880, 3

29. *Rocky Mountain News*, 27 November 1885, 2. Accounts evolving out of the *Santa Cruz (California) Surf* include *Sacramento Daily Record-Union*, 10 April 1886, 6; *Omaha Daily Bee*, 11 June 1886, 5; and *McCook (Nebraska) Tribune*, 26 May 1887, 6.

30. The *American Journal Examiner's* "Cowboy Jo—Was a Woman!" appeared in, for example the *Rocky Mountain News*, 23 March 1904, clipping in Joe Monahan File, Idaho State Historical Society.

31. A good introduction to the western dime novel is Daryl Jones, *The Dime Novel Western* (Bowling Green, OH: Bowling Green University Popular Press, 1978).

32. Edward L. Wheeler, *Deadwood Dick on Deck; or, Calamity Jane, The Heroine of Whoop-Up. A Story of Dakota* (New York: Beadle and Adams Publishers, 1878).

33. On Martha Jane Canary's dress as a man, see James D. McLaird, *Calamity Jane: The Woman and the Legend* (Norman: University of Oklahoma Press, 2005), 4–5, 23, 32, 37, 42, 57, 164, 209; Richard W. Etulain, "Calamity Jane: The Making of a Frontier Legend," in *Wild Women of the Old West*, ed. Glenda Riley and Richard W. Etulain (Golden, CO: Fulcrum Publishing, 2003), 187.

34. Wheeler, *Deadwood Dick on Deck*, 1.

35. Ibid., 11.

36. Ibid., 1–2.

37. Ibid., 13.

38. Philip S. Warne, *Hard Crowd; or, Gentleman Sam's Sister* (New York: Beadle and Adams, 1878), 1 (quoted).

39. Ibid., 24.

40. *Anaconda (Montana) Standard*, 12 December 1908, 1.

41. *Grand Forks (North Dakota) Herald*, 16 December 1908, 1.

42. For example, *Idaho Statesman*, 19 December 1908, 2, and *Oakland (California) Tribune*, 20 December 1908, 21.

43. *Placerville (California) Mountain Democrat*, 27 November 1875, 1.

44. An eastern news correspondent first encountered Mountain Charley in the Gregory diggings of Colorado's Pike's Peak gold rush. His story appeared in the *Rocky Mountain News Weekly*, 10 September 1859, 2. There he recounted an interview with Charley, who claimed her name was Eliza Jane Forrest (a name remarkably similar to "Jane Forrest," which reportedly was Calamity Jane's true name in *Deadwood Dick on Deck*). She explained that she was born on a Louisiana plantation a few miles above New Orleans. She was "a wife at fourteen and left a widowed mother at sixteen." Finding it difficult to earn a living for her and her child, she took

to male clothing and headed West, meanwhile consigning her child to a private school in Tennessee. She drove cattle across the plains to California on three occasions and then turned to gold mining.

The *Fort Collins (Colorado) Standard*, 22 July 1874, 1, reports an 1860s Gregory diggings saloon called "Mountain Charley's" kept by "Charley, a woman who was buck-skinned in male attire." Next, the *Leadville (Colorado) Daily Chronicle*, 15 July 1879, 3, told of the name and history of "Mountain Charley," who at sixteen, "to avoid an unsatisfactory marriage demanded by her parents" somewhere in the East, ran away, enlisted in the army, served for several weeks before being discovered, and then headed to Colorado. She worked for a winter there under the name Charley Walworth and then drove a mule team over the mountains to Cheyenne, Wyoming, where in 1868 she bought a gambling house. The only reason the Leadville newspaper had for reporting this somewhat dated story was that Mountain Charley had reportedly just taken up residence in town.

45. *Mountain Charley, or the Adventures of Mrs. E.J. Guerin, Who Was Thirteen Years in Male Attire, an Autobiography Comprising a Period of Thirteen Years Life in the States, California, and Pike's Peak*, edited with an introduction by Fred W. Mazzulla and William Kosktka (Norman: University of Oklahoma Press, 1968).

46. Guerin's autobiography, though originally published in Dubuque, Iowa, in 1861, is reprinted in *Mountain Charley*, 3–61.

47. George West's serialized story, "Mountain Charley, A Colorado Story of Love, Lunacy and Revenge," appeared in the 14 January, 25 February, 4 March, and 11 March 1885 editions of Golden's *Colorado Transcript*. I am using the reprint in *Mountain Charley*, 63–112. Quotations are from pages 72 and 73. Some discussion of the popular success of West's Mountain Charley saga can be found in the *Colorado Transcript*, 21 January 1885, 3.

48. Denver, *Field and Farm*, 31 August 1912, 8.

49. *Washington (D.C.) Times*, Magazine Section, 1 October 1905, 12.

50. *Idaho Falls Times*, 15 December 1898, 7.

51. Reno, *Nevada State Journal*, 4 January 1880, 2.

52. Edward L. Wheeler, *Deadwood Dick's Doom; or, Calamity Jane's Last Adventure, a Tale of Death Notch* (New York: Beadle and Adams, 1899); David Butler, director, *Calamity Jane*, Warner Brothers Pictures, 1953.

53. Dianne Dugaw, *Warrior Women and Popular Balladry, 1650–1850* (Cambridge: Cambridge University Press, 1989), 5. See also Tania Modleski, "A Woman's Gotta Do . . . What a Man's Gotta Do? Cross-Dressing in the Western," *Signs* 22, no. 3 (Spring 1997): 522.

54. Moving female-to-male cross-dressers East and to the post-frontier may have also helped preserve the frontier as, in the words of historian Elizabeth Jameson, a male's "adolescent fantasyland." See Elizabeth Jameson, "Where Have All the Young Men Gone? The Social Legacy of the California Gold Rush," in *Riches for All: The California Gold Rush and the World*, ed. Kenneth N. Owens (Lincoln: University of Nebraska Press, 2002), 202–29 (203 quoted).

55. *San Francisco Bulletin,* 15 May 1878, 1.

56. *Nevada State Journal,* 16 May 1878, 2.

57. *Easton (Maryland) Gazette,* 1 June 1878, 2.

58. *Owyhee Avalanche,* 3 September 1881, 2.

59. *San Francisco Call,* 3 December 1905, 22.

60. *Washington Times,* Magazine Section, 1 October 1905, 12.

61. Portland, *Morning Oregonian,* 4 June 1912, 12; *Portland Evening Telegram,* 4 June 1912, 8; *Portland News,* 10 June 1912, 1, and 12 June 1912, 1; *Seattle Post-Intelligencer,* 28 December 1922, sec. 2, 16.

62. *Portland News,* 10 April 1912, 3.

63. Ibid., 10 June 1912, 1.

64. *Mountain Charley,* 63–78.

65. Ibid., 30 (quoted).

66. *Washington Times,* Magazine Section, 1 October 1905, 12; *Baltimore American,* 18 September 1905, 4.

67. *San Francisco Chronicle,* 2 January 1880, 3.

68. On the remarkable violence of the Middle Border, see Richard White, "Outlaw Gangs of the Middle Border: American Social Bandits," *Western Historical Quarterly* 12, no. 4 (Winter 1981): 387–408.

69. *Nevada State Journal,* 29 December 1879, 2.

70. *Field and Farm,* 1 September 1894, 6 (quoted); *Lincoln Evening News,* 18 September 1896, 6.

71. *Idaho Falls Times,* 15 December 1898, 7.

72. Ibid.

73. *Decatur (Iowa) Daily Republican,* 29 August 1895, 4.

74. *Idaho Statesman,* 12 August 1897, 5.

75. *Helena (Montana) Independent,* 30 August 1882, 4.

76. *Atchison (Kansas) Daily Globe,* 14 January 1898, 2 (quoted). The *Idaho Statesman,* 26 January 1898, 5, printed the exact same dispatch.

77. *Atchison Daily Globe,* 14 January 1898, 2; *Idaho Statesman,* 26 January 1898, 5.

78. *Atchison Daily Globe,* 14 January 1898, 2; *Idaho Statesman,* 26 January 1898, 5.

79. *Lewiston (Idaho) Morning Tribune,* 8 March 1909, clipping in Joe Monahan Vertical File, Idaho State Historical Society, Boise, and *Lewiston Morning Tribune,* 9 March 1904, 5.

80. *Mountain Charley,* 57–58.

81. Ibid., 79–81, 112 (quoted).

82. *Owyhee Avalanche,* 3 September 1881, 2.

83. *Nevada State Journal,* 25 June 1884, 3; *Reno Evening Gazette,* 7 January 1886, 3. Stories of other fictional western cross-dressing women purported to be real also have them recovering full genteel womanhood back East. Along these lines was a romantic mining story purported to be true that appeared in the *Idaho Statesman,* 14 January 1900, 3. It told of John Evans, a young prospector who showed up in the Blue Gulch diggings of eastern Oregon in 1862. Though he looked rather effeminate and

had a womanly refinement, his sociability and his willingness to mind his own business kept him beyond serious suspicion. But a local theft with evidence that pointed to Evans landed him before a makeshift court that found him guilty and sentenced him to death. In the wake of his trial, a small group of men appointed with the task of searching his cabin discovered evidence that revealed Evans to be a woman. Thinking of their "sisters and mothers and wives somewhere back in civilization," the miners could no longer believe their prisoner guilty of the supposed crime. They questioned Evans again. He admitted to being a woman by the name of Rachel McHenry. Now transformed into a she, McHenry explained that some people back in Missouri, whence she came, unlawfully got hold of her property and committed her to an asylum. To escape, she donned male clothing and then fled to "the most obscure place she could find" in the West. She pleaded once again her innocence of the crime for which she had been convicted and this time the men believed her, determining instead that some other rough miner among them had been responsible.

McHenry resumed women's clothing and "at once every mother's son of the miners fell in love with her." Demonstrating true feminine care and forgiveness, she even interceded to save the man who had committed the theft, and who also had actually been the one to accuse her in the first place. In explaining then that "as Auburn was then no place for a woman, [and she] resolved to return to civilization," the teller of this fanciful narrative kept to the notion of the West in 1862 as not a proper place for one of the fairer sex (at least when not disguised as a man). Between her own work in the diggings and what the Blue Gulch miners could secure for her, McHenry was able to return to Missouri with $5,000. She soon recovered her property, and because she was forever thankful for the help she had received in Oregon, McHenry also put a good portion of her "money and life to the cause of humanity . . . educating many a poor waif among the poor of St. Louis."

84. *Anaconda Standard*, 13 August 1899, 11.

85. *San Francisco Call*, 24 May 1903, 18.

86. *Portland Oregonian*, 22 October 1905, 6.

87. On these and related themes, see *The Female Marine and Related Works*, 1–45; Dugaw, *Warrior Women and Popular Balladry, 1650–1850*; Tonkovich, "Guardian Angels and Missing Mothers," 240–64; White, "Outlaw Gangs of the Middle Border," 387–408 (White deals only with male social bandits).

88. Henry Nash Smith, *Virgin Land: The American West as Symbol and Myth* (Cambridge, MA: Harvard University Press, 1950), 112.

89. Ibid., 115.

CHAPTER 4

1. General Edward S. Godfrey, "General Sully's Expedition Against the Southern Plains Indians, 1868," 5–6, Bates Collection, Museum Collection, Little Bighorn Battlefield National Monument, Crow Agency, Montana; Elizabeth B. Custer, *"Boots and Saddles" or, Life in Dakota with General Custer* (Norman: University of

Oklahoma Press, 1961), 165; Willah Weddon and Marion Huseas, "Shocking 'Mrs.' Nash," *True West* 31, no. 3 (March 1984): 20; Chicago, *Inter Ocean*, 9 November 1878, 4 (quoted).

2. Katherine Gibson Fougera, *With Custer's Cavalry* (Caldwell, ID: Caxton Printers, 1940), 191.

3. Ibid.; Custer, *"Boots and Saddles,"* 164.

4. Gibson Fougera, *With Custer's Cavalry*, 191 (quoted), 223; Custer, *"Boots and Saddles,"* 165, 166; Godfrey, "General Sully's Expedition Against the Southern Plains Indians, 1868," 7.

5. Gibson Fougera, *With Custer's Cavalry*, 193.

6. Custer, *"Boots and Saddles,"* 166.

7. *Bismarck Tribune*, 11 November 1878, 6.

8. Ibid., 6 (quoted); Custer, *"Boots and Saddles,"* 166 (quoted).

9. Custer, *"Boots and Saddles,"* 165 (quoted), 84; *Bismarck Tribune*, 11 November 1878, 6 (quoted).

10. *Bismarck Tribune*, 11 November 1878, 6.

11. Godfrey, "General Sully's Expedition Against the Southern Plains Indians, 1868," 6.

12. Custer, *"Boots and Saddles,"* 166; Gibson Fougera, *With Custer's Cavalry*, 191–92; Glendolin Damon Wagner, *Old Neutriment* (Lincoln: University of Nebraska Press, 1989), 112, 113. On Mexican midwifery, see Fran Leeper Buss, *La Partera: Story of a Midwife* (Ann Arbor: University of Michigan Press, 1980), 5, 6; Margarita A. Kay, "Mexican, Mexican American, and Chicana Childbirth," in *Twice a Minority: Mexican American Women*, ed. Margarita B. Melville (St. Louis: C. V. Mosby Company, 1980), 53; and Grace Granger Keyes, "Mexican-American and Anglo Midwifery in San Antonio, Texas" (PhD diss., University of Wisconsin-Milwaukee, 1985), 33, 34, 36, 136, 141, 142.

13. On western army laundresses, prostitution, and children, see Miller J. Stewart, "Army Laundresses: Ladies of the 'Soap Suds Row,'" *Nebraska History* 6, no. 4 (1980): 430; Anne M. Butler, *Daughters of Joy, Sisters of Misery: Prostitutes in the American West, 1865–90* (Urbana: University of Illinois Press, 1985), 143. Custer, *"Boots and Saddles,"* 164, explains how dissatisfied officers' expectant wives were with Fort Lincoln's physician.

14. *Bismarck Tribune*, 11 November 1878, 6; Damon Wagner, *Old Neutriment*, 112 (quoted).

15. Gibson Fougera, *With Custer's Cavalry*, 191.

16. Marc Simmons, *Witchcraft in the Southwest: Spanish and Indian Supernaturalism on the Rio Grande* (Lincoln: University of Nebraska Press, 1974).

17. Damon Wagner, *Old Neutriment*, 112–13.

18. *Inter Ocean*, 1 November 1878, 4; *Army and Navy Journal*, 9 November 1878, 216; Custer, *"Boots and Saddles,"* 165.

19. Custer, *"Boots and Saddles,"* 165–66; Damon Wagner, *Old Neutriment*, 113. General Edward S. Godfrey, on the other hand, claimed that "when her husbands

were discharged she never accompanied them to their new fields of endeavor. She prefered [*sic*] to remain with the regiment"; Godfrey, "General Sully's Expedition Against the Southern Plains Indians, 1868," 6.

20. The *Bismarck Tribune*, 4 November 1878, 1, gives Nash's marriages to "Clifford in '69, and again in '71 to James Nash and in '73 to Corporal Noonan." Several newspaper accounts claimed she was a widow of the Battle of Little Bighorn, for example *Army and Navy Journal*, 9 November 1878, 216. This is in error. She had been married to Noonan before the battle. Nora L. Whitely, who has studied Nash extensively, believes Nash's first husband was James Nash and her second husband was Clifton; see Nora L. Whitely, "The Mysterious 'Mrs. Nash,'" *14th Annual Symposium Custer Battlefield Historical & Museum Association* (Hardin, MT: Custer Battlefield Historical & Museum Association, 2001), 31. John Burkman, who served in the Seventh Cavalry and witnessed events, called Nash by the name Mrs. Nash but mentioned only two marriages in his memoirs, one to Clifton and the other to John Noonan (or Nonan); see Damon Wagner, *Old Neutriment*, 113. While Whitely proposes James Nash as the first husband, I would designate Harry O. Clifton as such. In part this is in keeping with the news account noted above (though newspapers are notoriously misinformed), but also because of Elizabeth Custer's explanation in her memoir that she first came to know Nash when the Seventh Cavalry was stationed in Elizabethtown, Kentucky, which was in 1871. Custer recounted that Nash had three husbands over the years. The first deserted her in Kentucky and the second in Dakota Territory. My search through Seventh Cavalry muster rolls shows a Harry O. Clifton who enlisted from Philadelphia in 1866 (Burkman mentions that Clifton was from the East) and was working extra duty as a clerk in the "G.M. Dept" in Elizabethtown, Kentucky, when he deserted in the spring of 1871 (Burkman explained that Clifton was "actin' as quartermaster clerk" when he married Nash). See Custer, *"Boots and Saddles,"* 165–66, and Damon Wagner, *Old Neutriment*, 113. The muster rolls are "Muster Roll, Co. A of the Seventh Regiment of Cavalry, Army of the United States (Colonel A. E. Smith)," (1) from 31 October 1866 to 31 December 1861, (2) 28 February 1871 to 30 April 1871, (3) 30 April 1871 to 30 June 1871, all contained in Roll 1, "Muster Rolls—7th U.S. Cavalry, Field Staff & Band, Co. A, Co. B, 1866–1884," White Swan Memorial Library, Little Bighorn Battlefield National Monument, Crow Agency, Montana.

21. Custer, *"Boots and Saddles,"* 165–66 and 84–85 describe Nash's "artificial curls."

22. *Bismarck Tribune*, 4 November 1878, 1; Custer, *"Boots and Saddles,"* 165–66.

23. Custer, *"Boots and Saddles,"* 166.

24. Ibid., 166 (quoted); Paul Hutton, "Noonan's Last Stand," *True West* 52, no. 10 (November/December 2005): 118–19; James V. Schneider, *An Enigma Named Noonan* (Ft. Wayne, IN: by the author, 1988).

25. *Bismarck Tribune*, 4 November 1878, 1 (quoted); Custer, *"Boots and Saddles,"* 165–66; Corporal John Noonan, Personnel File, White Swan Memorial Library.

26. Schneider, *An Enigma Named Noonan*, n.p.; *Bismarck Tribune*, 11 November 1878, 6; Gibson Fougera, *With Custer's Cavalry*, 222; Custer, *"Boots and Saddles,"* 166.

27. *Bismarck Tribune*, 11 November 1878, 6; *Inter Ocean*, 9 November 1878, 4.

28. Godfrey, "General Sully's Expedition Against the Southern Plains Indians, 1868," 6–7.

29. *Davenport (Iowa) Daily Gazette*, 16 November 1878, 3 (quoted); *Bismarck Tribune*, 2 December 1878, 1.

30. Damon Wagner, *Old Neutriment*, 114.

31. *Inter Ocean*, 1 November 1878, 4; *Army and Navy Journal* 16, no. 14 (9 November 1878): 216.

32. Damon Wagner, *Old Neutriment*, 114.

33. *Bismarck Tribune*, 4 November 1878, 4.

34. Damon Wagner, *Old Neutriment*, 114; *Bismarck Tribune*, 2 December 1878, 1; Terry Mangan, "The Gay West" (unpublished paper at the Colorado Historical Society, Denver), 16–17.

35. New York, *National Police Gazette*, 15 February 1879, 2.

36. Damon Wagner, *Old Neutriment*, 114–15.

37. *Bismarck Tribune*, 2 December 1878, 1. Several times during Nash's years with the Seventh, the issue of her childbearing came up, usually raised by some indelicate officer or his wondering wife. Always Nash responded that fate did not allow for all women to become mothers. On occasion these same sources mentioned that Nash was not young, but they never seemed to think that her age might have something to do with her barrenness. See Gibson Fougera, *With Custer's Cavalry*, 191, 192; *Bismarck Tribune*, 4 November 1878, 1; Custer, *"Boots and Saddles,"* 166.

38. *Bismarck Tribune*, 4 November 1878, 1 (quoted); Sandy Barnard, ed., *Ten Years with Custer: A 7th Cavalryman's Memoirs* (Terre Haute, IN: AST Press, 2001), 102; *National Police Gazette*, 15 February 1879, 2 (quoted).

39. *Bismarck Tribune*, 30 December 1878, 1.

40. *Inter Ocean*, 9 November 1878, 4.

41. Ryan, *Ten Years with Custer*, 102; *Davenport Daily Gazette*, 16 November 1878, 3.

42. *Atchison (Kansas) Daily Globe*, 17 December 1897, 1.

43. Denver, *Rocky Mountain News*, 2 July 1883, 1; Portland Police Department's Women's Auxiliary Reports, 24 August 1911, Lola G. Baldwin Papers, Portland Police Museum, Portland, Oregon.

44. *Oakland (California) Tribune*, 4 April 1908, 10; *Fort Worth Star-Telegram*, 30 March 1905, 10; *Albuquerque Journal*, 3 July 1908, 3.

45. *Galveston (Texas) Daily News*, 28 November 1883, 1.

46. Portland, *Morning Oregonian*, 14 March 1887, 3.

47. *Anaconda (Montana) Standard*, 21 November 1902, 2.

48. *St. Louis Globe-Democrat*, 6 June 1877, 5.

49. Phoenix, *Arizona Republican*, 3 October 1891, 1; *San Francisco Daily Evening Bulletin*, 28 September 1891, 1. On "wench" and cross-dressing and minstrelsy, see Laurence Senelick, "Boys and Girls Together: Subcultural Origins of Glamour Drag and Male Impersonation on the Nineteenth-Century Stage," in *Crossing the*

Stage: Controversies on Cross-Dressing, ed. Lesley Ferris (London: Routledge Press, 1993), 84–85; Marjorie Garber, *Vested Interests: Cross-Dressing and Cultural Anxiety* (New York: Routledge, 1992), 281.

50. *Portland Oregonian*, 21 May 1913, 1.

51. *Emporia (Kansas) Daily Gazette*, 25 July 1893, 1.

52. Damon Wagner, *Old Neutriment*, 112.

53. Godfrey, "General Sully's Expedition Against the Southern Plains Indians, 1868," 6; Custer, *"Boots and Saddles,"* 164; Gibson Fougera, *With Custer's Cavalry*, 222.

54. Gibson Fougera, *With Custer's Cavalry*, 191.

55. *Bismarck Tribune*, 4 November 1878, 1; *National Police Gazette*, 15 February 1879, 2; Ryan, *Ten Years with Custer*, 102.

56. Custer, *"Boots and Saddles,"* 164.

57. Gibson Fougera, *With Custer's Cavalry*, 224, 192.

58. *Bismarck Tribune*, 11 November 1878, 6

59. Custer, *"Boots and Saddles,"* 164, 165, 167. See also Godfrey, "General Sully's Expedition Against the Southern Plains Indians, 1868," 6; Gibson Fougera, *With Custer's Cavalry*, 191.

60. Gibson Fougera, *With Custer's Cavalry*, 223–24.

61. On this subject, see Patricia Albers and Beatrice Medicine, eds., *The Hidden Half: Studies of Plains Indian Women* (Washington, D.C.: University Press of America, 1983); Sabine Lang, *Men as Women, Women as Men: Changing Gender in Native American Cultures*, trans. John L. Vantine (Austin: University of Texas Press, 1998).

62. *Atchison Daily Globe*, 14 January 1898, 2.

63. Denver, *Field and Farm*, 1 September 1894, 6; *Emporia Daily Gazette*, 8 August 1894, 1.

64. Reno, *Daily Nevada State Journal*, 29 December 1879, 2.

65. *Galveston Daily News*, 4 September 1886, 2. Also see *Galveston Daily News*, 12 February 1884, 1.

66. An excellent exploration of Anglo Americans' long-developing negative stereotypes of Mexicans is Cecil Robinson, *Mexico and the Hispanic Southwest in American Literature* (Tucson: University of Arizona Press, 1977).

67. On this issue, see, for example, Robinson, *Mexico and the Hispanic Southwest in American Literature*, 47–49.

68. For more on this issue, see Shelley Streeby, *American Sensations: Class, Empire, and the Production of Popular Culture* (Berkeley: University of California Press, 2002), 119–23, 120 (quoted). On American racialized views of Mexicans more generally, see David J. Weber, "'Scare More Than Apes': Historical Roots of Anglo-American Stereotypes of Mexicans in the Border Region," chapter 9 in David J. Weber, *Myth and the History of the Hispanic Southwest* (Albuquerque: University of New Mexico Press, 1988), 153–67.

69. On this subject, see Marcienne Rocard, "The Mexican-American Frontier: The Border in Mexican-American Folklore and Elitelore," *Aztlán: A Journal of Chicano Studies* 18, no. 1 (Spring 1987): 83–94; and Robert McKee Irwin, *Bandits, Captives,*

Heroines, and Saints: Cultural Icons of Mexico's Northwest Borderlands (Minneapolis: University of Minnesota Press, 2007).

70. San Francisco, *Daily Alta California*, 30 August 1889, 5; *San Jose (California) Mercury News*, 31 August 1889, 3 (quoted); *Sacramento (California) Daily Record-Union*, 2 September 1889, 1, and 7 September 1889, 1; *St. Paul (Minnesota) Daily Globe*, 15 January 1889, 1; *Sacramento Daily Record-Union*, 9 September 1889, 1.

Also consider the case of Billy the Kid in the 1880s when he yet carried a heinous reputation. While he was not Mexican, dime novels in the 1880s conflated his reported barbarism and cowardice with his Mexican surroundings. The same dime novels also occasionally feminized and cross-dressed him. See John-Michael Rivera, "Miguel Antonio Otero II, Billy the Kid's Body, and the Fight for New Mexican Manhood," *Western American Literature* 35, no. 1 (Spring 2000): 47–57; Stephen Tatum, *Inventing Billy the Kid: Visions of the Outlaw in America, 1881–1981* (Albuquerque: University of New Mexico Press, 1982), 48, 50.

71. For example, see Mae M. Ngai, *Impossible Subjects: Illegal Aliens and the Making of Modern America* (Princeton, NJ: Princeton University Press), 111–16; Margot Canaday, *The Straight State: Sexuality and Citizenship in Twentieth-Century America* (Princeton, NJ: Princeton University Press, 2009), 27–29; David Anthony Tyeeme Clark and Joane Nagel, "White Men, Red Masks: Appropriations of 'Indian' Manhood in Imagined Wests," in *Across the Great Divide: Cultures of Manhood in the American West*, ed. Matthew Basso, Laura McCall, and Dee Garceau (New York: Routledge, 2001), 113; Karen J. Leong, "'A Distinct and Antagonistic Race': Constructions of Chinese Manhood in the Exclusionist Debates, 1869–1878," in *Across the Great Divide: Cultures of Manhood in the American West*, 131–48; Peggy Pascoe, "Race, Gender, and the Privileges of Property: On the Significance of Miscegenation Law in the U.S. West," in *Over the Edge: Remapping the American West*, ed. Valerie J. Matsumoto and Blake Allmendinger (Berkeley: University of California Press, 1999), 215–30; and Peggy Pascoe, *What Comes Naturally: Miscegenation Law and the Making of Race in America* (New York: Oxford University Press, 2009), 30–40.

Other historians have shown how blackface minstrelsy in its depiction of African-American men as silly, childlike, comical, and essentially innocuous rendered them essentially nonmasculine at the very time, in the wake of the Civil War, that they attempted to push for political and legal rights (that is, manhood) in the American West. See Lynn M. Hudson, "Entertaining Citizenship: Masculinity and Minstrelsy in Post-Emancipation San Francisco," *Journal of African American History* 93, no. 2 (Spring 2008): 174–97.

72. See Gary Y. Okihiro, *Common Ground: Reimagining American History* (Princeton, NJ: Princeton University Press, 2001), 55–113; Victor Jew, "'Chinese Demons': The Violent Articulation of Chinese Otherness and Interracial Sexuality in the U.S. Midwest, 1885–1889," *Journal of Social History* 37, no. 2 (Winter 2003): 389–410; Floyd Cheung, "Anxious and Ambivalent Representations: Nineteenth-Century Images of Chinese American Men," *Journal of American Culture* 30, no. 3 (September 2007), 293–309.

73. Ronald Takaki, *Strangers from a Different Shore: A History of Asian Americans*, rev. ed. (Boston: Bay Back Books, 1998), 124.

74. Pascoe, *What Comes Naturally*, 84–85.

75. Robert G. Lee, *Orientals: Asian Americans in Popular Culture* (Philadelphia: Temple University Press, 1999), 88; Okihiro, *Common Ground*, 104.

76. Quoted in Jonathan Ned Katz, *Gay American History: Lesbians & Gay Men in the U.S.A., A Documentary History*, rev. ed. (New York: Meridian, 1992), 51.

77. Canaday, *The Straight State*, 28–29; Lee, *Orientals*, 29.

78. Okihiro, *Common Ground*, 102.

79. Ibid., 76, 102; Canaday, *The Straight State*, 28.

80. *Oakland Tribune*, 22 July 1908, 3. As a relevant aside, like "the little Chinese" noted earlier in this chapter, Chin Ling exemplifies the press's penchant for racializing men who were duped by males who masqueraded as women of the same minority group. Another example comes from 1902, when "one of the most sensational robberies that has ever occurred in the history of western Montana took place" near Camas Prairie on the Flathead Reservation. A white man "dressed as a squaw" diverted attention at the door of his victim, a man named Matchell, while accomplices made off with his $22,000 hidden in an outbuilding. The papers described Matchell as "the wealthiest full-blood Indian on the reservation." He did not trust banks and thus kept his savings stashed on his property. See *Kalamazoo (Michigan) Gazette*, 4 November 1902, 1.

Okihiro has pointed to the description of a Chinese female impersonator at Chicago's world fair in 1893, contained in a caption to his promotional photograph, that "his dress and 'shrill Chinese female voice' ... underscored the period's feminization of Chinese men." See *Common Ground*, 77.

81. *Rocky Mountain News* 2 July 1883, 1 (quoted); Robinson, *Mexico and the Hispanic Southwest in American Literature*, 42–43, 88–89.

82. *St. Louis Globe-Democrat*, 30 January 1877, 2. The story actually takes place in Tennessee.

83. *Albany (New York) Evening Journal*, 30 July 1874, 2; *Reno (Nevada) Evening Gazette*, 13 November 1888, 3 (quoted); *Harrisburg (Pennsylvania) Patriot*, 17 March 1898, 7 (quoted). Another male-to-female Indian, though not in the classic West, who came to light in the press was "Peg Leg Ann," a Pottawatomie who lived "in the woods" alone near Watervliet, Michigan. She died in 1904, was discovered to be a male, and thus made the papers. She reportedly arrived in the vicinity in about 1860, wore a "long skirt and a sunbonnet," and operated a sawmill and a blacksmith shop for twenty-five years. Because of her noticeable limp, people called her Peg Leg. Having "extended all the chivalry of a rural community" to Ann for some four decades, the community was "dumbfounded" when they learned of her mystery. See *San Jose Mercury News*, 30 April 1904, 8.

84. *Reno Evening Gazette*, 13 November 1888, 3.

85. *Anaconda Standard*, 27 March 1898, 13.

86. *Rocky Mountain News*, 2 July 1883, 1.

87. *Oakland Tribune*, 22 July 1908, 3; *Emporia Daily Gazette*, 25 July 1893, 1.

88. *Morning Oregonian*, 31 August 1891, 5. For a brief consideration of the issue of Chinese women's feet, see Okihiro, *Common Ground*, 73, 75, 78.

89. On the issues of racializing sexuality and gendering race in the American West, see Pablo Mitchell, *Coyote Nation: Sexuality, Race, and Conquest in Modernizing New Mexico, 1880–1920* (Chicago: University of Chicago Press, 2005); and in America more generally, Okihiro, *Common Ground*.

90. Traditionally, anthropologists have termed such people "berdache," a word derived from Arabic and Persian roots that in original form means something along the lines of a "kept boy" or "male prostitute." French explorers first began employing it. It then found its way into common and scholarly usage. But because of its derogatory meaning and colonial implications, anthropologists, other scholars, and Native Americans who see themselves in the tradition of this individual have more recently taken to using terms such as "third gender" and "two-spirit" instead of "berdache," though these designations have their own problems. For more on these various terms, see Will Roscoe, "The Life and Times of a Crow Berdache," *Montana* 40, no. 1 (Winter 1990): 48; Sue-Ellen Jacobs, Wesley Thomas, and Sabine Lang, eds., *Two-Spirit People: Native American Gender Identity, Sexuality, and Spirituality* (Urbana: University of Illinois Press, 1997), 3–4; Evan B. Towle and Lynn M. Morgan, "Romancing the Transgender Native: Rethinking the Use of the 'Third Gender' Concept," *GLQ* 8, no. 4 (2002): 469–97; Wesley Thomas and Sue-Ellen Jacobs, "'. . . And We Are Still Here': From *Berdache* to Two-Spirit People," *American Indian Culture and Research Journal* 23, no. 2 (1999): 91–107. For considerations of the problem of these terms, see Towle and Morgan, "Romancing the Transgender Native," 469–97; Carolyn Epple, "Coming to Terms with Navajo 'Nádleehí': A Critique of 'Berdache,' 'Gay,' and 'Alternate Gender,' and 'Two-Spirit,'" *American Ethnologist* 25, no. 2 (May 1998): 267–90; Stephen O. Murray, "On Subordinating Native American Cosmologies to the Empire of Gender," *Current Anthropology* 35, no. 1 (February 1994): 59–61.

More appropriately, each North American tribe that countenanced alternative gender roles, and one recent count places the number at 133, had its own term for such people, for example, *nadle* (Navajo), *winkte* (Lakota), *bo-te* (Crow), *joya* (Chumash), *ko'thlama* (Zuñi), *i-coo-coo-a* (Sauk and Fox), and *he-man-eh* (Cheyenne), to name but a few. See Lang, *Men as Women, Women as Men*, 6 (gives the figure of 133); Maurice Kenny, "Tinselled Bucks: A Historical Study in Indian Homosexuality," *Living the Spirit: A Gay American Indian Anthology*, ed. Will Roscoe (New York: St. Martin's Press, 1988), 19; Paula Gunn Allen, *The Sacred Hoop: Recovering the Feminine in American Indian Traditions* (Boston: Beacon Press, 1992), 197–98.

91. For a brief consideration of varied European and Euro-American responses to the "berdache," see Will Roscoe, "Was We-Wha a Homosexual? Native American Survivance and the Two-Spirit Tradition," *GLQ* 2, no. 3 (1995): 197–201.

Particularly negative descriptions of Native Americans who, in the eyes of Europeans, mixed male and female attributes include the following. As early as about 1530 in Florida, Alvar Núñez Cabeza de Vaca "saw a devilish thing . . . impotent, effeminate men [*amarionados*] and they go about dressed as women, and do women's tasks." Quoted in Katz, *Gay American History*, 285. At the end of the seventeenth century, Louis Hennepin wrote of some interior Native people as being "so lascivious as to be guilty of Sodomy, and keep Boys, whom they clothe with Women's Apparel, because they make of them that abominable use." See Louis Hennepin, *A New Discovery of a Vast Country in America* (London: M. Bentley, I. Tonson, H. Bonwick, and S. Manschip, 1698), 133. A few years later Pierre Liette, who had lived for some time in the Illinois country about Lake Michigan, similarly described Indian boys there who "omit nothing that can make them like the women" and among whom the "sin of sodomy prevails. . . . There are men sufficiently embruted to have dealings with them on the same footing." Quoted in Katz, *Gay American History*, 288. A Jesuit missionary in California in the 1770s remarked on the indigenous men there "dressed like women . . . [who] were sodomites, dedicated to nefarious practices." Quoted in Katz, *Gay American History*, 291. Also in the eighteenth century, Father Juan Agustín de Morfi from the Southwest wrote of "boys" there whom Spaniards had called "hermaphrodites" and whose principal duty seems to have been accompanying warriors on campaign and there "lend their bodies to infamous and nefarious uses." See Father Juan Agustín de Morfi, *Excerpts from the Memorias for the History of the Province of Texas*, with a prologue, appendix, and notes by Frederick C. Chabot (San Antonio, TX: Naylor, 1932), 55.

92. On European and U.S. reasons for and efforts at conquest and assimilation of Native Americans due to the presence among them of the berdache and of same-sex sexual practices (actual or otherwise), see Richard C. Trexler, *Sex and Conquest: Gendered Violence, Political Order, and the European Conquest of the Americas* (Ithaca, NY: Cornell University Press, 1995); Rudi C. Bleys, *The Geography of Perversion: Male-to-Male Sexual Behavior Outside the West and the Ethnographic Imagination, 1750–1918* (New York: New York University Press, 1996); Walter L. Williams, *The Spirit and the Flesh: Sexual Diversity in American Indian Culture* (Boston: Beacon Press, 1992), 134–40, 175–83; Will Roscoe, *Changing Ones: Third and Fourth Genders in Native North America* (New York: St. Martin's Griffin, 1998), 34–36, 195–96; Will Roscoe, *The Zuni Man-Woman* (Albuquerque: University of New Mexico Press, 1991), 171–94.

93. Richard C. Trexler explores this with regard to Spanish encounters with the indigenous peoples of Latin American and specifically with regard to sodomy in *Sex and Conquest*, 142–55.

94. Quoted in Katz, *Gay American History*, 291.

95. Alexander P. Maximilian, Prince of Wied, *Travels in the Interior of North America: 1832–1834*, vol. 22 of *Early Western Travels, 1748–1846*, edited with notes, introduction, and index by Reuben Gold Thwaites (Cleveland, OH: A. H. Clark, 1904–7), Part I, 354.

96. See Edwin Thompson Denig, *Five Indian Tribes of the Upper Missouri*, edited with an introduction by John C. Ewers (Norman: University of Oklahoma Press, 1961), 187–88, 195–200 (187 and 199 quoted).

97. It might be that newspapers did not report on Indian female-to-male traditions, for as Evelyn Blackwood explains, this cross-gender role had pretty much disappeared by the end of the nineteenth century. See Evelyn Blackwood, "Sexuality and Gender in Certain Native American Tribes: The Case of Cross-Gender Females," in *Theorizing Feminism: Parallel Trends in the Humanities and Social Sciences,* ed. Anne C. Herrmann and Abigail J. Stewart (Boulder, CO: Westview Press, 1994), 309–10.

98. Roscoe, "Was We-Wha a Homosexual?" 203.

99. William A. Hammond, "The Disease of the Scythians (Morbus Feminarum) and Certain Analogous Conditions," *American Journal of Neurology and Psychiatry* 1, no. 3 (August 1882): 339–55 (345–46 quoted). Subsequent citations of Hammond's consideration of the *mujerado* include A. B. Holder, "The Bote: Description of a Peculiar Sexual Perversion Found Among North American Indians," *New York Medical Journal* 50, no. 23 (7 December 1889): 624–25; R. von Krafft-Ebing, *Psychopathia Sexualis,* trans. Charles Gilbert Chaddock from the 7th German ed. (Philadelphia: F. A. Davis Co., 1893), 201; C. H. Hughes, "Erotopathia—Morbid Eroticism," *Alienist and Neurologist* 14, no. 4 (October 1893): 554; James Weir, *Religion and Lust,* 3rd ed. (Chicago: Chicago Medical Book Company, 1905), 43–45.

100. Hubert Howe Bancroft, *The Works, The Native Races* (San Francisco: A. L. Bancroft, 1883), vol. 1, 81, 82 (quoted).

101. Holder, "The Bote," 623. Subsequent citations of this piece include Hughes, "Erotopathia—Morbid Eroticism," 553; Weir, *Religion and Lust,* 45; Havelock Ellis, *Studies in the Psychology of Sex, Vol. 2, Sexual Inversion* (Philadelphia: F. A. Davis, 1908), 9–10, 122.

Other examples in keeping with this come from Alexander Henry and David Thompson, who in 1801 encountered a youth, whose name they thought was "Berdash," from the Assiniboine tribe, "a curious compound between a man and a women. He is a man both as to members and courage, but pretends to be womanish, and dresses as such. His walk and mode of sitting, his manners, occupation, and language are those of a woman." Quoted in Katz, *Gay American History,* 292.

John Treat Irving, while traveling in Pawnee country in the 1830s, chanced upon a "strange being . . . clad in the garb of a female, and performing the most menial of their offices, [who] was in reality a man." See John Treat Irving, *Indian Sketches Taken During an Expedition to the Pawnee Tribes,* edited and annotated by John Francis McDermott (Norman: University of Oklahoma Press, 1955), 93.

102. Historians have noted the curious historical event of the American West becoming masculinized at the very moment when the region ceased to be so disproportionately male. See Susan Lee Johnson, "'A Memory Sweet to Soldiers': The Significance of Gender in the History of the 'American West,'" *Western Historical Quarterly* 24, no. 4 (November 1993): 497.

103. Michael Kimmel, *Manhood in America: A Cultural History* (New York: Free Press, 1996), 135, 136, 147, 150–52, 182; Daryl Jones, *The Dime Novel Western* (Bowling Green, OH: Popular Press, 1978); Sarah Watts, *Rough Rider in the White House:*

Theodore Roosevelt and the Politics of Desire (Chicago: University of Chicago Press, 2003), 145, 146–50. A somewhat different view of masculinity in dime novels is offered by Daniel Worden, "Masculinity for the Million: Gender in Dime Novel Westerns," *Arizona Quarterly* 63, no. 3 (Autumn 2007): 35–60.

104. Gail Bederman, *Manliness & Civilization: A Cultural History of Gender and Race in the United States, 1880–1917* (Chicago: University of Chicago Press, 1995), 170–84; Douglas Brinkley, *The Wilderness Warrior: Theodore Roosevelt and the Crusade for America* (New York: Harper, 2009), 152–65, 167–81.

105. Watts, *Rough Rider in the White House*, 155.

106. Bederman, *Manliness & Civilization*, 178 (quoted), 179–81.

107. Joane Nagel, "Masculinity and Nationalism: Gender and Sexuality in the Making of Nations," *Ethnic and Racial Studies* 21, no. 2 (March 1998): 242–69, 251 (quoted). See also Okihiro, *Common Ground*, 65–68.

108. Frederick J. Turner, "The Significance of the Frontier in American History," in *Annual Report of the American Historical Association for the Year 1893*, Congress, Senate, Miscellaneous Document No. 104, 53rd Cong., 2d sess., 1894 (Washington: Government Printing Office, 1894), 199–227.

109. Ibid., 199.

110. For a fuller meditation on westward expansion in myth and history as a heteronormative enterprise, see Peter Boag, "Thinking Like Mount Rushmore: Sexuality and Gender in the Republican Landscape," in *Seeing Nature Through Gender*, ed. Virginia J. Scharff (Lawrence: University Press of Kansas, 2003), 40–59.

111. Theodore Roosevelt to Frederick Jackson Turner, 10 February 1894, photostatic copy, Frederick Jackson Turner Collection, TU Box 1, Correspondence, 1879–1894, Huntington Library, San Marino, California.

112. For an incisive consideration of the relationship between gender and sexuality and the creation of the nation, see Mrinalini Sinha, "Gender and Nation," in *Women's History in Global Perspective*, ed. Bonnie G. Smith (Urbana: University of Illinois Press, 2004), vol. 1, 229–74.

113. *Bismarck Tribune*, 2 December 1878, 1.

114. *New York Herald*, 1 December 1878, 8.

115. See Custer, *"Boots and Saddles,"* 167, and Gibson Fougera, *With Custer's Cavalry*, 223–24. Though Gibson was a witness to these events, she understood Sergeant Nash, rather than Noonan, to be the last husband and did not note the suicide.

116. Damon Wagner, *Old Neutriment*, 115–16.

117. Scholarly and other somewhat academic books and articles that consider or mention Nash include Evan S. Connell, *Son of the Morning Star* (San Francisco: North Point Press, 1984); L. Whitely, "The Mysterious 'Mrs. Nash,'" 29–44; Don Rickey Jr., *Forty Miles a Day on Beans and Hay: The Enlisted Soldier Fighting the Indian Wars* (Norman: University of Oklahoma Press, 1963); Ronald H. Nichols, ed., *Men with Custer: Biographies of the 7th Cavalry*, rev. ed. (Hardin, MT: Custer Battlefield Historical & Museum Association, 2000).

In addition to the scholarly treatment of Nash, popular articles on her have even appeared in *True West*, a magazine that commenced in 1953 and has since then catered to aficionados of the classic Old West. It persistently offers articles on cattle trails, gunslingers, and Indian battles, and it always advertises miniature sculptures of cowboys, replica firearms, western clothing, and reenactments of shootouts. These pieces on Nash are Weddon and Huseas, "Shocking 'Mrs.' Nash," 19–21, 59–60; and Hutton, "Noonan's Last Stand," 118–19.

To be sure, the magazine has made offhanded attempts at being somewhat more multicultural, including in terms of sexuality, though one example is the lamentably titled article "Homos on the Range." That piece, in fact, perpetuated old myths of the West and sexuality, pushing transgressive sexuality and gender ever to the region's margins: it concludes, for instance, with the statement that these were not "something you spoke about in polite society. . . . In those clearer, calmer days, cowboys and townsfolk alike were more comfortable with the attitude: 'Don't ask, don't tell.'" See Jana Bommersbach, "Homos on the Range," *True West* 52, no. 10 (November/December 2005): 41–45 (45 quoted).

118. Custer, *"Boots and Saddles."* Other firsthand accounts are Gibson Fougera, *With Custer's Cavalry*; Damon Wagner, *Old Neutriment*; and Ryan, *Ten Years with Custer*.

119. Rickey Jr., *Forty Miles a Day on Beans and Hay*, 170–71.

120. In popular literature, for example, as recently as 2004, W. W. Norton & Company produced the slick volume *Men of the West: Life on the American Frontier*. The last and shortest chapter is devoted to Native Americans. It is also the only chapter in the book to which the issue of "homosexuality" is indexed. Its treatment of homosexuality here is in reference to the berdache. See Cathy Luchetti, *Men of the West: Life on the American Frontier* (New York: W. W. Norton, 2004), 225–26.

121. The critical eye of later-day filmmakers has also captured the racialization and marginalization of transgressive sexuality in the West. In their 2005 film *Brokeback Mountain*, for example, screenwriters Diana Ossana and Larry McMurtry and director Ang Lee masterfully depicted this theme, though Annie Proulx, who wrote the short story on which the film is based, alluded to this as well. The film concerns a long-term, though never entirely fulfilled, love and sex affair between two otherwise masculine and white Wyoming cowboy types (they are actually sheepherders) named Ennis del Mar and Jack Twist. Although Jack wants a more sustained relationship, Ennis is never able to commit to it. Neither of the two claim to be "queer." In the film, queer sexuality is rather most prominently associated with Mexico. It is to a Mexico border town, in fact, that Jack turns when he is unable to get all he needs from Ennis. Near the end of the film during a heated disagreement between the two, in fact Ennis accuses Jack, "Well, you've been in Mexico, Jack Twist? Cause I hear what they got in Mexico for boys like you."

The suggestion is, of course, that the type of sexuality evinced by a boy like Jack Twist is not associated with Wyoming, portrayed here as the heart of the American West. Wyoming is of course also a place and a state of mind in the film, something that Ennis cannot and never does leave. It renders him apoplectic in his personal relationships and pushes him to what might be argued as the most "American" and therefore "non-queer" places—a lonely trailer court, in a lonely field, almost smack-dab in the middle of lonely Wyoming.

The geographical and therefore racial metaphor for sexuality in the film is also apparent in two juxtaposed scenes. One is when Jack goes to Juarez and finds something of a lispy male prostitute—this is after Ennis spurns Jack's attempt to create a more permanent relationship between the two. Not only is this scene the real depiction of "what they got in Mexico for boys like you," but the scene does not take place in some back alley: children, what appear to be families, single people, male and female prostitutes, a few chickens and other animals running hither and thither, as well as other elements of carnival-like nightlife more generally are all integrated into the scene, evincing the idea that queer sexuality is part of everyday life—indeed *is* everyday life—in Mexican border towns.

Compare this to the 4th of July scene in Riverton, Wyoming, in something like 1967, where multigenerational white American families are shown gathering, sitting pleasantly on the lawn with blankets, and all there to commemorate the most patriotic, and thereby most American, of celebrations. Then two uncouth, foulmouthed, perhaps inebriated hippie biker buddies invade the space and start spouting off about all the "Pussy on the hoof" in Riverton and how the sex scene there compares to the West and East Coasts. In a sense, it is within the embodiment of the hippie bikers that a form of queer sexuality invades this middle-American heteronormative place. But it is quickly extinguished: Ennis defends the honor of heteronormativity and, specifically family, by warning the two undesirables to shut their traps because he has his two little girls there. He then proceeds to knock the two in the chops, while fireworks go off behind him. The two interlopers recede from the setting. With bombs bursting in air, the atmosphere is a contemporary rendering of what the original 4th of July commemorates—the protection from invaders of what is truly American.

The subtly clever way in which the filmmakers of *Brokeback Mountain* comment on popular racial and sexual visions of the West speaks volumes about hegemonic American visions of the region. See Ang Lee, director, *Brokeback Mountain*, Focus Features, 2005; Annie Proulx, "Brokeback Mountain," *New Yorker*, 13 October 1997, 74–80, 82–85.

CHAPTER 5

1. My biography of Lobdell is based on various clippings in the "Lucy Ann Lobdell: Wild Woman of Manannah" vertical file at the Meeker County Historical Society, Litchfield, Minnesota; A. C. Smith, *A Random Historical Sketch of Meeker County, Minnesota* (Litchfield, MN: Belfoy & Joubert, 1877), 98–111; L. A. Lobdell, *Narrative of Lucy Ann Lobdell: The Female Hunter of Sullivan and Delaware Counties, N.Y.* (New York: Published for the Authoress, 1855); "A Mountain Romance," Chicago, *Inter Ocean*, 14 April 1877, 9; "Death of a Modern Diana," *New York Times*, 7

October 1879, 2; "A Woman's Strange Career," *New York Sun*, 18 October 1880, 1; "A Queer Married Couple," *New York Sun*, 3 November 1883, 3; "Two Strange Lives," *New York Sun*, 17 June 1885, 4; *St. Paul (Minnesota) Daily Globe*, 23 November 1890, 8; "Woman as Man and Wife," *Omaha Daily Bee*, 22 December 1890, 6; P. M. Wise, "Case of Sexual Perversion," *Alienist and Neurologist* 4, no. 1 (January 1883): 87–91; James G. Kiernan, "Sexual Perversion and the Whitechapel Murders," *Medical Standard* 4, no. 6 (December 1888): 170–71; James G. Kiernan, "Sexual Perversion," *Detroit Lancet* 17, no. 11 (May 1884): 481-84; Detroit U.S. Department of Commerce, Bureau of the Census, Seventh Census, 1850, Manuscript Population Census Returns, Westerlo, Albany County, NY, page 75[a], lines 11–16; U.S. Department of Commerce, Bureau of the Census, Eighth Census, 1860, Manuscript Population Census Returns, Hancock, Delaware County, NY, page 42, lines 29–32.

These and other sources are wildly divergent and contradictory in their information; what I offer here does not pretend to be exact, but rather combines verifiable fact with undoubtedly more apocryphal information that news reports relayed at the time. In writing Lobdell's biography, I mainly cite direct quotations but occasionally additional material when relevant. Although *A Random Historical Sketch of Meeker County, Minnesota*, uses the name La-Roi Lobdell, I have chosen to use the name "Joseph," as it is more common in the other literature.

2. "Lucy Ann Lobdell, Female Hunter," photostatic copy [n.p.] in "Lucy Ann Lobdell: Wild Woman of Manannah" vertical file.

3. Smith, *A Random Historical Sketch of Meeker County Minnesota*, 102–5 (104 and 105 quoted).

4. Ibid., 102–4 (102 quoted).

5. Ibid., 105–6 (106 quoted).

6. "Lucy Ann Lobdell, Female Hunter," photostatic copy [n.p] in "Lucy Ann Lobdell: Wild Woman of Manannah" vertical file; Lobdell, *Narrative of Lucy Ann Lobdell*, 36–38.

7. Lobdell, *Narrative of Lucy Ann Lobdell*, 42–45 (44 and 45 quoted).

8. Kiernan, "Sexual Perversion," 482–83.

9. "Death of a Modern Diana," *New York Times*, 7 October 1879, 2.

10. "A Woman's Strange Career," *New York Sun*, 18 October 1880, 1.

11. "Death of a Modern Diana," *New York Times*, 7 October 1879, 2, and "A Woman's Strange Career," *New York Sun*, 18 October 1880, 1.

12. Wise, "Case of Sexual Perversion," 89. At the time of his commitment, Lobdell was residing with his brother who, along with some other locals and a physician, testified about Lobdell's insanity. That testimony is available online at www.oneonta.edu/library/dailylife/family/lucytest1.html, www.oneonta.edu/library/dailylife/family/lucytest2.html, www.oneonta.edu/library/dailylife/family/lucytest3.html, www.oneonta.edu/library/dailylife/family/lucytest4.html, and www.oneonta.edu/library/dailylife/family/lucytest5.html (each accessed 7 March 2011).

13. "Two Strange Lives," *New York Sun*, 17 June 1885, 4; Lillian Faderman, "Lucy Ann Lobdell," in *Encyclopedia of Lesbian, Gay, Bisexual, and Transgender History in*

America, vol. 2 (New York: Charles Scribner's Sons, 2004), 202; Carolyn Dinshaw, "Born Too Soon, Born Too Late: The Female Hunter of Long Eddy, *circa* 1855," in *21st Century Gay Culture*, ed. David A. Powell (Newcastle, UK: Cambridge Scholars Press, 2008), 5.

14. *New York Sun*, 3 November 1883, 3; *Omaha Daily Bee*, 22 December 1890, 6 (quoted); *St. Paul Daily Globe*, 23 November 1890, 8. Marie's exchange with the news editor is described and quoted in Dinshaw, "Born Too Soon," 11.

15. Smith, *A Random Historical Sketch of Meeker County, Minnesota*, 110; "A Mountain Romance," *Inter Ocean*, 14 April 1877, 9; "Death of a Modern Diana," *New York Times*, 7 October 1879, 2; "A Woman's Strange Career," *New York Sun*, 18 October 1880, 1; "A Queer Married Couple," *New York Sun*, 3 November 1883, 3; "Two Strange Lives," *New York Sun*, 17 June 1885, 4. At the time of her mother's commitment to Willard, Helen already had two children, her uncle John providing for them all. See John F. Lobdell's testimony at Lobdell's 1880 commitment hearing, www.oneonta .edu/library/dailylife/family/lucytest1.html (accessed 7 March 2011).

16. Smith, *A Random Historical Sketch of Meeker County, Minnesota*, 104.

17. Wise, "Case of Sexual Perversion," 88–89, 90.

18. James G. Kiernan, "Insanity," *Detroit Lancet* 7, no. 11 (May 1884): 482–83; Kiernan, "Sexual Perversion and the Whitechapel Murders," 170–71; and James G. Kiernan, "Sexology: Increase of American Inversion," *Urologic and Cutaneous Review* 20, no. 1 (January 1916): 45.

19. Kiernan, "Sexology," 45.

20. Wise, "Case of Sexual Perversion," esp. 90–91; Kiernan, "Sexual Perversion and the Whitechapel Murders," 170–71; Kiernan, "Insanity," 481–84.

21. Wise, "Case of Sexual Perversion," 91.

22. Frederick J. Turner, "The Significance of the Frontier in American History," in *Annual Report of the American Historical Association for the Year 1893*, Congress, Senate, Miscellaneous Document No. 104, 53rd Cong., 2d sess., 1894 (Washington: Government Printing Office, 1894), 199–227.

23. A standard treatment is John D'Emilio and Estelle B. Freedman, *Intimate Matters: A History of Sexuality in America*, 2nd ed. (Chicago: University of Chicago Press, 1997).

24. Harry Oosterhuis, *Stepchildren of Nature: Krafft-Ebing, Psychiatry, and the Making of Sexual Identity* (Chicago: University of Chicago Press, 2000), 38–43.

25. Ibid., 32; Jay Hathaway, *The Gilded Age Construction of Modern American Homophobia* (New York: Palgrave MacMillan, 2003), 105, 109.

26. See especially George W. Stocking Jr., "Lamarckianism in American Social Science: 1890–1915," *Journal of the History of Ideas* 23, no. 2 (April–June 1962): 239–56; Oosterhuis, *Stepchildren of Nature*, 52–53; Hathaway, *The Gilded Age Construction of Modern American Homophobia*, 86–87.

27. See Modris Eksteins, "History and Degeneration: Of Birds and Cages," 1–23, Robert A. Nye, "Sociology and Degeneration: The Irony of Progress," 49–71, and Sander L. Gilman, "Sexology, Psychoanalysis, and Degeneration: From a Theory of

Race to a Race to Theory," 72–96, all in *Degeneration: The Dark Side of Progress*, ed. J. Edward Chamberlain and Sander L. Gilman (New York: Columbia University Press, 1985); R. B. Kershner Jr., "Degeneration: The Explanatory Nightmare," *Georgia Review* 40, no. 2 (Summer 1986): 416–44.

28. E. C. Spitzka, "Gynomania," *Medical Record* 19, no. 13 (March 28, 1881): 359. Examples of American sexologists elevating Krafft-Ebing to the role of principal authority are J. C. Shaw and G. N. Ferris, "Perverted Sexual Instinct," *Journal of Nervous and Mental Disease* 10, no. 2 (April 1883): 203; George F. Shady, "Perverted Sexual Instinct," *Medical Sentinel* 26, no. 3 (July 19, 1884): 71; and Kiernan, "Insanity," 483–84. I might note that while some American physicians, namely James G. Kiernan and G. Frank Lydston, did make key contributions to the field and had an impact on Europeans, in fact European sexologists had a far greater influence on their American counterparts.

29. Hathaway, *The Gilded Age Construction of Modern American Homophobia*, 103; Vern L. Bullough, *Science in the Bedroom: A History of Sex Research* (New York: Basic Books, 1994), 40.

30. Frank J. Sulloway, *Freud, Biologist of the Mind: Beyond the Psychoanalytic Legend* (New York: Basic Books, 1979), 284, 288 fn. 7; George Chauncey, "From Sexual Inversion to Homosexuality: Medicine and the Changing Conceptualization of Female Deviance," in *Passion and Power: Sexuality in History*, ed. Kathy Peiss and Christina Simmons with Robert A. Padgug (Philadelphia: Temple University Press, 1989), 99. It should be said, however, that Krafft-Ebing did maintain that one could still acquire sexual perversions through vicious activities, but in most cases it was an inborn condition.

31. R. von Krafft-Ebing, *Psychopathia Sexualis*, trans. Charles Gilbert Chaddock from the 7th German ed. (Philadelphia: F. A. Davis Co., 1893), 6–7.

32. Examples of its acceptance are Spitzka, "Gynomania," 359; Shaw and Ferris, "Perverted Sexual Instinct," 185–204; and Kiernan, "Insanity," 481–84.

33. John Higham, "The Divided Legacy of Frederick Jackson Turner," in *Writing American History: Essays on Modern Scholarship* (Bloomington: Indiana University Press, 1970), 93, 88.

34. Turner, "The Significance of the Frontier in American History," 199, 200 (quoted), 201 (quoted), 221, 226–27.

35. Quoted in two parts in James G. Kiernan, "Are Americans Degenerates? A Critique of Nordau's Recent Change of View," *Alienist and Neurologist* 18, no. 3 (1896): 446, 456.

36. Examples with direct reference to Krafft-Ebing are James Weir Jr., "Viraginity and Effemination," *Medical Record* 44, no. 12 (September 16, 1893): 359; James Weir Jr., "Is It the Beginning of the End?" *Medical Record* 46, no. 26 (December 29, 1894): 801; Bukk G. Carleton, "The Causes and Treatment of the So-Called Sexual Neuroses of the Male," *Medical Times* 25 (March 1897): 70; James Weir Jr., *Religion and Lust*, 3rd ed. (Chicago: Chicago Medical Book Co., 1905), 124.

37. G. Frank Lydston, *Addresses and Essays* (Louisville, KY: Renz & Henry, 1892), 100–101; Weir Jr., "Viraginity and Effemination," 359, 360; C. H. Hughes,

"Erotopathia—Morbid Eroticism," *Alienist and Neurologist* 14, no. 4 (October 1893): 535, 540, 563; Weir Jr., "Is It the Beginning of the End?" 801, 802; E. Stuver, "Would Asexualization of Chronic Criminals, Sexual Perverts and Hereditary Defectives Benefit Society and Elevate the Human Race?" *Texas Medical Journal* 12, no. 5 (November 1896): 231; Orpheus Everts, "Degeneracy," *American Journal of Insanity* 57 (1900): 120–21; Weir Jr., *Religion and Lust*, 124, 132, 149–51, 209; G. Frank Lydston, *The Diseases of Society (The Vice and Crime Problem)*, 5th ed. (Philadelphia: J. B. Lippincott, 1908), 19; Kiernan, "Sexology," 44.

38. William Lee Howard, "Sexual Perversion in America," *American Journal of Dermatology and Genito-Diseases* 8, no. 1 (January 1904): 9.

39. Weir Jr., "Viraginity and Effemination," 360; Sturver, "Would Asexualization of Chronic Criminals, Sexual Perverts and Hereditary Defectives Benefit Society and Elevate the Human Race?" 231.

40. G. Frank Lydston, *Addresses and Essays*, 100.

41. Weir Jr., "Viraginity and Effemination," 360.

42. A. J. Bloch, "Sexual Perversion in the Female," *New Orleans Medical and Surgical Journal* 22, no. 1 (July 1894): 1.

43. Charles Gilbert Chaddock, "Sexual Crimes," in Allan McLane Hamilton and Lawrence Godkin, *A System of Legal Medicine* (New York: E. B. Treat, 1894), vol. 2, 570. A smaller group of sexologists, however, argued that homosexuality was purely a result of viciousness. Morton Prince from the Harvard Medical School strongly supported this view, in turn detracting from the arguments Kiernan made and that I note in the text below. See Morton Prince, "Sexual Perversion or Vice? A Pathological and Therapeutic Inquiry," *Journal of Nervous and Mental Disease* 24, no. 4 (April 1898): 237–56.

44. Lydston, *The Diseases of Society*, 78.

45. Kiernan, "Sexual Perversion and the Whitechapel Murders,", 129–30; James G. Kiernan, "Psychological Aspects of the Sexual Appetite," *Alienist and Neurologist* 12, no. 2 (1891): 195–96.

46. Weir Jr., "Viraginity and Effemination," 359.

47. George M. Beard, *American Nervousness: Its Causes and Consequences. A Supplement to Nervous Exhaustion (Neurasthenia)* (New York: G. P. Putnam's Sons, 1881), vii–viii, 172.

48. Turner, "The Significance of the Frontier in American History," footnote on page 227.

49. Beard, *American Nervousness*, vi.

50. For example, John D. Quakenbos, "Causes and Recent Treatment of Neurasthenia," *Medical Times* 26 (March 1898): 65; Everts, "Degeneracy," 118, 120; Howard, "Sexual Perversion in America," 9; Lydston, *The Diseases of Society*, 50, 78–79, 359; and the American correspondent for Havelock Ellis, *Studies in the Psychology of Sex, vol. II: Sexual Inversion*, 3rd ed. (Philadelphia: F. A. Davis, 1917), 261, fn. 3.

51. Beard, *American Nervousness*, vi, 96–97.

52. S. Weir Mitchell, *Nurse and Patient, and Camp Cure* (Philadelphia: J. B. Lippincott & Co., 1877); S. Weir Mitchell, *Wear and Tear, or Hints for the Overworked* (Philadelphia: J. B. Lippincott & Co., 1871), 6.

53. George M. Beard, *Sexual Neurasthenia: Its Hygiene, Causes, Symptoms and Treatment*, 5th ed., edited with notes and additions by A. D. Rockwell (New York: E. B. Treat & Company, 1898), 102–3.

54. "Correspondence," letter to the editor by E. J. H., *Alienist and Neurologist* 5, no. 2 (1884): 352; G. Frank Lydston, "Sexual Perversion, Satyriasis and Nymphomania," *Medical and Surgical Reporter* 61, no. 10 (September 7, 1889): 245, 256; Irving C. Rosse, "Sexual Hypochondriasis and Perversion of the Genesic Instinct," *Journal of Nervous and Mental Disease*, whole series vol. 19, new series vol. 17, no. 11 (November 1892): 805, 807 (quoted); G. J. Monroe, "Sodomy—Pederasty," *Saint Louis Medical Era* 9 (1899): 432; Charles H. Hughes, "Homo Sexual Complexion Perverts in St. Louis," *Alienist and Neurologist* 28, no. 4 (November 1907): 487–88; Weir Jr., *Religion and Lust*, 125. See also Lydston, *The Diseases of Society*, 275, 308–9.

Jennifer Terry, in *An American Obsession: Science, Medicine, and Homosexuality in Modern Society* (Chicago: University of Chicago Press, 1999), 90, found that rumors even spread internationally that American cities "fostered perversion and were resorts for sex perverts."

55. See A. K. Gardner, "Causes of Physical Degeneracy," *Popular Science Monthly* (August 1872): 484, 485 (quoted), 486; Henry Childs Merwin, "On Being Civilized Too Much," *Atlantic Monthly*, June 1897, 838, 839.

56. Terry, *An American Obsession*, 87–97.

57. See, for example, "Proceedings of Societies," *New York Medical Journal* 49 (January 5, 1889): 21; E. Hubbell, "Sexual Neurasthenia," *Journal of Orificial Surgery* 7 (1898): 28; Philip Zenner, "Neurasthenia," *Cincinnati Lancet-Clinic* 40 (June 25, 1898): 648–49; Joseph Collins and Carlin Phillips, "The Etiology and Treatment of Neurasthenia. An Analysis of Three Hundred and Thirty-Three Cases," *Medical Record* 55, no. 12 (March 25, 1899): 415, 420.

58. Mitchell, *Nurse and Patient, and Camp Cure*.

59. Ibid., 46, 57.

60. See specifically ibid., 60, although *Wear and Tear, or Hints for the Overworked*, 32–33, suggests exercise as well. Mitchell's book *Fat and Blood: And How to Make Them* (Philadelphia: J. B. Lippincott & Co., 1877) refers to the rest cure. See also Barbara Will, "The Nervous Origins of the American Western," *American Literature* 70, no. 2 (June 1998): 293–316.

61. William Lee Howard, "Effeminate Men and Masculine Women," *New York Medical Journal* 77 (May 5, 1900): 687. Also see James Weir Jr., "The Effect of Female Suffrage on Posterity," *American Naturalist* 29, no. 345 (September 1895): 815–25; Lydston, *The Diseases of Society*, 50; T. H. Evans, "The Problem of Sexual Variants," *St. Louis Medical Review* 54, no. 10 (September 8, 1906): 213–15; Havelock Ellis, *Studies in the Psychology of Sex*, vol. II, 261 fn. 3.

62. Rollin Lynde Hartt, "A New England Hill Town," *Atlantic Monthly*, April 1899, 572, and May 1899, 714 (quoted). See also "Rural Degeneracy in New England," *Public Opinion*, 1 June 1899, 685–86.

63. Eugene S. Talbot, "A Study of the Stigmata of Degeneracy Among the American Criminal Youth," *Journal of the American Medical Association* 30 (April 1898): 849–56, 851 (quoted).

64. Weir, "Is It the Beginning of the End?" 804; Lydston, *The Diseases of Society*, 129.

65. Frederick Jackson Turner also lamented the new immigration in a series he wrote on the subject for the *Chicago Record-Herald* in 1901. He declared the southern Italians, Poles, Russian Jews, and Slovaks who replaced the British and German immigrants of an earlier era as "a loss to the social organism of the United States." They had also "made New York City," in Turner's view, "a great reservoir for the pipe lines that run to the misery pools of Europe." Like G. Frank Lydston, he attributed to the new immigrants increasing rates of crime and pauperism. Finally, Turner expressed considerable anxiety about how they would be absorbed into the nation now that the frontier was gone. "The immigration of the preceding period," Turner wrote, "was assimilated with comparative ease.... But the free lands that made the process of absorption easy have gone. The immigration is becoming increasingly more difficult of assimilation . . . the effects upon American social well-being are dangerous in the extreme." See Frederick J. Turner, "Studies of American Immigration. XV.—The Stream of Immigration into the United States," *Chicago Record-Herald*, 25 September 1901, 7 (quoted); Frederick Jackson Turner, "Studies of American Immigration. XVIII.—Jewish Immigration," *Chicago Record-Herald*, 16 October 1901, 7 (quoted). Others in Turner's series are "Studies of American Immigration. XI.—German Immigration in the Colonial Period," *Chicago Record-Herald*, 28 August 1901, 7; "Studies of American Immigration. XII.—German Immigration into the United States, II," *Chicago Record-Herald*, 4 September 1901, 7; and "Studies of American Immigration. XIV.—French and Canadian Immigration to the United States," *Chicago Record-Herald*, 18 September 1901, 7. See also Edward N. Saveth, *American Historians and European Immigrants* (New York: Russell & Russell, 1965), 122–49; Allan G. Bogue, *Frederick Jackson Turner: Strange Roads Going Down* (Norman: University of Oklahoma Press, 1998), 55, 185–86; Lee A. Benson, "The Historical Background of Turner's Frontier Essay," *Agricultural History* 25, no. 2 (April 1951): 77–80.

66. Beard, *Sexual Neurasthenia*, 103.

67. William A. Hammond, "The Disease of the Scythians (Morbus Feminarum) and Certain Analogous Conditions," *American Journal of Neurology and Psychiatry* 1, no. 3 (August 1882): 347–48.

68. A. B. Holder, "The Bote: Description of a Peculiar Sexual Perversion Found Among North American Indians," *New York Medical Journal* 50, no. 23 (7 December 1889): 625.

69. C. G. Seligmann, "Sexual Inversion Among Primitive Races," *Alienist and Neurologist* 23, no. 1 (January 1902):, 15. Seligmann speaks specifically of North American Indians on pages 11–12.

70. Hughes, "Erotopathia–Morbid Eroticism," 553, 554 (quoted); Beard, *Sexual Neurasthenia*, 104.

71. Rosse, "Sexual Hypochondriasis and Perversion of the Genesic Instinct," 802. See also Weir Jr., *Religion and Lust*, 124–25; Seligmann, "Sexual Inversion Among Primitive Races," 11.

72. Hammond, "The Disease of the Scythians (Morbus Feminarum) and Certain Analogous Conditions," 339, 343, 347 (quoted).

73. See George Catlin, *North American Indians*, edited and with an introduction by Peter Matthiessen (New York: Viking, 1989), 445.

74. Will Roscoe, "Was We'Wha a Homosexual?" *GLQ* 2, no. 3 (1995): 193–235, argues that European encounters with Native American sexuality, including what Europeans would view as deviant same-sex sexualities, profoundly influenced European and American conceptualization of sexual inversion and homosexuality. My argument is not that Indian sexuality had no effect on American sexologists, but rather that it had little effect on how they understood the frontier's sexually transformative nature. I also contend that sexologists linked heterosexuality, something the frontier secured, to whiteness, as the frontier process was specifically about Europeans and Euro-Americans. This view adds to the various studies that have examined the concomitant historical developments of sexual deviance and a racialized blackness and that argue that the events were intrinsically connected beyond matters of their coincidence in timing at the end of the nineteenth century. On these issues of race and sexuality, see Siobhan B. Somerville, *Queering the Color Line: Race and the Invention of Homosexuality in American Culture* (Durham, NC: Duke University Press, 2000); Lisa Duggan, *Sapphic Slashers: Sex, Violence, and American Modernity* (Durham, NC: Duke University Press, 2000).

75. Kiernan, "Sexology," 44–46.

76. Ibid., 44.

77. Ibid., 44. On eighteenth-century London, see Randolph Trumbach, "London's Sodomites: Homosexual Behavior and Western Culture in the 18th Century," *Journal of Social History* 11, no. 1 (Autumn 1977): 1–33; Randolph Trumbach, "Sodomitical Assaults, Gender Role, and Sexual Development in Eighteenth-Century London," in *The Pursuit of Sodomy: Male Homosexuality in Renaissance and Enlightenment Europe*, ed. Kent Gerard and Gert Hekma (New York: Harrington Park Press, 1989), 407–29; Clare A. Lyons, "Mapping an Atlantic Sexual Culture: Homoeroticism in Eighteenth-Century Philadelphia," *William and Mary Quarterly* 60, no. 1 (January 2003): 124-28.

78. Kiernan, "Sexology," 44.

79. Ibid.

80. Ibid.

81. Kiernan, "Are Americans Degenerates?" 456.

82. Kiernan, "Is the Race Degenerating?" 406 (quoted); Kiernan, "Are Americans Degenerates?" 456.

83. Kiernan, "Is the Race Degenerating?" 407.

84. Quoted both in Kiernan, "Is the Race Degenerating?" 406; and Kiernan, "Are Americans Degenerates?" 456.

85. Kiernan, "Is the Race Degenerating?" 408–9 (409 quoted). See also Kiernan, "Are Americans Degenerates?" 457.

CONCLUSION

1. Bret Harte, "The Luck of Roaring Camp," *Overland Journal* 1, no. 2 (August 1868): 183–89. On Harte's life, see, for example, Axel Nissen, *Bret Harte: Prince and Pauper* (Jackson: University Press of Mississippi, 2000); and Gary Scharnhorst, *Bret Harte: Opening the American Literary West* (Norman: University of Oklahoma Press, 2000).

Susan Lee Johnson, *Roaring Camp: The Social World of the California Gold Rush* (New York: W. W. Norton, 2000), 333–40, 343, uses Bret Harte and his writings on the California gold rush to demonstrate how they provided space for intimate, perhaps even sexual, male–male relationships.

2. Contained in Bret Harte, *Mrs. Skaggs's Husbands, and Other Sketches* (Boston: James R. Osgood, 1873), 153–70 (hereafter cited as Bret Harte, "The Poet of Sierra Flat").

3. Bret Harte, "The Poet of Sierra Flat," 154.

4. Ibid., 162.

5. Ibid., 164.

6. Ibid.

7. Ibid., 165.

8. Ibid., 167.

9. Ibid., 170.

10. Ibid., 157.

11. Ambrose Bierce, "The Haunted Valley," in *Ghost and Horror Stories of Ambrose Bierce*, selected and introduced by E. F. Bleiler (New York: Dover Publications, 1964), 150–59 (hereafter cited as Ambrose Bierce, "The Haunted Valley").

12. On Bierce's life, see, for example, Carey McWilliams, *Ambrose Bierce: A Biography* (Hamden, CT: Archon Books, 1967); Roy Morris Jr., *Ambrose Bierce: Alone in Bad Company* (New York: Crown Publishers, 1995).

13. Ambrose Bierce, "The Haunted Valley," 150.

14. Ibid., 150–51.

15. Ibid., 152.

16. Ibid., 152–53.

17. Ibid., 158.

18. Ibid., 159.

19. Ibid.

20. Bret Harte, "The Poet of Sierra Flat," 167.

21. Ibid., 168.

22. Ibid., 159.

23. Helen Lee-Keller, who has analyzed "The Haunted Valley," explains that the late nineteenth-century "obsession with the perceived deviancy of Chinese immigrants, registered in the story as gender fluidity, allowed white U.S.-Americans to avoid confronting homosociability as well as homosexuality" among themselves. Feminizing Ah Wee and more generally Chinese immigrant males made it possible for white masculinity to express its own homosexual desires. Helen Lee-Keller, "Civilizing Violence: 'The Haunted Valley,'" *Ambrose Bierce Project Journal* 2, no. 1 (Fall 2006), www.ambrosebierce.org/journal2lee-keller.html (accessed 1 September 2010).

INDEX

Ackerman, Samuel, 13

Adams, Freddie, 45

Ah Wee (fictional character in "The Haunted Valley"), 191, 192, 195

Albany, OR, 10, 12, 16

Albany College (Lewis & Clark College), 10

Albuquerque, NM, 14, 140

Alexander, Henrietta, 140

Alexander, Henry, 140

Allen, Harry, 23–31, 24*fig.*, 35, 45, 46, 53–54, 57, 117; death of, 30; feminizing of, 27–28; fictionalizing of, 117; gender of, 25–26, 29–30, 48, 50, 52; masculinizing of, 26–27, 46; name of, 202n2; newspaper responses to, 25–27; reasons to cross-dress, 27, 28–29; sexuality of, 26, 28–29; transgenderism and, 29, 48, 50; transsexuality and, 29, 50

Altman, CO, 79–80

American Journal Examiner, 102–3

Anaconda, MT, 68, 71

Apache, 144

Arizona, 116, 125, 144

Ashland, NE, 87, 89

Ashton, Nicholas, 68

Aspen, CO, 43

Atchison, KS, 46, 68, 75–77

Austin, TX, 69

Avery, Alida C., 50

Baker, Alice, 85

Baker, Arthur J., 84–86, 90, 141

Baker, James Arthur, 84–86, 90, 141

Baker, Mabel, 84, 86

Baker, Madeline, 84, 86

Baldwin, Lola G., 29, 45

Ballad of Little Jo, The (1993), 102

Bancroft, Hubert Howe, 151

Beard, George M., 174–76; and heterosexualizing the frontier, 185; on Native Americans, 181

Belle, 43

Bender, Kate, 123

"berdache," 149, 150, 156, 182, 233n90; relationship to western history, 156–57

Bethany, PA, 162

Bettie, Net, 118, 121–22, 123, 144

Beunon, Blanche, 36

Bierce, Ambrose, 191, 192, 193, 195. *See also* "Haunted Valley, The"

Billings, MT, 179

Billman, Roscoe, 78

Billy the Kid, 44, 120, 121, 231n70

Birch, Billy, 65

Bisbee, AZ, 61

Bismarck, ND, 66, 71, 130, 132, 135, 138

blackface minstrelsy, 65, 66, 76, 141, 214n10, 231n71

Black Hills, SD, 78, 135, 136, 141

Blanche, 43, 44

Bloch, A. J., 174

Boise, ID, 14, 101

Boise Basin, ID, 65

Bonnet, Jeanne, 35–36

Boone, Daniel, 2, 152, 167
"Boots and Saddles" or, Life in Dakota with General Custer (1885), 156
Bossu, Jean Bernard, 150
bo-te, 151, 182
Boulton-Park case, 217n77
Bowdre, Charles, 44, 121
Brenham, TX, 140
Broadhead, WI, 88
Brockman, Henry, 83
Brokeback Mountain (film, 2005), 2, 3, 237n121
"Brokeback Mountain" (short story, 1997), 2
Bronco Liz, 39–40
Brown, Elmer, 82
Brown, Nympha, 146
Browne, Bothwell, 75
Brownell, Winnie, 37–38
Buchanan, James, 76
Buffalo, NY, 97–98, 103
Buffalo Bill's Wild West, 81, 167
Buffalo Soldiers, 34
Burkman, John, 134, 136, 137, 141, 155
Burnham, Edgar, 88–89
Burnham, Ellen, 88–89
Butcher, Frank, 73, 74
Butler, Judith, 16–17
Butte, MT, 45, 46

Calamity Jane: as dime-novel heroine, 107–8; feminizing of, 124; gender identity of, 108; heterosexualizing of, 114–15, 124; reasons to cross-dress, 108, 109
Calamity Jane (1953), 115
Calaveras, CA, 189
California, 1, 31, 32, 33, 46, 50, 64, 73, 85, 86, 99, 106, 107, 112, 117, 118, 146, 147, 189, 191, 193, 195
California Pet (fictional character in "The Poet of Sierra Flat"), 189, 190–91, 193, 194
Campbell, Harry, 71
Canary, Martha Jane, gender identity of, 108. See also Calamity Jane
Cariboo, CA, 35
Carson, Emma, 32
Carson City, NV, 37
Cathay, William, 34
Catlin, George, 182–83
Chaddock, Charles Gilbert, 170, 174
Chinese Exclusion Act (1882), 141, 147

Chinese men: feminizing of, 147–48, 192, 195; homosexualizing of, 147, 149; racializing of, 141, 142, 194–95
Chinese theaters, 66
Chin Ling, 148
Choctaw, 150
Choteau, MT, 39
Chubbuck, Milton (fictional character in "The Poet of Sierra Flat"), 189, 190, 191, 193, 194, 195
Clark, Lizzie, 110–11
Coe, Henry Waldo, 13, 16
Coeur d'Alene district, ID, 39, 40, 41, 105
Cole, Otto, 70
Colfax, WA, 38, 74, 79
Colorado, 1, 44, 61, 86, 111, 116, 117, 148, 173
Comanche, 144
Cook, Henry Thomas, 68
Copeland, E. J., 70
Corrister, W. D., 65–66
Council Bluffs, IA, 45
Cox, Dora, 114, 118, 119
cross-dressers, relationship to frontier myth, 6, 8, 104–26, 194. See also female-to-male cross-dressers; male-to-female cross-dressers
Crow, 150, 151, 182
Cushman, Eva, 10–11
Custer, Elizabeth, 131, 132, 133, 134, 135, 141, 142, 156
Custer, George, 2, 135, 136

Dakota badlands, 152
Dakotas, 110, 155
Dakota Territory, 130, 142
Dalton, Bill, 120
Dalton gang, 118, 120
Damascus Township, PA, 163
Dawson, Nancy, 76
Day, Doris, 115
Deadwood Dick on Deck; or, Calamity Jane, The Heroine of Whoop-Up (1878), 107–8, 109, 115
Deadwood Dick's Doom; or, Calamity Jane's Last Adventure (1899), 115
Dean, Lena, 87, 89
De Forest, Eugene, 50, 129
degeneration theory, 169, 170, 171, 172, 186–87; applicability to the United States, 172, 173
DeLamar, ID, 33
Delaware Valley, NY, 161
de Martina, John, 68

de Martina, Paul, 68
Deneve, Arthur, 36
Denig, Edwin, 150
Dennison, TX, 122
Denver, CO, 56, 63, 66, 68, 71, 74, 79, 82–83,
    112, 124, 140, 148, 149
dime novels, 4, 6, 104, 128, 129, 152; and
    female-to-male cross-dressers, 107–9, 111,
    114
Donovan, Ed, 114, 117, 126–27
Doolin, Bill, 120
Doolin gang, 118, 120
Dornin, George, 64
Doyle, John, 68, 69
Duggan, Lisa, 45
Dunfer, Jo. (fictional character in "The
    Haunted Valley"), 191, 192, 193
Dusty Dick (fictional character in Deadwood
    Dick on Deck), 108, 114
Duxsted, Anna, 39

Eagle Pass, TX, 145
Edwards, Edgar, 69
Ellis, Henry Havelock, 184, 185
Eltinge, Julian, 66, 75
Evans, Robert, 71, 74

Fairweather, Helen, 49
Fargo, ND, 68
Farquhar, Sandy (fictional character in The
    Undaunted), 14, 15
Fells, Carmen, 45, 140
female impersonation, 63, 65–66, 70–71, 74;
    blackface minstrelsy and, 65; Chinese
    theaters and, 66; homosexuality and,
    75–80; local western, 70–71; Nance and,
    75–76
female-to-male cross-dressers: community
    response to, 16, 18, 31, 52–57, 96–97,
    100–101, 101–2; defenses of, 28, 31–32,
    160fig.; dime novels, 107–9, 114; feminizing
    of, 27–28, 43–45; fictionalizing of, 105–29;
    frontier myth and, 104–29, 194; gender of,
    9–10, 12, 15, 16, 24, 25–26, 29–30, 43–46,
    48–49, 50, 51, 52–54, 57; gold mining and,
    1, 32, 33, 35, 98, 112; hermaphroditism and,
    88–89; heterosexualizing of, 6, 43–45;
    hoboes as, 34; horse stealing and, 38; jokes
    about, 54–56; masculinizing of, 26–27, 43,
    45–46; newspaper response to, 18, 25–27,
    31–32, 41–42, 45–46, 47–48, 54–55; New

Woman and, 47; one-sex model and, 17;
    progress narrative and, 19, 30, 32, 40, 57,
    58; prostitutes and, 28, 35–36; race and,
    140–41, 142–43, 144, 145; sentimental
    seduction novel and, 106, 107; sexuality of,
    10, 11, 15, 16, 26, 28–29, 42–43, 46–47, 48,
    49, 50, 184; the Middle Border and, 115,
    118, 120, 123; the southern plains and, 115,
    118, 123, 144; the Southwest and, 115, 118,
    121–22, 123, 144; transgenderism and, 29,
    48, 49, 50; transsexuality of, 15, 29, 50,
    200n38; two-sex model and, 17; ubiquity
    of, 32, 57, 101; war and, 13, 32, 52, 118, 145;
    western American context of, 30–31,
    32–33, 37, 38, 39, 40, 57, 117–22; western
    military and, 34
female-to-male cross-dressers (fictional):
    female-warrior tale and, 115; feminizing
    of, 102–15, 124; heterosexualizing of,
    102–15, 124, 194; in dime novels, 107–9,
    114–15; restoration of genteel womanhood
    to, 115–17, 124–26; sentimental seduction
    novel's influence on, 106, 107
female-to-male cross-dressers (fictional),
    reasons for: ease of tracking down man,
    109; gender identity and sexuality, 41–58;
    relationships with men, 106–7, 108–9, 110;
    vengeance, 109, 111–13, 128
female-to-male cross-dressing, reasons for:
    adventure, 34, 37, 205n40; crime, 37–38,
    207nn56,59; ease of travel, 33; employ-
    ment, 26, 28, 34, 36, 205n44; gambling, 37,
    207n54; prostitution, 35, 36, 206n45;
    relationships with men, 27, 38–40,
    208nn61,62,63; safety, 33, 205n39
female-warrior tale, 115
feminizing racial minority males, 145–49
Ferrell, Minnie, 140–41
Flagstaff, AZ, 122
Forslund, Helen, 44–45, 46, 209n80
Fort Abraham Lincoln, DT, 130, 131, 132, 133,
    135, 136, 138, 142
Fort Bayard, NM, 34
Fort Gibson, OK, 121, 144
Fort Harker, KS, 34
Fort Hays, KS, 133
Fort Morgan, CO, 56
Fort Riley, KS, 34
Fort Sumpter, NM, 120
Fort Union, NM, 34
Fort Worth, TX, 140

Fostelle, Charles, 66
Foucault, Michel, 157–58
Fox, 182
Frankfort, DT, 35
Fraser, A. A., 33
frontier: closing of, 3–4, 167; effects on
    sexuality of, 7–8, 167–68, 175–76, 178–79,
    181, 183; influence on sexology, 167, 168,
    171–72, 173–76; neurasthenia and, 175,
    176–77; as term, 19–20. See also West
frontier myth: creation of, 4, 7; cross-dressers
    and, 6, 104–29, 194; heteronormalizing of,
    104, 109, 167–68, 175–76, 178–79, 181, 183,
    184–87, 194; heterosexual nature of, 7–8,
    157, 195–96; masculinity and, 152–55, 157;
    whiteness and, 153–55, 157, 178

Garber, Marjorie, 19
Gardiner, OR, 13
Garland, Jack, 50–52, 51fig., 53
George Christy Minstrels, 65
Georgetown, CO, 67
Gibson, Katherine, 131, 134, 141, 142, 143, 146
Gilbert, J. Allen, 12, 15, 16
Gilligan, Joseph, 82–83, 90
Girard, Emet, 36
Goodwin, George, 78
Gopher (fictional character in "The Haunted
    Valley"), 191, 192, 193
Grand Island, NE, 59, 73
Graves, Davis, 68
Greeley, Horace, 1, 2, 20
Greenwald, Maggie, 102
Gribbel, Edwin, 160
Guerin, Mrs. E.J., 111–12, 117, 124

Haisch, Ferdinand, 71–72
Hall, Jack, 125–26
Halls Summit, KS, 9
Hamada, Hikozo, 65
Hamilton, John, 69–70
Hamilton, Louis McLane, 130
Hammond, William, 150–51, 181, 182, 219n92
Hard Crowd; or, Gentleman Sam's Sister (1878),
    108–9
Harrah, OK, 84
Harrington, Charles, 78, 80, 90
Hart, Alan, 9–16, 52, 129; at Albany College,
    10; attempted suicide of, 11; begins
    cross-dressing, 11; birth of, 9; career of,
    13–14; childhood, 9–10; death of, 14;
    education, 10; employment difficulties of,
    13–14; gender of, 9–10, 12, 16, 52; marriage to
    Edna Ruddick, 14; marriage to Inez Stark,
    14; in Portland, 11–12, 13; reactions to sex
    change of, 12, 13; relationship with Eva
    Cushman, 10–11; in San Francisco, 11, 13; sex
    change of, 12; sexuality of, 10, 11, 15, 16; at
    Stanford, 11; transsexuality of, 15, 16, 52,
    200n38; under care of J. Allen Gilbert, 12; at
    University of Oregon Medical School, 11;
    writing The Undaunted (1936), 14
Hart, Albert, 9
Hart, Edna Bamford, 9
Hart, Lucile Alberta. See Hart, Alan
Hart, Pearl, 113fig.
Harte, Bret, 189, 190, 191, 193, 195. See also
    "Poet of Sierra Flat, The"
Harvey daughters, 37
Harwood, Gypsy, 46
"Haunted Valley, The" (1871), 191, 195;
    feminizing racial minority males and, 195;
    racializing male-to-female cross-dressers
    and, 195
hermaphroditism, 83–89, 137, 149, 174, 182, 191,
    192, 195, 219n92
heterosexuality: emergence of, 5, 42; frontier
    myth and, 7–8, 104–29, 167–68, 157,
    175–76, 178–79, 181, 183, 184–87, 194,
    195–96. See also homosexuality
Hickok, Wild Bill, 115
Higham, John, 171
Hill, John, 56–57, 129
Hilsher, Helen, 56–57
Hirschfeld, Magnus, 147
Holder, A. B., 151, 182
homosexuality: American West and, 3, 156;
    emergence of, 5–6, 16, 42; frontier and, 6;
    racializing of, 147, 155–56. See also
    heterosexuality
homosexualizing racial minority men, 147,
    149–52
Honesdale, PA, 163, 164
Hopps, Mazie, 71
Houston, TX, 68
Howard, Eleanor, 37
Howard, Frank, 76
Howard, William Lee, 173, 179
Hughes, Charles H., 177, 182
Hughes, Joe, 70
Hughes, Marancy, 54, 55, 116
Hunter, Alice, 141

Idaho, 39, 44, 85, 95, 97, 98, 99, 102, 123
Independence, MO, 118
Iola (character in *Hard Crowd; or, Gentleman Sam's Sister*), 108, 109
Iowa, 85, 88, 112, 124

Jackson, Andrew, 76
Jacksonville, TX, 68
James gang, 118
Jameson, Elizabeth, 80
Johnson, Tom, 37
Jordan Valley, OR, 99

Kandiyohi, MN, 160–61, 165
Kansas, 9, 34, 84, 123, 133
Kansas City, KS, 85, 86, 119
Kansas Jayhawkers, 118
Keya Paha County, NE, 86
Kiernan, James G., 173, 174; and creation of sexual inversion, 165–66; and heterosexualizing the frontier, 184–86; on mollies, 184; writings on Joseph Lobdell of, 165–66
King, Nellie, 35
King, Rufus, 76
King, Tom, 119–20, 119*fig.*, 144
Kinsey, Alfred, 3
Krafft-Ebing, Richard von, 169–70, 171, 172, 173; influence on American sexology of, 169–70, 172

"Lady Jim," 148
La Junta, CO, 61
Lake County, CO, 38
Lake Minnetonka, MN, 159, 160, 179
Laqueur, Thomas, 4
Laramie County, WY, 39
La Secher, Madame, 138, 139
Lease, Mary, 46
Leavenworth, KS, 130
Lebanon, OR, 54
Lebow, Barbara, 102
LeCroft, 140
Lee, Robert G., 147
Lee Hoo, 66
Lee Ping, 66
Leisher, Florence, 46–47
Leonard, Ray, 54, 211n110
Lind, Earl, 81, 83, 90, 91
Lind, Eva, 74, 79
Livenash, Edward, 141
Livingston, MT, 72–73

Livingstone, Harry. *See* Allen, Harry
Lobdell, Helen, 164–65
Lobdell, Joseph Israel, 159–66; in almshouse, 162; arrest of, 163; commitment to Willard Asylum, 163–64; childhood, 159; death of, 163–64; engagement of, 162; as hunter, 159, 160, 161; insanity of, 164; marriage to George W. Slater, 161; in Minnesota Territory, 159–61; as musician, 162; in Pennsylvania, 162, 163; pet cat of, 160, 165; relationship with Marie Louise Perry, 162, 163; role in medicalization of homosexuality, 165–66; sex discovery in Minnesota, 161; in sexological literature, 165–66; sexuality of, 165; writing of *Narrative of Lucy Ann Lobdell, The Female Hunter of Delaware and Sullivan Counties, N.Y.* (1855), 161–62
Lobdell, Lucy Ann. *See* Lobdell, Joseph Israel
Long Eddy, NY, 159, 162
Los Angeles, CA, 45, 50, 73, 74, 81–82
Loveland, Willie, 68
"Luck of Roaring Camp, The" (1868), 189
Lydston, G. Frank, 173, 174, 177, 180

"M," 59–62, 73, 91; childhood, 59–61; decision to head West, 59; gender of, 60–61; western American context of, 61–62
Madame Stanley's Female Mastodons, 77
Maguire, Tom, 65
Maher, Kate, 114, 116–17, 126–27
male-to-female cross-dressers: community response to, 72, 80–81, 84–85, 87–88, 89; hermaphroditism and, 83–89; homosexualizing of, 75–83, 149–52; jokes and, 80; in mining regions, 63, 64–65, 79, 214n7; newspaper response to, 68, 76–77, 79, 80; progress narrative and, 138–39, 157; race and, 6–7, 139–40, 141–42, 143–44, 146, 155, 194–95; reasons to go to the American West, 59, 73–74, 80; sanity of, 73; sexuality and, 62–63, 74–83, 90, 139; ubiquity of, 63–64, 67–68, 73–74; western American context of, 61–62, 63–64; working classes and, 78, 80–81. *See also* female impersonation
male-to-female cross-dressing, reasons for: crime, 70, 138, 143–44, 216n45; dances, 63, 64–65, 214n7; disguise, 69; employment, 74; gender identity, 59–60; health, 71; hermaphroditism, 83–89; joking, 69–70,

male-to-female cross-dressing (continued)
215n42; masquerade balls, 65, 214n8;
mental state, 73; parental decision, 61, 88;
transvestism, 62–63. See also female
impersonation
Malloy, Barney, 95
Malloy, Kate, 95
Manannah, MN, 159, 161
Mandan, ND, 77, 81
"man-girl," 30
Manhattan, MT, 31, 52, 109
Manley, Helen, 78
Mann Act (1910), 23
"man-woman," 16, 50, 57, 137
Martin, Bert, 60fig., 86–89
Martin, Bertha, 60fig., 86–89
Martin, Nancy, 88
Martin, Shirley, 46
Martinez, CA, 14
Martini, Bessie, 36
Martino, Edward, 79, 140, 148, 149
Mason, TX, 69
Matson, Milton, 48–49, 49fig., 50, 129
Maximilian, Alexander, Prince of Wied, 150,
219n92
Maxwell, Isabelle, 23
McAfferty, John, 105
McNish, Johnson & Slavin minstrels, 76
McPherson, Douglass, 79–80, 81, 218n82
McRay, Mrs. Georgie, 34
Meeker, CO, 56
Merwin, Henry Childs, 177
Mexican-American War, 145
Mexican borderlands, 19, 34, 118, 122, 133, 134,
143–44, 144–46, 149
Mexican men, feminization of, 145
Mexico, 122, 123, 133, 144, 145
Mills, Ezra, 100–101
Minnesota, 35, 159, 160, 161, 162, 164, 168, 187
Missoula, MT, 71
Mitchell, Alice, 45
Mitchell, Pearl, 140
Mitchell, Silas Weir, 176, 178–79; camp cure
of, 178–79
M'Keene, Annie Harris, 43–44, 118–19,
144
M'Keene, John, 118–19
Monahan, Joe, 95–104, 96fig., 105, 109, 129;
arrival in Silver City, 98, 100; childhood,
98, 99; community response to, 100–102;
death of, 95; feminizing of, 102–3, 124;

fictionalized life of, 102–3, 107, 116; funeral
service for, 96–97; heterosexualizing of,
102–3; as Kate Bender, 123; newspaper
response to, 100
Monroe, G. J., 177
Monroe County, PA, 163
Montana, 31, 34, 40, 45, 105, 110, 155, 180
Morales, Sylvestro, 146
Moret, Jack, 45, 46, 50
Moscow, ID, 39, 40
Mountain Charley, 111–12, 114, 117, 124, 129
Moynihan, 61
Moynihan, Irene, 61, 213n2
Mugarietta, Elvira Virginia, 45, 46, 50, 52
mujerado, 151, 181–82
Murphy, Lucille, 45
Myer, Ruth, 46

Namaste, Ki, 8
Nance, 75–76, 149
Narrative of Lucy Ann Lobdell, The Female
Hunter of Delaware and Sullivan Counties,
N.Y. (1855), 160fig., 161–62
Nash, Mrs., 130–40, 131fig.; as Carlos
Marillo, 139; as cook, 131–32; death of,
135; discovery of male body of, 135;
domestic skills, 132–33; feelings toward
children, 133; as fugitive, 143; hermaphroditism of, 137; husbands, 134–35, 143, 155,
228n20; as Joseph Drummond, 138, 139;
as laundress, 130–31; as midwife, 133–34;
pregnancy of, 137; racialization of,
139–40, 141–43, 146, 155, 156; as
seamstress, 133; sexuality of, 137; wealth
of, 134; and witchcraft, 134
Nash, Sergeant, 134, 143, 228n20
Native American men: feminizing of, 148–49;
homosexualizing of, 150–52
Native Americans: cross-gender traditions,
63, 181–83; hermaphroditism, 149, 182,
219n92, 234n91; sexology and, 150–52, 167,
168
Native American sexuality and the frontier,
181–83
Nebraska, 61, 62, 88, 116, 117
Nebraska Larry (character in Hard Crowd; or,
Gentleman Sam's Sister), 109, 114
Nebraska State Penitentiary, 70, 86–87
Nelson, Robert, 68
neurasthenia: connections to the American
West of, 175; Frederick Jackson Turner's

views on, 175; and sexual inversion, 174, 175; and the United States, 174–75

Nevada, 55, 67, 116

New Mexico, 34, 44, 117, 130

New Woman, 47, 120, 179, 193

Nodaway County, MO, 88

Noonan, John, 134–35, 136–37; rehabilitation of, 155; sexual relations with Mrs. Nash, 137; suicide of, 136–37; treatment of, 136, 154–55

Nordau, Max, 171–72, 173, 179, 185

Oakland, CA, 47, 48, 69

Oklahoma, 84, 85, 119–20

Oklahoma City, OK, 84, 86

Omaha, NE, 69, 71, 77, 79, 83

one-sex model, 4–5; cross-dressers and, 17

Oosterhuis, Harry, 168

Orange County, CA, 146

Oregon, 9, 10, 11, 52, 86, 95, 97, 99, 123

Overland Monthly, 189, 191

Owens, George, 77, 81

Owyhee Mountains, ID, 95, 99, 99*fig.*, 100, 101

Ozark Mountains, MO, 119

Paine, Mr., 77

Palmer, Fred, 98–99

Pardee, Irene, 84

Parker, Alice, 38

Parkhurst, Charley, 46, 52–53, 54, 109, 114, 116, 117–18, 129; feminizing of, 124; heterosexualizing of, 106–7; masculinizing of, 46; sentimental seduction novel and, 106–7

Pellet, Louis, 68

Perry, Marie Louise, 162–63, 164

Pickerell, Nell. *See* Allen, Harry

Pickett, Nellie, 44, 118, 120–21

Pickett, Tom, 44, 120

Piedras Negras, MX, 145

Pike's Peak Express, 1, 2, 20

"Poet of Sierra Flat, The" (1873), 189, 190, 191, 195; feminizing racial minority males and, 195; racializing male-to-female cross-dressers and, 195

Poland, Phil, 74, 79, 80

Pollard, Samuel M., 54–55, 101, 116, 124–25

Portland, OR, 10, 11, 12, 13, 23, 25, 27, 29, 30, 45, 66, 68, 81–82, 85, 86, 117, 126, 140, 149, 200n38

Pray, Charles, 23

progress narrative, 19, 30, 32, 40, 57, 58, 126, 138–39, 157, 194; applied to male-to-female cross-dressers, 138–39, 157; defined, 19

Proulx, Annie, 2

Providence, RI, 53

Pueblo, 151, 181, 182

Pueblo, CO, 66

Puget Sound, WA, 14

Pyramid Lake War (1869), 148

Quantrill's raiders, 43, 118, 144

Quappe, Dolly, 26, 203n8

"queer," 41, 72, 82, 209n69

Quick, Flora, 118, 119–20, 119*fig.*, 144

race: female-to-male cross-dressers and, 140–41, 142–43, 144, 145; male-to-female cross-dressers and, 6–7, 139–40, 141–42, 143–44, 146, 155, 194–95

Redding, CA, 140

Remington, Frederic, 152, 179

Renfrow's Jolly Pathfinders, 66

Reno, NV, 67, 73

Rice, W. Henry "Billy," 76

Richardson, Albert, 33

Roberts, John, 67

Roosevelt, Theodore, 62, 152–53, 154, 179

Rosse, Irving C., 177, 182

Runk, John, ii*fig.*

Ryan, John, 137, 140

Sac, 182

Sadler, Geneva, 44

Salmon, ID, 37

San Francisco, 11, 13, 35–36, 37, 47, 50, 52, 64, 65–66, 67–68, 69, 71–72, 73, 78, 126, 141, 191, 192; Barbary Coast, 37; Chinatown, 37; masquerade balls of, 65, 214n8; Tenderloin, 11

San Jose, CA, 48

San Luis Valley, CO, 47

San Miguel, CA, 36

Santa Cruz, CA, 53

Santa Fe Trail, 34

Schnabel, Frederica, 97

Schnabel, William, 97, 100, 101–2

Seattle, WA, 23, 30, 117

Segundo, CO, 84–85

Seligman, C. G., 182

sentimental seduction novel, 106, 107
Seventh Cavalry, 90, 130, 131, 132, 133, 134, 135, 137, 139, 140, 142, 143, 154, 156
Seventh Missouri Militia, 119
sexologists: degeneration and, 173; frontier and, 167, 172, 176, 178–79, 184–87, 195–96; Native Americans and, 168, 181–83; neurasthenia and, 174–76; Richard von Krafft-Ebing's influence on American, 170–71, 172; views on the city, 175, 176; views on immigrants, 178, 180; views on modernity, 175. *See also individual sexologists by name*
sexual inversion, 5, 6, 8, 15, 16, 29, 30, 41, 47, 50, 52, 57, 63, 74, 75, 83, 90, 102, 109, 128, 129, 154, 165, 166, 167, 168, 169, 170, 173–74, 175, 176, 177, 179, 182, 183, 184, 187, 193, 196; acquired, 166, 169, 173; appearance and spread in the United States, 166, 167–68, 173–74, 175–76; the city and, 176–77; congenital, 166, 173; creation of, 166; degeneration and, 169, 170, 173; frontier's effects on, 167–68, 173, 176–77, 181; modernization and, 169; neurasthenia and, 174, 175
sexuality, modern emergence of, 4–5
Sierra County, TX, 38
"Significance of the Frontier in American History, The" (1893), 7, 153, 154, 195; as heterosexual story, 7, 153; influence on Theodore Roosevelt, 154; whitening frontier and, 153. *See also* Turner, Frederick Jackson
Silver City, ID, 54, 97, 100, 101
Sioux, 182
Skeels, Charles, 39–40
Slater, George W., 161, 164
Slifka, Anna, 56–57
Slifka, Victor, 56–57
Smith, Bill, 148
Smith, Henry Nash, 127–28
Snell, Henry, 71
South Dakota, 78
Span, Thomas, 73
Spanish-American War, 52
Spokane, WA, 14, 23, 39
Springer daughters, 33, 42
"Squaw Charley," 148–49
St. Albans, ME, 78
Stephens, Jennie, 118, 120, 121*fig.*, 123
Stockton, CA, 51, 52, 53

Streeby, Shelley, 145
Stroudsburg, PA, 163
Stuver, Emanuel, 173
Susie, Marie, 36
Sutton, Edna (fictional character in *Deadwood Dick on Deck*), 108
Sweethome, OR, 123

Talbot, Eugene S., 180
Talmey, Bernard S., 59, 60, 62–63, 73
Tekoa, WA, 32
Terry, Jennifer, 178
Texas, 118, 120, 122
Thatcher, Prinsrose & West's minstrels, 76
Thomas, William, 67
Todd, George, 79, 80, 90
Tombstone, AZ, 66
Topeka, KS, 79
transgender, 15, 19, 57, 29, 48, 80, 90, 128, 156, 194
transsexual, 15, 16, 19, 29, 52, 57, 90, 128, 165, 200n38
transvestism, 15–16, 62–63
Treaty of Guadalupe Hidalgo (1848), 145
Trinidad, CO, 53
Tunnel City, WA, 25–26
Turner, Frederick Jackson, 7, 126, 153–54, 167, 168, 170, 171, 172, 173, 175, 179, 183–84, 186, 195; influence on Theodore Roosevelt, 154; scholarly criticism of, 184; views on immigrants, 244n65; views on neurasthenia, 175
Tuscarora, NV, 54, 55, 101, 116, 124
two-sex model, 5, 16, 42; cross-dressers and, 17

Ullman, Sharon R., 75
Undaunted, The (1936), 14
University of Oklahoma Press, 111
University of Oregon Medical College, 11
Utah, 44

Van Waters, Miriam, 27–29
Victor, CO, 61
viragint, 47, 50, 174
Virgin Land: The American West as Symbol and Myth (1950), 127–28
Vosbaugh, Charles, 53–54

Waco, TX, 37, 39, 43
Walker, Mary, 32
Walter, Anna, 98

Walter, Katherine, 98, 99
Walters, Hazel, 26, 203n8
Warne, Philip S., 108
Washington State, 23, 25, 44
Waterloo, IA, 88
Watsonville, CA, 53
Weber, Helene Marie, 42
Weir, James, 173, 174, 177, 180
Weiser, ID, 32
West: masculinity and, 2, 62, 152–54;
   homosexuality and, 3; as term, 20;
   whiteness and, 153–54. *See also* frontier
West, George, 112
Western Federation of Miners, 80
"What-Is-It?," 55, 56, 57
Wheeler, Edward, 107
White, Noah, 165
Wichita, KS, 68
Wilde, Oscar, 83
Willard, Mose, 68

Williams, Cathy, 34
Williams, Sammy, 31–32, 42, 45, 52, 53; death
   of, 31; feminizing of, 124; heterosexual-
   izing of, 109–10; as Ingeborge Wekan, 110;
   masculinizing of, 45; newspaper
   responses to, 31
Winning of the West, The, 62, 152–53;
   influenced by Frederick Jackson Turner,
   154
Winslow, J. B., 68
Wisconsin, 34, 110
Wise, Peter M., 165, 166, 167
Wister, Owen, 152, 179
"woman-man," 16
Woodhull, Frank, 32
Wyman, Alf, 66
Wyoming, 14, 44, 173

Yarick, Percy, 71
Yellowstone bather, 72–73

TEXT
10.5/14 Jenson

DISPLAY
Jenson Pro

COMPOSITOR
Westchester Book Group

PRINTER AND BINDER
Sheridan Books, Inc.